Colorado Quilters' Cookbook

Written and Compiled by
Gail Tibbetts

ISBN No. 0-9648381-0-9

Copyright © 1995 by Innovative Designs Plus+

All other referenced trademarks and registered trademarks are the property of their respective owners.

All rights reserved. No part of this book may be reproduced or utilized in any form or by any means, electronic or mechanical, including photocopying and recording, or by any information storage and retrieval system, without permission in writing from the publisher.

How To Order

To order additional copies of the *Colorado Quilters' Cookbook*, send $18.95* per copy plus $3.00 each to cover postage and handling (Colorado residents add 3% sales tax) to:

Innovative Designs Plus+
PO Box 24005
Denver, CO 80224-0005

For faster service on credit card orders, call:
(303) 692-1880

*Payable in U.S. funds only. Prices subject to change.

First Printing—2,500 copies, September 1995

Contents

Appetizers & Beverages 5
 Appetizers 7
 Dips 15
 Beverages 19
Sauces, Marinades, Dressings, Relishes, Pickles 23
Brunch 33
 Rolls, Coffee Cakes, & Muffins 35
 Main Dishes 45
Breads & Rolls 57
Soups, Salads, Vegetables, Side Dishes 83
 Soups 85
 Salads 109
 Vegetables & Side Dishes 140
Main Dishes & Casseroles 163
 Poultry 165
 Beef 194
 Pork 227
 Fish & Seafood 238
 Other Main Dishes & Casseroles 244
Cakes, Cookies, Brownies & Other Bars 259
 Cakes 261
 Frostings 301
 Cookies 304
 Brownies & Other Bars 328
Pies, Puddings, & Other Desserts 345
 Pies 347
 Puddings 363
 Cobblers, Crisps, Crumbles, & Crunches 369
 Cheesecakes 376
 Trifles & Tortes 384
 Other Desserts 388
Index 407

This spool is used as a symbol throughout the book to indicate a quilting or sewing tip.

Dedication

To Jay,

When you least expect it, miracles do happen. I have received many blessings in my life, but you are the best blessing of them all.

In Appreciation

Thanks to all who contributed recipes. This book would not be possible without your generosity.

A very special "Thanks" to Barb Durland for her generosity of time and her valued editorial expertise. Your friendship and your desire to make this book a success are appreciated more than words can say.

Every effort has been made to maintain accuracy while providing clarity and consistency on the material in this book. Please let us know if an error has been made, and we will gladly make the necessary changes in subsequent printings.

Appetizers & Beverages

Special Notes:

Hot Canapes

  1 12-ounce package ground sausage (not links)
  8 ounces very sharp Cheddar cheese, grated
1 1/2 cups buttermilk baking mix

Preheat oven to 400 degrees. Mix all ingredients together well. Knead with hands until it sticks together. Make small balls, 1 inch in diameter. Place on a greased cookie sheet. Bake 20 minutes or until brown. Serve hot.

Notes:
I prefer Jimmie Dean sausage. The canapes do not reheat well.

Peggie Notarianni
Wheat Ridge, Colorado

Yield: 50 canapes

Cheddar Chutney Cheese Snacks

  8 ounces grated Cheddar cheese
      chutney, to taste (use a quality brand)
      chopped onions, to taste
      crackers

Preheat oven to 350 degrees. Melt cheese, chutney, and onion together. Spread on crackers and reheat in oven for approximately 10 minutes. Take it out of the oven when cheese starts to melt. You do not want the cheese to run. Serve warm.

Deborah Smith
Greeley, Colorado

Glazed Baked Brie

Glaze:
- 2 cups packed brown sugar
- 1 cup water
- 2 eggs
- 4 tablespoons cream sherry
- 4 tablespoons half and half

Baked Brie:
- 1 1-pound package phyllo leaves, thawed
- 8 4½-ounce packages Brie
- 1½ cups (3 sticks) melted margarine

Preheat oven to 375 degrees. In a saucepan boil the brown sugar and water for 8 minutes, stirring constantly. Cool 10 minutes. Meanwhile, beat eggs on high for 3 minutes. While still beating, add a constant stream of brown sugar mixture to eggs. Mix well. Mixing on low speed, add sherry and half and half. Continue cooking to reduce for 10 minutes on medium heat. Set aside until Brie has been placed in oven for baking, then slowly reheat.

Unwrap phyllo leaves and keep covered with damp tea towel. There are approximately 20 leaves per package. Working on a sheet of foil, stack five sheets of phyllo, one at a time, brushing each with melted margarine (not too generously).

With a sharp knife, cut stacked sheets in half widthwise. Place one brie in center of each half and fold each to enclose, tucking ends securely underneath. Brush top with margarine. Continue until all of the brie is wrapped. Place wrapped Brie on an ungreased cookie sheet. Bake for approximately 25 minutes, until dough is golden brown. Immediately place on serving plates and drizzle with warmed glaze.

Notes:
You can halve the recipe, but use remaining phyllo sheets immediately. Serve half as appetizer—whole as dessert.

Diane Schlagel
Strasburg, Colorado

Chicken Nacho Supreme

- 2 chicken breasts, boiled, boned, and shredded
- 1 16-ounce can refried beans
- 1/2 cup picante sauce
- 1 tablespoon butter or margarine
- 2 bunches green onions, chopped fine (with greens)
- 1/2 sweet pepper, chopped
- 3 avocados, peeled, seeded, and mashed smooth
- 1 pint sour cream
- 1 16-ounce package Cheddar cheese, shredded
- 1 6-ounce can black olives, halved
-   corn chips

Preheat oven to 350 degrees. Combine chicken, refried beans, and picante sauce and spread over the bottom of a 9x13x2-inch baking pan. Sauté green onions and sweet pepper in butter and sprinkle over the chicken layer. Spread the mashed avocados over the sautéed onions and peppers. Spread the sour cream over the avocados. Spread the cheese over the top of the sour cream and then place the black olives over the cheese. Top with drizzles of picante sauce. Bake until bubbly—30 to 35 minutes. Serve with corn chips for dipping.

Helen Alden
Boulder, Colorado

Sesame Chicken Wings

- 1/2 cup soy sauce
- 1/3 cup water
- 1/4 cup sugar
- 2 tablespoons sesame or olive oil
- dash pepper
- 4 green onions with tops, sliced
- 1/2 medium onion, sliced
- 2 garlic cloves, minced
- 1 to 2 tablespoons sesame seeds
- 2 1/2 pounds chicken wings

In a large plastic bag or glass dish, combine everything but the chicken. Add chicken wings; coat well. Cover and refrigerate 2 to 3 hours or overnight, turning occasionally. Place chicken on a shallow rack in a baking pan; discard marinade. Bake in a preheated 350-degree oven, uncovered, for 30 minutes. Turn and bake about 20 minutes longer or until tender.

Gwen Moore
Littleton, Colorado

Yield: 6 to 8 appetizer servings

Party Swedish Meatballs

Meatballs:
- 2 pounds ground beef
- 1 cup fine bread crumbs
- 2 eggs
- 1 1/2 cups milk
- 2 tablespoons grated onion
- 2 teaspoons salt
- 1/4 teaspoon pepper
- 1/4 teaspoon ground nutmeg

Sauce:
- 1/2 cup prepared yellow mustard
- 3/4 cup red currant jelly
- 1 10 1/2-ounce can beef gravy

Preheat oven to 400 degrees. Mix all ingredients together and gently roll into small balls. Put on jelly-roll pans and bake for 20 minutes.

Mix sauce ingredients in a saucepan and heat until jelly is melted and mustard is blended in. Place meatballs in serving dish or casserole. Pour sauce over meatballs.

Notes:
Can be made ahead and frozen.

Kristine Scerbo
Fort Collins, Colorado

Tortilla Rollups

     2 8-ounce packages cream cheese
     2 4-ounce cans diced green chilies
     1 4$\frac{1}{2}$-ounce can chopped black olives
6 to 8 large flour tortillas

Allow the cream cheese to reach room temperature. Drain the green chilies and black olives. Mix the cream cheese, green chilies, and black olives together. Put a layer of cream cheese mixture on each flour tortilla, spreading all the way to the edges. Spread as thick or thin as you desire. Roll the tortillas up, and put the tortillas in the refrigerator for 1 to 2 hours or overnight. Slice the rolls into narrow pieces ($\frac{1}{4}$ inch).

Deanna Naumann
Aurora, Colorado

Crisp Spiced Walnuts

2$\frac{1}{2}$ cups walnuts
  1 cup sugar
$\frac{1}{2}$ cup water
  1 teaspoon ground cinnamon
$\frac{1}{2}$ teaspoon salt

Preheat oven to 300 degrees. Place walnuts in a shallow pan and heat in oven for 15 minutes. In a saucepan, cook sugar, water, cinnamon, and salt to the soft-ball stage. Then add nuts and stir until creamy and well-coated. Lay on a cookie sheet or waxed paper to dry. Store in covered container.

Jan Shuping
Pueblo, Colorado

Vegetable Bars

- 2 8-ounce packages refrigerated crescent roll dough
- 1 8-ounce package cream cheese, softened
- 3/4 cup mayonnaise
- 1/2 cup sour cream
- 1 4-ounce envelope ranch dressing mix
- 3/4 cup chopped sweet peppers
- 1/4 cup chopped green onion
- 3/4 cup chopped tomatoes
- 3/4 cup chopped broccoli
- 3/4 cup chopped cauliflower
- 3/4 cup grated Cheddar cheese

Preheat oven to 350 degrees. Shape crescent roll dough to fit bottom of 11x17-inch jelly roll pan. Bake for 7 to 8 minutes or until browned. Allow crust to cool completely. Mix cream cheese, mayonnaise, sour cream, and dry ranch dressing mix until smooth. Spread this mixture on top of crust, covering completely. In a large bowl, combine vegetables and toss. Spoon evenly over cream cheese mixture. Sprinkle with shredded cheese. Refrigerate for 3 to 4 hours. Cut into bars.

Kathlyn Thompson
Colorado Springs, Colorado

Praline Quaker Oat Squares

  1 16-ounce package Quaker Oat Squares cereal
  2 cups chopped pecans or walnuts
$1/2$ cup packed brown sugar
$1/2$ cup light corn syrup
$1/4$ cup margarine
  1 teaspoon vanilla
$1/2$ teaspoon baking soda

Preheat oven to 250 degrees. Combine cereal and nuts together, mixing well. Set aside. Combine brown sugar, corn syrup, and margarine in a microwaveable bowl. Microwave on high for $1^{1}/2$ minutes. Stir and cook on high for $1/2$ to $1^{1}/2$ minutes more, until it comes to a boil. Stir in vanilla and baking soda. Pour over cereal and nuts. Coat evenly. Bake in a greased and floured 9x13x2-inch baking pan for 1 hour, stirring about every 20 minutes. Spread on baking sheet to cool. Break apart. While baking, keep an eye on this to make sure it does not scorch.

Jo Silkensen
Longmont, Colorado

Fruit Dip

 1 8-ounce package cream cheese, softened
 1 pint marshmallow cream

Mix cream cheese and marshmallow cream together until smooth. Serve with your favorite fruit cut into bite-sized pieces.

Notes:
Can be refrigerated for several days.

Shirley Franzen
Thornton, Colorado

Chili Con Queso

 1 $10^{3}/_{4}$-ounce can cream of mushroom soup
 1 32-ounce package of processed cheese
 $^{1}/_{2}$ pound pork sausage
 1 10-ounce package frozen broccoli pieces
 1 chopped onion
 1 green chili, chopped, to taste, or $^{1}/_{2}$ cup salsa, to taste

Fry sausage into "chunks"; drain grease after frying. Melt cheese in microwave. Add all remaining ingredients and heat through. Serve with chips for dipping.

Notes:
This recipe works great in a slow cooker.

Melody Munson
Colorado Springs, Colorado

Hot "Chili" Dip

    1/2 1.25-ounce package onion soup mix
      1 8-ounce container sour cream
      1 pound ground beef
      1 cup chili sauce
1 1/2 to 2 teaspoons chili powder
         corn chips

Combine onion soup mix with sour cream, blending well. In a skillet brown ground beef; drain fat. Add chili sauce and chili powder to ground beef. Mix well. Stir in sour cream/soup mixture. Heat. Serve with corn chips.

Peggie Notarianni
Wheat Ridge, Colorado

Chili Cheese Dip

  1 pound lean ground beef
  1 pound processed cheese, cut in 1-inch cubes
  1 8-ounce can green chilies with tomato sauce
  2 teaspoons worcestershire sauce
1/2 teaspoon chili powder
  3 ounces jalapeño chili sauce
     tortilla chips or corn chips

Brown ground beef well and drain off excess fat. Put all ingredients in slow cooker and stir will. Cover and cook on high for 1 hour, stirring until cheese is melted. Serve immediately or turn to low to keep warm. Serve with tortilla chips or corn chips.

Barbara Shie
Colorado Springs, Colorado

Hot Artichoke Dip

- 1   14-ounce can artichokes
- 1   green sweet pepper, chopped
- 1   red sweet pepper, chopped
- 1   clove garlic, sliced
- 1/2 cup Parmesan cheese
- 1   8-ounce package cream cheese, softened

Drain the artichokes and place in food processor. Add green sweet and red peppers, garlic, and Parmesan. Add the cream cheese to the other ingredients and mix well.

Place the cold dip in a microwave dish and heat for about 2 minutes.

Serve dip with crackers or bread sticks that have been heated.

Notes:
This is a delicious and easy dip for any gathering.

Cynthia Rothbard
Longmont, Colorado

Ranch Dip—Low Calorie

- 1 24-ounce container 1% fat cottage cheese
- 8 tablespoons fat-free sour cream
- 1 4-ounce package reduced-fat ranch dressing mix

Place all ingredients in a blender or food processor and process until creamy.

Notes:
Great dip for pretzels or vegetables. Each 1/4 cup serving containes approximately 1 gram fat and 88 calories.

Deana Lovelace
Littleton, Colorado

Yield: 12 to 14 servings

Orange Julius

- 1 cup orange juice
- 1 cup milk
- 1/4 cup sugar
- 1 egg
- 1 teaspoon vanilla
- 6 ice cubes

Mix in blender on high speed.

Helen Alden
Boulder, Colorado

Yield: 2 servings

Juice Shake

- 3 ounces unsweetened frozen (1/2 small can) concentrated fruit juice
- 2 cups milk, divided
- ground nutmeg or cinnamon

In a blender, whip concentrated fruit juice and 1 cup milk until frothy. Add 1 cup more milk and blend quickly. Sprinkle with nutmeg or cinnamon, and serve in chilled glasses, adding ice cubes made from unsweetened fruit juice.

Notes:
Recommended frozen fruit juice concentrates: apple, grapefruit, orange, or pineapple.

Jeanne Arnoldy
Littleton, Colorado

Yield: 3 servings

Hot Buttered Lemonade

       grated peel of 1/2 lemon
- 1/2 cup freshly squeezed lemon juice
- 3 cups water
- 1/2 cup sugar
- 1/4 cup light rum (optional)
- 1 tablespoon butter

Combine all ingredients in a saucepan. Heat.

Notes:
While this can't make any claims for cures, little can comfort a virus victim more than a big mug of hot lemonade.

Jamee Rogers Chambers
Morrison, Colorado

Yield: 4 cups or five 6-ounce servings

Fireside Coffee

- 2 cups instant cocoa
- 2 cups powdered coffee creamer
- 1 cup instant coffee (fine grind)
- 1 1/2 cups sugar
- 1 teaspoon ground cinnamon
- 1/2 teaspoon ground nutmeg

Mix all ingredients together. Place 2 to 4 tablespoons of the mixture in a mug and pour in boiling water. Mix well with a teaspoon.

Notes:
This drink is lovely on a cold day in winter.

Cynthia Rothbard
Longmont, Colorado

Fruit Slush

1¼ cups fruit, fresh or canned in unsweetened juice, chopped
8 to 10 ice cubes

In a food processor or blender, blend fruit until smooth. Gradually add ice cubes and blend until mixture reaches a thick, slushy consistency. Serve immediately.

Notes:
Recommended fruit: apples, bananas, blueberries, peaches, pears, or pineapple.

Jeanne Arnoldy
Littleton, Colorado

Yield: 3 servings

Special Notes:

Sauces, Dressings, Relishes, Pickles

Special Notes:

Hot Fudge Sauce

- 1 cup sugar
- 3 tablespoons cornstarch
- 5 tablespoons cocoa
- 1/4 teaspoon salt
- 1 cup boiling water
- 1 tablespoon butter or margarine
- 1 teaspoon vanilla

Mix sugar, cornstarch, cocoa, and salt together. Stir in boiling water and mix well. Add butter and cook for a few minutes, stirring constantly until mixture thickens.

Transfer to a glass microwaveable bowl; cover tightly with plastic wrap. Cook in microwave for 1 to 2 minutes on high. Blend in vanilla and mix well. Store in a covered jar.

Variations:
Two extra tablespoons of butter makes it taste really yummy.

Notes:
The microwaving process allows this to be kept for several weeks on a cabinet shelf.

Edytha Vickers
Aurora, Colorado

Pesto

- 1/2 cup freshly grated Parmesan or Romano cheese
- 1 cup olive oil
- 2 cups fresh coarsely chopped basil
- 2 teaspoons chopped garlic cloves
- 1 teaspoon salt
- 1/2 teaspoon pepper
- 2 tablespoons pine nuts

Place all ingredients in a blender and pulse for 1 minute. Pour into ice cube tray, freeze, and pop out to store in freezer bags. Just take out what you need for pasta, chicken, etc.

Chris Mooney
Longmont, Colorado

Bug Juice

- 1/2 cup molasses
- 1/2 cup beer
- 1/2 cup chili sauce
- 1/2 cup chopped onion
- 1/4 cup mustard
- 1 teaspoon worcestershire sauce
- salt and pepper to taste

Combine all ingredients in a saucepan and simmer for 5 minutes. Brush onto hamburgers and then barbeque.

Notes:
We have used this recipe for years. It is easy and quick to make and makes your barbequed hamburgers taste so good.

Winnie Lane
Northglenn, Colorado

Marinade for Chicken

1½ cups soy sauce
¾ cup dry sherry or sake
1⅓ tablespoons mild honey
2 teaspoons finely minced garlic
1½ teaspoons finely minced fresh ginger root
1 teaspoon Oriental sesame oil
1 cup toasted sesame seeds

Combine all ingredients and mix well. Add chicken and marinade for several hours, then grill until done. Discard any remaining marinade.

Teresa Mensch
Evergreen, Colorado

Yield: 8 servings

Honey Dressing for Spinach Salad

1/2 cup sugar
1 teaspoon dry mustard
1 teaspoon paprika
1 teaspoon celery seeds
1/4 teaspoon salt
1/2 cup honey
1/2 cup vinegar
1 tablespoon lemon juice
3/4 cup vegetable oil

Mix sugar, mustard, paprika, celery seeds, and salt. Add honey, vinegar, and lemon juice. Pour vegetable oil into mixture very slowly, beating constantly with electric mixer or rotary beater.

Notes:
This dressing is particularly good on a spinach salad with mushrooms, bacon, hard-boiled eggs, and green onions.

Jeanne Creighton
Denver, Colorado

Piquant Italian-Style Dressing

1 1/4 cups olive oil
1/2 cup red wine vinegar
1 tablespoon dry mustard
2 teaspoons fructose
1 teaspoon salt
1 teaspoon celery seeds
1/2 teaspoon fresh ground pepper
1/2 teaspoon crushed tarragon
1/2 teaspoon crushed basil
1/2 teaspoon crushed parsley
1/4 teaspoon ground paprika
1/4 teaspoon garlic powder
grated Parmesan

Thoroughly mix all ingredients. Chill at least 1/2 hour before use. Pour over any green, chicken, or fish salad. Top with freshly grated Parmesan cheese.

Delia Molloy da Cunha
Boulder, Colorado

Wesport Cranberry Relish

- 3 cups fresh whole cranberries
- 1 orange, unpeeled, quartered and seeded
- 1 tart apple, unpeeled, quartered and cored
- 3/4 cup sugar
- 1/8 teaspoon salt
- 1/4 teaspoon ground cinnamon
- 1/2 cup water
- 1/2 cup golden seedless raisins
- 1/2 cup chopped dried apricots
- 1/2 cup chopped pecans

Coarsely grind cranberries, orange, and apple. Stir in sugar, salt, and cinnamon. Set aside. In a saucepan combine water, raisins, and apricots. Cook over medium heat until raisins are plump—about 5 minutes. Drain. Stir raisins, apricots, and pecans into relish. Refrigerate overnight to allow flavors to blend.

Notes:
This recipe is from my mother's recipe collection.

Kristine Scerbo
Fort Collins, Colorado

Yield: 3 1/2 cups

Garlic Dill Pickles

    2 cups water
    1 cup vinegar
    3 tablespoons pickling salt
       pickling cucumbers (enough to fill one-quart jar)
  2 1/2 garlic cloves
       dill
       grape leaf (optional for firmness)

Bring to boil water, vinegar, and pickling salt. Pack pickling cucumbers that are at room temperature into sterilized canning jar. Place garlic, dill, and grape leaf into jar. Pour boiling solution over packed cucumbers and seal.

Notes:
No need to process with hot water bath. Let sit for 6 months before eating.

Jerry Goddard
Loveland, Colorado

Cucumbers

    8 cups sliced cucumbers
       salt, to taste
    1 cup vinegar
    2 cups sugar
    1 teaspoon celery seeds
    1 cup sliced onions

Place sliced cucumbers in a large bowl and sprinkle salt over them. Let cucumbers sit for a couple of hours at room temperature. In a separate bowl, combine vinegar, sugar, celery seeds, and onions. Pour over cucumbers. Chill for four hours before serving.

Judy Hying
Denver, Colorado

Brunch

Special Notes:

Easy Caramel Rolls

- 2 dozen frozen prepared dinner rolls (dough)
- 1 4-ounce package butterscotch pudding (not instant)
- 1/2 cup packed brown sugar
- 1/2 cup (1 stick) margarine, softened
- 1/2 cup chopped nuts

Place frozen rolls in a greased bundt pan. Thoroughly mix pudding, brown sugar, margarine, and nuts. Sprinkle over top of frozen dough. Allow dough to rise overnight in the refrigerator. Preheat oven to 350 degrees. Bake for 40 minutes. Turn upside down on a plate to allow hot caramel to run down over rolls.

Sissi Williams
Westminster, Colorado

 Use old x-ray film for templates.

Prussian Cinnamon Rolls

Rolls:
- 1 1/2 cups warm water
- 3 packets active dry yeast
- 1/2 cup safflower or sunflower oil
- 1 egg
- 3/4 cup baked, mashed yam or sweet potato
- 1 to 3 teaspoons salt (to taste)
- 3 tablespoons nonfat dry milk powder
- 3 cups spelt or barley flour
- 3 cups whole wheat pastry flour
- 1/2 cup (1 stick) butter or margarine, softened and cut into 6 slices
- 1/2 cup (1 stick) butter or margarine, softened and set aside
- 3/4 to 1 cup packed brown sugar
- 2 tablespoons ground cinnamon
- 1 tablespoon ground nutmeg
- 1 teaspoon ground cardamom

Frosting:
- 3/4 cup butter or margarine, softened
- 1 cup powdered sugar
- 3 tablespoons flour
- 2 teaspoons vanilla extract
- 1/4 teaspoon orange essence or 1/8 cup orange juice (optional)

In a large mixing bowl, dissolve yeast in warm water. Add the safflower oil and stir with wooden spoon. Lightly beat the egg and add in. Add the cooked yam and mix well.

In a separate bowl, sift salt and nonfat dry milk powder into the 3 cups of barley flour. Add these to the first mixture and beat well. Gradually add the wheat pastry flour. When dough is workable, transfer to lightly floured surface and knead for 10 to 15 minutes. Let rest for 5 minutes.

(continued)

Prussian Cinnamon Rolls
(continued)

Grease a very large bowl with half the butter, smooth the dough, and place in the bowl. Grease the dough with butter as well. Cover the bowl with a tea towel and let dough rise in a warm place until doubled in size, about 2 hours.

After the dough has doubled, punch it down thoroughly to remove air bubbles. Smooth dough again and place back in regreased bowl. Grease dough with butter again as well, and let rise 1 hour.

After 1 hour has passed, punch down dough and transfer to lightly floured work surface. Roll out into a rectangle about 12 inches wide and 18 inches long. Dough should be at least 1 1/2 inches thick. Shorten rectangle if dough is not thick enough.

Spread the leftover softened butter over the dough all the way to the edges. Mix the brown sugar, cinnamon, nutmeg, and cardamom together well and sprinkle over the butter. Roll the dough up from one of the ends, forming a large roll. Using a very sharp, serrated, floured knife, cut this large roll into eight to ten approximately 2-inch-thick slices.

Place slices about 1 1/2 to 2 inches apart in a greased, 10x10x2-inch or 11x7x2-inch pan. Cover and let rise in warm place for 1 hour.

Bake 15 to 18 minutes in a preheated 350-degree oven. Remove from oven and cool rolls completely on wire rack lined with waxed paper.

For frosting, place butter and powdered sugar in a mixing bowl and beat well. Whisk in flour, then vanilla and orange essence (if desired). Beat until smooth and creamy. Spread onto cooled cinnamon rolls. After rolls are frosted, store in tightly sealed container lined with waxed paper.

Loree L. M. De La Cuadra
Colorado Springs, Colorado

Yield: 8 to 10 rolls

Breakfast/Brunch Rolls

Rolls:
- 1 cup (2 sticks) margarine, softened
- 1 12-ounce container cottage cheese
- 2 cups flour

Frosting: (optional)
- 1 cup powdered sugar
- 1 tablespoon margarine, softened
- 1/4 teaspoon vanilla
- 1 tablespoon milk

Filling: (optional)
- brown sugar
- raisins
- ground cinnamon

Cream margarine and cottage cheese. Add flour, gradually. Batter will be very thick. Refrigerate batter for 4 hours or longer. Divide batter into three equal parts. Roll onto floured surface like a pie crust. Each circle should be about 12 inches in diameter. Cut each circle into 16 parts. Roll each roll from outside to inside. Place on a greased cookie sheet and bake in a preheated 350-degree oven for 20 minutes.

Choose either the frosting or filling option above. For frosting, combine powdered sugar, margarine, vanilla, and milk. Blend and frost rolls while they are still hot.

For filling, sprinkle brown sugar, raisins, and cinnamon on dough before cutting. Cut and roll up. Bake. Do not frost.

Notes:
My favorite option is the filling. I often serve these for a special luncheon with chicken fruit salad.

Janet Mount
Longmont, Colorado

Yield: 48 rolls

Quick Coffee Cake

Cake:
- 1 cup packed brown sugar
- 1/2 cup (1 stick) margarine, softened
- 2 eggs
- 3 cups flour
- 2 1/2 teaspoons baking powder
- 1 teaspoon salt
- 1 1/2 cups milk

Topping:
- 3/4 cup granulated sugar
- 3/4 cup flour
- 1/2 cup (1 stick) margarine, softened
- 1 tablespoon ground cinnamon

Preheat oven to 350 degrees. For cake, cream brown sugar and margarine; add eggs and mix well. Add flour, baking powder, salt, and milk. Mix well. Pour into a greased and floured 9x13x2-inch pan.

For topping, mix all ingredients until crumbly. Sprinkle over top of cake. Bake for 20 to 30 minutes.

Notes:
I like this recipe because it is easily and quickly prepared from items you usually have in your cupboard and it tastes great.

Sandia Hayes
Lakewood, Colorado

Quick Cinnamon Coffee Bread

Coffee Bread:
- 1/4 cup vegetable shortening or butter, softened
- 1 cup sugar
- 2 eggs
- 1 cup sour milk*
- 1 teaspoon vanilla
- 1/2 teaspoon salt
- 1/2 teaspoon baking soda
- 1 teaspoon baking powder
- 2 cups flour

Filling:
- 6 tablespoons brown sugar
- 2 tablespoons ground cinnamon
- nuts (optional)

Preheat oven to 350 degrees. In a large bowl, combine vegetable shortening, sugar, and eggs; mix well. Mix in eggs, sour milk, and vanilla. Combine salt, baking soda, baking powder, and flour together. Add to mixture, blending well. In a greased 9x5x3-inch loaf pan add half the bread mixture, then sprinkle half the filling over batter. Add remaining batter, then sprinkle on remaining filling for top of coffee cake. Bake for 1 hour.

Notes:
*To make sour milk, add 1 tablespoon vinegar to 1 cup milk.

Donna Preston
Denver, Colorado

Yield: 1 loaf

Blueberry Coffee Cake

Cake:
- 1/2 cup vegetable shortening
- 1 cup sugar
- 2 eggs
- 1 teaspoon vanilla
- 2 1/4 cups flour
- 1 tablespoon baking powder
- 2/3 cup milk

Topping:
- 2 cups fresh or frozen blueberries
- 2/3 cup sugar
- 2/3 cup flour
- 1/2 cup (1 stick) margarine or butter, softened
- 1/4 teaspoon almond extract

Preheat oven to 350 degrees. For cake, beat the vegetable shortening and sugar until light and fluffy. Add eggs and vanilla and beat well. Mix flour and baking powder and add to beaten mixture alternately with milk. Spread into two greased and floured 9-inch cake pans. For topping, sprinkle 1 cup blueberries on each cake. Mix the sugar and the flour and cut in the margarine and almond extract until crumbly. Sprinkle over the blueberries. Bake for 35 minutes. Cool slightly and cut into wedges.

Mae Jane Keller
Aurora, Colorado

Yield: 16 servings (two 9-inch cakes)

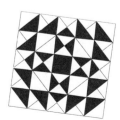

Streusel Coffee Cake

Filling:
- 1/2 cup packed brown sugar
- 2 tablespoons flour
- 2 teaspoons ground cinnamon
- 2 tablespoons butter or margarine, melted
- 1/2 cup chopped nuts

Cake:
- 1 1/2 cups flour
- 3 teaspoons baking powder
- 1/2 teaspoon salt
- 3/4 cup granulated sugar
- 1/4 cup vegetable shortening
- 1 egg, beaten
- 1/2 cup milk
- 1 teaspoon vanilla

Preheat oven to 350 degrees. To make topping, mix brown sugar, flour, and cinnamon together. Blend in the melted butter; stir in the nuts.

To make the cake, sift flour once before measuring. Then sift flour, baking powder, salt, and sugar together. Cut in vegetable shortening until mixture is like fine cornmeal. Blend in well-beaten egg, mixed with milk and vanilla, and beat just enough to mix well. Pour half the batter into a well-greased 8-inch square pan. Sprinkle with half of the filling; then add remaining batter and put the remainder of the filling on top. Bake about 25 minutes or until done.

Notes:
Can double ingredients and bake in a 9x13x2-inch pan.

Nancy Orth
Kiowa, Colorado

Raw Apple Coffee Cake

Cake:
- 1 cup sugar
- $2/3$ cup vegetable shortening
- 1 large egg
- $1\ 2/3$ cups unsifted flour
- 1 teaspoon baking soda
- $1/2$ teaspoon ground cinnamon
- $1/2$ teaspoon salt
- $1/2$ cup warm coffee
- $1\ 1/4$ cups ground raw apple, unpeeled

Topping:
- $1/2$ cup packed brown sugar
- $1/2$ cup chopped pecans

Preheat oven to 350 degrees. Mix sugar, vegetable shortening, and egg together. Add flour, baking soda, cinnamon, and salt. Mix well. Add warm coffee and ground apple and mix well. Pour into a greased and floured 9x13x2-inch pan. In a separate bowl, combine brown sugar and pecans. Sprinkle over top of cake. Bake for 45 minutes or until cake tests done. Do not over bake.

Notes:
This cake is best when it is made 1 or 2 days before serving. Great with coffee and tea. This recipe is perfect for your guild meeting.

Diane Schlagel
Strasburg, Colorado

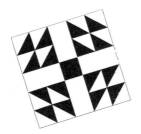

Cinnamon Coffee Cake

  1 cup (2 sticks) butter or margarine, softened
2¾ cups sugar, divided
  2 teaspoons vanilla extract
  4 eggs
  3 cups all-purpose flour
  2 teaspoons baking powder
  1 teaspoon baking soda
  1 teaspoon salt
  2 cups (16 ounces) sour cream
  2 tablespoons ground cinnamon
½ cup chopped walnuts (optional)

Preheat oven to 350 degrees. In a large mixing bowl, cream butter and 2 cups sugar until fluffy. Add vanilla. Add eggs, one at a time, beating well after each addition. Combine flour, baking powder, soda, and salt; add alternately with sour cream, beating just enough after each addition to keep batter smooth. Spoon one-third of batter into a greased 10-inch tube pan. Combine cinnamon, nuts, and remaining ¾ cup sugar; sprinkle one-third over batter in pan. Repeat layers two more times. Bake for 70 minutes or until cake tests done. Cool for 10 minutes. Remove from pan to a wire rack to cool completely.

Notes:
Freezes well.

Gail Tibbetts
Denver, Colorado

Yield: 16 to 20 servings

Blender Pancakes

- 1 cup buttermilk
- 1 egg
- 1 tablespoon sugar
- 1 cup flour
- 1 teaspoon baking soda
- 1/2 teaspoon salt
- 2 tablespoons vegetable oil

Combine all ingredients and blend in blender until thoroughly mixed. Heat skillet or griddle over medium-high heat until drop of water sizzles. Brush lightly with vegetable oil. Pour batter by scant 1/4 cupfuls onto hot skillet or griddle, making a few pancakes at a time. Cook until bubbly and bubbles burst; edges will look dry. With pancake turner, turn and cook until underside is golden brown.

Serve with bacon, eggs, hash browns, and orange juice.

Christine Sitzman
Fort Lupton, Colorado

Overnight Apple French Toast with Spiced Applesauce

French Toast:
- 3/4 cup packed brown sugar
- 6 tablespoons butter
- 3 tablespoons light corn syrup
- 3 to 4 large tart apples, peeled and thickly sliced
- 4 large eggs
- 2 cups milk
- 1 1/2 teaspoon vanilla
- 1 loaf sheepherder's bread or French bread, cut into 1-inch slices

Spiced Applesauce:
- 1 cup chunky applesauce
- 3/4 cup (6 ounces) apple jelly
- 1/2 teaspoon ground cinnamon
- 1/8 teaspoon ground cloves

Place brown sugar, butter, and corn syrup into microwaveable bowl. Microwave on high for 3 minutes. Stir to mix. Pour over the bottom of a large 11x17-inch jelly roll pan. Arrange apple slices over syrup in pan.

Break eggs into a small square baking pan and beat well. Beat in milk and vanilla. Dip both sides of each bread slice into the egg mixture. Arrange bread slices over apples. Slowly pour remaining egg mixture over the bread slices. Cover with plastic wrap and refrigerate overnight.

One hour before serving, preheat oven to 350 degrees. Uncover French toast and bake for 35 to 40 minutes. Make sauce while French toast is baking by combining applesauce, apple jelly, cinnamon, and cloves in a small saucepan. Heat slowly on top of stove. It will make your house smell good! Also cook sausage or bacon to serve with French toast and applesauce.

Martha Thompson
Lakewood, Colorado

Yield: 6 generous servings

Pineapple-Cream Cheese Sandwiches

- 2 8-ounce packages cream cheese, softened
- 2 tablespoons finely chopped sweet pepper
- 2 tablespoons finely chopped onion
- 1/4 cup crushed pineapple, drained
- 2 teaspoons seasoning salt
- 1 cup chopped pecans
  white bread, crusts removed
  mayonnaise (optional)

Beat cream cheese until smooth. Add other ingredients and spread on trimmed white bread or bread that has been cut with various cookie cutters. You may use a little mayonnaise to thin consistency, if desired.

Notes:
Good for a luncheon or brunch sandwich.

Sharon Hoffman
Charlotte, North Carolina

Overnight Breakfast

- 12 eggs, lightly beaten
- salt and pepper, to taste
- 8 ounces grated Cheddar cheese, divided
- 1 cup whipping cream
- 1 sweet pepper, chopped (optional)
- 1 onion, chopped (optional)
- 1 cup sliced mushrooms (optional)
- 2 medium-sized baked potatoes, cooled, crumbled
- 1 1/2 pounds lean bacon, sausage, or ham, cut up

Pour beaten eggs into a well-greased 9x13x2-inch baking dish. Add salt and pepper and mix well. Sprinkle half of grated cheese over top of eggs. Pour in whipping cream. Sprinkle sweet peppers, onions, and mushrooms over top of cheese. Sprinkle on potatoes. Sprinkle cut up bacon, sausage, or ham over potatoes. Sprinkle with remaining grated cheese. Do not stir. Refrigerate for 10 or more hours. Bake in a pre-heated 350-degree oven for 50 to 60 minutes.

Notes:
This is an easy way to give your family breakfast on those days when your husband has promised to take the kids fishing while you spend the day working on your quilt.

Lori Worrell
Grand Junction, Colorado

Egg Baskets with Hollandaise Sauce

Egg Baskets:
- 6 purchased frozen pastry patty shells
- 6 eggs
- 6 slices Canadian bacon

Hollandaise:
- 3 egg yolks
- 2 tablespoons fresh lemon juice
- dash cayenne
- 1/2 cup (1 stick) butter or margarine

Garnishes:
- parsley
- pimento
- black olives

Preheat oven to 325 degrees. Bake patty shells according to directions on package, but undercook slightly so shells are light brown (half cooked). Cool. Cut off tops and scoop out middle dough, being careful not to make holes in the sides of the shells. Place shells on a large cookie sheet. Carefully crack a raw egg into each shell. Bake until egg is set, about 20 to 25 minutes. Serve each shell on top of a slice of Canadian bacon that has been heated.

To make Hollandaise, place egg yolks, lemon juice, and cayenne in blender. Pulse on and off for 2 to 3 seconds. Heat butter until almost boiling. With blender on high speed, slowly pour in butter. Blend for 30 seconds, until thick. Place in a double boiler over warm, but not boiling, water until ready to serve. Pour Hollandaise over egg baskets and garnish with parsley, pimento, or black olives.

Notes:
If making more than six baskets, make two separate batches of Hollandaise; do not double recipe. Pepperidge Farm makes the pastry patty shells that I use.

Marcia Potter
Denver, Colorado

Yield: 6 servings

Egg and Ham or Sausage Brunch

6 to 7 slices of bread, cubed
    1 pound precooked ham or 1 pound sausage, browned
    8 ounces Old English cheese, cubed
    6 eggs, beaten
    2 cups milk
    1/2 teaspoon dry mustard
    1/2 teaspoon salt
    1/2 cup (1 stick) butter or margarine, melted

Grease a 9x13x2-inch pan using a non-stick aerosol spray. In pan, mix bread and ham or sausage. Sprinkle cubed cheese over this mixture. In a separate bowl, thoroughly mix eggs, milk, dry mustard, and salt. Pour over the bread mixture. Pour melted butter over the top. Cover and refrigerate overnight. Uncover and bake in a preheated 325-degree oven for 45 minutes.

Ruby Hill Davis
Clifton, Colorado

Yield: 6 servings

Breakfast Casserole

- 8 slices white bread, crusts removed
- 1 pound breakfast sausage, browned and crumbled
- 1 12-ounce can evaporated milk plus enough whole milk to equal 2 cups
- 12 eggs, beaten
- 1 1/2 cups grated cheese

Grease a 9x13x2-inch pan. Place bread so it covers the bottom of the pan. Sprinkle cooked sausage over bread. Mix milk and eggs and pour over sausage. Sprinkle cheese over the top. Refrigerate overnight. Bake in a preheated 375-degree oven for 35 to 45 minutes until casserole is firm in the center.

Toni Fitzwater
Pine, Colorado

Kitchen Scrambler and Country Fries

Scrambler:
- 1 teaspoon vegetable oil
- 1 tablespoon butter
- 1 medium onion, chopped
- 1 cup frozen peas
- 4 tablespoons chopped chives or green onions
- 8 eggs
- 1/2 cup grated cheese (any flavor or mix flavors)
- 1 cup bean sprouts
- 1 tomato, chopped

Country Fries:
- 2 tablespoons vegetable oil
- 4 medium potatoes, unpeeled, cut into bite-sized pieces
- salt and pepper to taste

For scrambler, heat vegetable oil and butter in skillet. Sauté onion, frozen peas, and chives or green onions. In a separate bowl, lightly beat eggs with a fork. Pour eggs over vegetables. Cook over medium heat until eggs are set. Frequently stir eggs as they are cooking to keep them from forming a solid mass. Remove from heat, sprinkle grated cheese over eggs, and place cover on pan for about 30 seconds until cheese melts. Place eggs on plates and top with bean sprouts and tomatoes.

For country fries, heat vegetable oil in a skillet. Add potatoes and salt and pepper. Fry until brown, stirring potatoes periodically.

Notes:
This recipe is from the Summer Kitchen in Door County, Wisconsin.

Doris Graf
Fort Collins, Colorado

Yield: 4 servings

Ham and Swiss Breakfast

- 3 English muffins
- 3 tablespoons butter or margarine
- 12 ounces Swiss cheese, divided
- 6 slices ham
- 3 eggs, beaten
- 2 cups milk
- 1 teaspoon salt
- 1/4 teaspoon pepper
- 1 teaspoon dry mustard

Spread muffin halves with butter. Place split side up in a 9x13x2-inch baking dish. Cut cheese in half, reserving half for topping. Slice the first half of cheese into six pieces, and lay one piece of cheese on top of each English muffin. Cover cheese with ham slices. Mix eggs, milk, salt, pepper, and dry mustard. Pour over ham slices. Grate reserved cheese. Sprinkle on top of egg mixture. Refrigerate overnight. Bake in a preheated 350-degree oven for 40 minutes. Mixture should be set but not dry.

Sissi Williams
Westminster, Colorado

Yield: 4 to 6 servings

Choose a print first, then pick colors from the print to match the solids or the smaller design prints.

Egg Casserole

      Texas toast
- 2 pounds meat (sausage, bacon, or ham)
- 1 cup grated cheese
- 1/3 cup chopped onion
- 1/3 cup diced sweet pepper
- 12 eggs
- 1 1/3 cups milk, divided
- 1 teaspoon dry mustard
- 1 10 3/4-ounce can cream of mushroom soup
- 1 4-ounce can/jar sliced mushrooms
- 1/3 cup milk

Line a 9x13x2-inch greased pan with Texas toast. In a skillet, brown meat. Drain grease. Spread cooked meat over bread. Sprinkle grated cheese over meat. Sauté onion and sweet pepper and spread over meat. In a separate bowl, mix eggs, 1 cup milk, and dry mustard thoroughly. Pour over casserole. Cover and refrigerate overnight. Mix cream of mushroom soup, sliced mushrooms, and 1/3 cup milk. Spread evenly over casserole. Cover and bake in a preheated 350-degree oven for 1 1/2 hours. Remove cover during last 15 minutes of baking.

Variations:
You can substitute two slices of regular toast for each slice of Texas toast.

Shirley Franzen
Thornton, Colorado

Greek Spinach Pie

- 1 10-ounce package frozen chopped spinach
- 1/2 pound Feta cheese or New York sharp Cheddar cheese
- 1 pint (2 cups) small-curd cottage cheese
- 4 eggs, beaten
- 6 tablespoons flour
- 1/2 teaspoon salt, or to taste
- 1/2 teaspoon pepper
- dash of bottled hot pepper sauce
- 1 tablespoon butter or margarine

Thaw spinach (takes 1 hour at room temperature) and drain. Crumble Feta cheese with a fork (or grate the Cheddar). Mix Feta or Cheddar with thawed, drained spinach and the cottage cheese. In another bowl, mix eggs, flour, salt, pepper, and hot pepper sauce. Grease a round quiche pan with 1 or 2 teaspoons of butter. (This actually makes the cheeses/egg mixture form the "crust" so it is a necessary amount.) Pour into pan and spread evenly. Bake in a preheated 350-degree oven for 1 hour or until knife inserted in center comes out clean. Cool a few minutes and cut into pie shape.

Variations:
This versatile recipe can be the base for any number of variations: add chopped green or regular onion, chopped or diced Anaheim peppers, etc.

Notes:
This is wonderful for a brunch with a fruit salad and muffins. I usually make the full recipe so I have "planned-overs." Temperature and time given for baking are at 5700 feet—does not work at sea-level elevations.

Jamee Rogers Chambers
Morrison, Colorado

Cheesy Spinach (or Broccoli) Quiche

  1/2 cup flour
  1/2 tablespoon baking powder
  1/2 teaspoon salt
    4 eggs or egg substitute
    4 tablespoons butter or margarine, melted
  1/2 cup milk
  3/8 cup minced onion
  3/8 cup (1/8 pound) shredded Cheddar cheese
  3/8 cup (1/8 pound) shredded Swiss cheese
  3/8 cup (1/8 pound) shredded Mozzarella cheese
    1 8 to 12-ounce package frozen spinach or broccoli, thawed
    1 unbaked 9-inch pie crust

Preheat oven to 350 degrees. Toss together flour, baking powder, and salt. In a separate bowl, combine eggs, melted butter, milk, and onion. Stir in Cheddar, Swiss, and Mozzarella cheeses; add spinach or broccoli. Add flour mixture. Stir until combined. Pour into prepared pie crust. Bake for 45 to 60 minutes. Cool 5 minutes before cutting.

Cardwell Spiller
Colorado Springs, Colorado

Snip the selvedges of a full width of fabric (that has been folded in half, selvedges together) every 4 inches or so when you are cutting lots of strips. This helps keep the angle between the fold and the cut edge closer to 90 degrees so that there is less squaring up needed as each strip is cut.

Breads & Rolls

Special Notes:

Mandarin Scones

- 1/3 cup margarine or butter, softened
- 4 tablespoons sugar, divided
- 2 tablespoons grated orange rind
- 1 egg
- 1/4 cup milk
- 1 11-ounce can mandarin oranges, drained and chopped
- 2 cups flour
- 2 1/2 teaspoons baking powder

Preheat oven to 400 degrees. Cream the butter and 3 tablespoons of sugar. Mix in the orange rind, egg, milk, and mandarin oranges. Combine the flour and baking powder and lightly fold into the other mixture. Knead on a floured board 10 times. Dough will be sticky. Shape into a 9-inch circle and place on a greased cookie sheet. Score into eight wedges. Sprinkle top with remaining 1 tablespoon of sugar. Bake for 20 minutes.

Mae Jane Keller
Aurora, Colorado

Yield: 8 servings

Butter Dips

- 1/3 cup butter or margarine
- 2 1/4 cups sifted all-purpose flour
- 1 teaspoon sugar
- 3 1/2 teaspoons baking powder
- 1 1/2 teaspoon salt
- 1 cup milk

Preheat oven to 450 degrees. Melt butter in a 9x13x2-inch pan. Remove pan from oven when butter is melted. Sift together flour, sugar, baking powder, and salt. Add milk. Stir with fork until dough just clings together. Turn onto floured bread board. Roll to coat with flour and knead gently about 10 times. Roll out 1/2-inch thick into an 8x12-inch rectangle. With a floured knife, cut in half lengthwise, then cut each half crosswise into 16 strips. Roll each strip in the melted butter and place in rows in the same pan the butter was melted in. Bake for 15 to 20 minutes.

Notes:
I roll dough to the size suggested above. Then I use a pizza cutter to cut dough into strips close to size suggested above. This goes together real fast. The rolls go great with soups! They have a delicious biscuit taste with a strong buttery flavoring.

Gail Tibbetts
Denver, Colorado

Yield: 32 biscuit strips

Corn Muffins

- 1 cup unsifted flour
- 1 cup yellow cornmeal
- 3 tablespoons sugar
- 4 teaspoons baking powder
- 1 teaspoon salt
- 1 cup milk
- $1/2$ cup mayonnaise

Preheat oven to 400 degrees. Grease twelve $2^{1}/_{2} \times 1^{1}/_{4}$-inch muffin cups. Stir together flour, cornmeal, sugar, baking powder, and salt. Stir milk into mayonnaise; stir into flour mixture just until moistened. Batter may be lumpy. Fill cups two-thirds full. Bake for 20 minutes.

Notes:
These corn muffins are quick to mix up and are delicious with chili, beans, or soup that has been cooking all day.

Alice Del Dosso
Monte Vista, Colorado

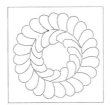

Pumpkin Muffins

1 2/3	cups flour
1	cup sugar
2 to 3	teaspoons pumpkin pie spice*
1	teaspoon baking soda
1/4	teaspoon baking powder
1/4	teaspoon salt
2	large eggs
1	cup canned pumpkin
1/2	cup (1 stick) butter or margarine, melted
1	tablespoon grated lemon peel
1	cup chopped walnuts
1/2	cup raisins

Preheat oven to 350 degrees. In large bowl combine flour, sugar, pumpkin pie spice, baking soda, baking powder, and salt. In medium bowl whisk eggs, pumpkin, melted butter, and lemon peel. Stir in walnuts and raisins. Pour pumpkin mixture into dry ingredients. Stir just until mixed. Spoon batter evenly into 12 greased or paper-lined muffin cups. Bake for 20 to 25 minutes until golden brown.

Notes:
*Pumpkin pie spice: 2 teaspoons ground cinnamon, 1 teaspoon ground ginger, 1/2 teaspoon ground nutmeg or allspice, and 1/4 teaspoon ground cloves.

Lori Erickson
Denver, Colorado

Yield: 12 muffins

Guadelupe Oatmeal Muffins

Muffins:
- 1 1/3 cup old-fashioned rolled oats
- 1 cup skim milk
- 2/3 cup dark raisins
- 3 tablespoons honey
- 3 tablespoons canola or safflower oil
- 2 teaspoons vanilla
- 2 1/2 tablespoons light brown sugar
- 1 large egg white
- 3/4 cup white flour
- 1/2 cup whole wheat flour
- 1 1/2 teaspoons baking powder
- 1 teaspoon ground cinnamon
- 1/2 teaspoon baking soda
- 1/4 teaspoon salt

Mexican Vanilla Butter: (optional)
- 1 1/2 cups confectioners sugar
- 2 tablespoons soft butter
- 2 tablespoons light cream
- 1 teaspoon vanilla

Preheat oven to 425 degrees. In a medium bowl, thoroughly mix rolled oats, milk, raisins, honey, canola oil, vanilla, brown sugar, and egg white. In a large bowl, stir together the white and whole wheat flours, baking powder, cinnamon, baking soda, and salt. Pour the oat mixture into the flour mixture. Stir just until dry ingredients are moistened; do not over mix. Spray 12 standard size muffin cups with non-stick cooking spray or line with paper cups. Divide the batter evenly among the muffin cups. Bake for 13 to 16 minutes, or until the muffins are nicely browned and spring back when touched lightly. Transfer the pan to a wire rack and let cool for 5 minutes before removing the muffins. For the butter, combine all the ingredients and cream until smooth. Serve on the side.

Notes:
These muffins are low-fat but the Mexican Vanilla Butter is not!

Jan Magee
Denver, Colorado

Yield: 12 muffins

Cranberry Apple Bread

Bread:
- 3/4 cup unsweetened applesauce
- 1/3 cup vegetable oil
- 2 large eggs
- 1/4 cup water
- 2 cups unbleached white flour
- 1 teaspoon baking soda
- 2 teaspoons baking powder
- 1/2 teaspoon ground nutmeg
- 1 teaspoon ground cinnamon
- 1 fresh apple, peeled, cored, and chopped into 1/3-inch cubes
- 1/2 cup chopped fresh cranberries

Topping:
- 1 8-ounce package cream cheese, softened (optional)

Preheat oven to 325 degrees. In a mixing bowl beat together applesauce, vegetable oil, eggs, and water. Add flour, baking soda, baking powder, nutmeg, and cinnamon. Beat well. Stir in chopped apple and cranberries. Spoon batter into a greased and floured 9x5x3-inch loaf pan. Spread batter evenly in pan. Bake for 40 to 45 minutes or until a toothpick inserted into the center comes out clean. Cool on a wire rack. Serve plain or top each slice with softened cream cheese.

Jeanne Arnoldy
Littleton, Colorado

Yield: 6 servings

Pumpkin Bread

- 1 1/2 cups sugar
- 1/2 cup vegetable oil
- 1/2 cup water
- 2 eggs, beaten
- 1 cup canned pumpkin
- 1 teaspoon salt
- 1/2 teaspoon ground cinnamon
- 1/2 teaspoon ground cloves
- 1/2 teaspoon ground nutmeg
- 2 1/2 cups flour
- 1 teaspoon baking powder
- 1 teaspoon baking soda
- nuts (optional)

Preheat oven to 350 degrees. In a large bowl mix sugar, vegetable oil, water, eggs, canned pumpkin, salt, cinnamon, cloves, and nutmeg. Sift together and add flour, baking powder, and baking soda. Mix in nuts. Spray loaf pan with non-stick cooking spray and pour mixture into pan. Bake for 1 hour.

Notes:
This is a very old family recipe that started with Grandma Irene from Nebraska, the great sewer and quilter in the family. She made this bread every Christmas for each member of the family.

Barbara Dyer
Fort Collins, Colorado

Yield: 1 loaf

Orange Glazed Pumpkin Bread

Bread:
- 1 1/2 cups sugar
- 1 3/4 cups flour
- 1/2 teaspoon baking powder
- 1 teaspoon baking soda
- 1 teaspoon salt
- 1 teaspoon ground cloves
- 1 teaspoon ground cinnamon
- 2 eggs
- 1/2 cup vegetable oil
- 1/2 cup water
- 1 cup cooked, mashed pumpkin (can use canned)
- 1/2 cup pecans, chopped

Glaze:
- 1 cup powdered sugar, sifted
- 2 tablespoons orange juice

Preheat oven to 325 degrees. Mix all ingredients for the bread, except the nuts, until just moistened and then add the nuts. Bake the bread in a greased, floured 9x5x3-inch loaf pan for 1 hour or until done. While the bread is baking, mix the ingredients for the glaze. Cool the bread for 5 minutes and remove from the pan. While the bread is still hot, pour the glaze over the bread.

Mae Jane Keller
Aurora, Colorado

Yield: 1 loaf

Peachy Peach Bread

Bread:
- 1 1/2 cups flour
- 3/4 teaspoon salt
- 1/2 teaspoon baking soda
- 1 cup sugar
- 2 eggs or 1/2 cup egg substitute
- 1/2 cup vegetable oil
- 1 1/4 cups chopped ripe peaches
- 1 teaspoon vanilla extract
- 1 teaspoon almond extract
- 1/4 cup chopped toasted almonds

Glaze:
- 1 cup sifted powdered sugar
- 1/4 teaspoon almond extract
- 2 tablespoons fresh orange juice

Preheat oven to 350 degrees. Mix the flour, salt, baking soda, and sugar in a large bowl. Make a well in the center and add the eggs and vegetable oil; stir until just moistened. Mix the peaches and extracts and add to the other ingredients. Stir until all ingredients are moistened, but do not over mix. Stir in nuts. Pour into greased and floured 9x5x3-inch loaf pan and bake for 1 hour. While bread is baking, mix the glaze ingredients. Cool the bread for 5 minutes. Remove bread from pan. While the bread is still hot, with a fork poke holes into the bread and pour glaze over bread.

Mae Jane Keller
Aurora, Colorado

Yield: 1 loaf

Poppy Seed Tea Bread

Bread:
- 3 cups flour
- 1 1/2 teaspoons baking powder
- 1 teaspoon salt
- 3 eggs
- 1 1/2 cups milk
- 1 1/8 cups vegetable oil
- 2 1/3 cups sugar
- 1 1/2 tablespoons poppy seeds
- 1 1/2 teaspoons butter-flavored extract
- 1 1/2 teaspoons almond extract
- 1 1/2 teaspoons vanilla

Glaze:
- 2/3 cup sugar
- 1/4 cup orange juice
- 1/2 teaspoon butter-flavored extract
- 1/2 teaspoon vanilla
- 1/2 teaspoon almond extract

Preheat oven to 350 degrees. For bread, in a separate bowl, mix flour, baking powder, and salt. In a large bowl, beat eggs. Add milk, vegetable oil, sugar, poppy seeds, butter-flavored extract, almond extract, and vanilla, blending well. Add dry ingredients and mix well. Bake in two greased and floured loaf pans for 45 minutes. For glaze, combine all ingredients and boil until sugar is dissolved. While bread is still hot and in pans, prick bread generously with a toothpick and pour glaze over bread. Let cool 10 minutes and then remove from pans and cool completely.

Notes:
You can also use five mini-loaf pans or one bundt pan instead of the two loaf pans mentioned above.

Judy Brim
Steamboat Springs, Colorado

Yield: 2 loaves

Zucchini Bread

- 3 eggs
- 1 cup vegetable oil
- 1 1/2 cups sugar
- 1 teaspoon vanilla
- 3 cups sifted flour
- 1 teaspoon salt
- 3 teaspoons ground cinnamon
- 1 teaspoon baking soda
- 2 cups grated zucchini
- 1/2 cup chopped walnuts or pecans

Preheat oven to 350 degrees. Mix eggs, vegetable oil, and sugar together in a large bowl. Stir in vanilla. In a separate bowl, mix flour, salt, cinnamon, and baking soda. Stir flour mixture and grated zucchini alternately into the egg mixture. Stir in nuts. Pour into two greased 8 1/2 x 4 1/2-inch loaf pans and bake for 60 minutes. Cool on wire rack for 5 minutes. Turn out of pans and cool completely.

Linda Pace
Grand Junction, Colorado

Yield: 2 loaves

Whole Wheat Banana Bread

- 1 cup sugar
- 1/2 cup (1 stick) butter or margarine, melted
- 2 eggs, slightly beaten
- 1 cup (2 to 3) bananas, mashed
- 1/3 cup water
- 1 cup white flour
- 1 cup whole wheat flour
- 1 teaspoon baking soda
- 1 teaspoon salt
- 1/2 cup chopped walnuts (optional)

Preheat oven to 350 degrees. Cream sugar and margarine. Add eggs, bananas, and water. Mix well. Combine dry ingredients. Stir into banana mixture, mixing well. Add nuts if desired. Pour into greased and lightly floured 9x5x3-inch loaf pan. Bake for 50 to 55 minutes. Cool for 10 minutes, then remove from pan.

Evelyn Scott
Elizabeth, Colorado

Yield: 1 loaf

Eggnog Quick Bread

- 2 eggs
- 1 cup sugar
- 1 cup dairy eggnog (not canned)
- 1/2 cup (1 stick) butter or margarine, melted
- 2 teaspoons rum extract
- 1 teaspoon vanilla
- 2 1/4 cups flour
- 2 teaspoons baking powder
- 1/2 teaspoon salt
- 1/4 teaspoon ground nutmeg

Preheat oven to 350 degrees. Grease bottom only of 9x5x3-inch loaf pan. In a large bowl beat eggs. Add sugar, eggnog, margarine, rum extract, and vanilla; blend well. Lightly spoon flour into measuring cup; level off. Add flour, baking powder, salt, and nutmeg to moist ingredients. Stir just until dry ingredients are moistened. Pour into greased pan. Bake for 45 to 50 minutes. Cool 10 minutes. Remove from pan. Cool completely.

Lori Erickson
Denver, Colorado

Yield: 1 loaf

Rosemary Focaccia

1 loaf frozen white bread dough
3 tablespoons olive oil (approximately)
   cornmeal
   kosher salt
   fresh rosemary

Early in day, set frozen bread dough out to rise, covered loosely with a clean dish towel. When dough has doubled in size, place on a greased pizza pan or cookie sheet and work the dough gently with fingertips toward edges of pan. Sprinkle dough with cornmeal to make it easier to work. Prick the dough all over with a fork, then brush with olive oil. Sprinkle with salt and rosemary leaves. Bake in a preheated 400-degree oven until golden brown, about 15 minutes. Serve hot.

Barb Durland
Aurora, Colorado

Yield: 4 to 5 servings

Oatmeal Honey Bread
(Bread Machine)

  2 tablespoons butter or margarine, softened
  1 cup warm milk
  1 egg
  2 tablespoons honey
  1 cup uncooked oatmeal
1 1/2 cups flour
  1 teaspoon salt
1 1/2 teaspoon yeast

Place butter, milk, egg, and honey in bottom of the pan of your bread machine. Add oatmeal, flour, salt, and yeast. Bake according to manufacturer's instructions, selecting the light setting for the crust.

Susan Ragan
Salida, Colorado

Yield: 1 pound loaf

Best-Ever Dinner Rolls

- 3/4 cup warm water
- 1 package dry yeast
- 1/4 cup vegetable shortening
- 1/4 cup sugar
- 1 teaspoon salt
- 1 egg
- 2 1/2 cups flour, divided
-   margarine, softened

Dissolve yeast in warm water. Add vegetable shortening, sugar, salt, egg, and 1 cup of the flour. Beat until well blended. Stir in remainder of flour until mixed well. Dough will be sticky.

Cover with waxed paper and a cloth; let rise in a warm place until doubled—about 1 hour. Stir down by beating 25 strokes (or less). Turn dough out onto well-floured board. Roll into rectangle about 10x18 inches. Spread with softened margarine. Fold over so dough measures about 5x18 inches and cut into 3/4-inch strips. Twist strips and tie into knot. Place on a greased cookie sheet. Let rise until doubled—45 minutes to 1 hour. Bake in a preheated 375-degree oven for 20 minutes.

Variations:
This recipe makes excellent cinnamon rolls. Add sugar and cinnamon after spreading with margarine.

Notes:
You can shape these into any shape you desire.

Alice Griggs
Grand Junction, Colorado

Yield: 24 rolls

Family Reunion Rolls

- ²/₃ cup milk
- ²/₃ cup sugar
- ¹/₄ teaspoon salt
- ¹/₂ teaspoon ground nutmeg
- ¹/₃ cup butter or margarine, softened
- ²/₃ cup warm water
- 2 packages yeast
- 3 eggs
- 6³/₄ cups flour

Scald milk. Add sugar, salt, nutmeg, and margarine. Cool. Soften yeast in warm water. Add eggs, then the milk mixture, stirring well. Add flour 1 cup at a time and mix well. Knead until elastic. Place dough in a greased bowl and cover with a clean towel. Set aside to rise until doubled in size. Punch down. Divide into 24 equal pieces and place on a greased cookie sheet 2 inches apart. Cover with towel and let rise until doubled. Bake in a preheated 400-degree oven for 20 minutes.

Rita Hildred
Laporte, Colorado

Yield: 2 dozen

Landin's Pretzels

- 1¼ teaspoons dry yeast
- ¾ cup lukewarm water
- 1½ cups flour
- 1 teaspoon sugar
- ½ teaspoon salt
- 1 egg
- salt

Preheat oven to 450 degrees. In one bowl combine yeast and warm water. In a second bowl combine flour, sugar, and ½ teaspoon salt. Gradually add the flour to water and yeast mixture, mixing thoroughly after each addition. Let rise until doubled in size. Roll into eight 1-foot strands; fold into pretzel shape. Brush each pretzel with egg and sprinkle with salt. Bake 8 minutes.

Notes:
Recipe was given to me by my 12-year-old son.

Deana Lovelace
Littleton, Colorado

Yield: 8 pretzels

8:30 a.m. Bread

- 7 1/2 teaspoons (3 packages) yeast
- 2 2/3 cups warm water (120 to 140 degrees)
- 5 1/2 cups white bread flour
- 1 cup whole wheat flour
- 1/4 to 1/2 cup 7-grain cereal
- 3 tablespoons sugar
- 4 scant teaspoons salt
- 1/3 cup butter or margarine, softened

Dissolve yeast in warm water. In a separate bowl combine white flour, wheat flour, cereal, sugar, and salt. Add softened butter to the water and dissolved yeast. Start dough hook and add flour mixture 1 cup at a time. Knead 10 minutes with dough hook. Place the dough in a greased bowl and cover with plastic wrap. Let rise until doubled in size. Cut dough in half. On a floured surface, roll each half out and roll up to place into two greased loaf pans. Brush with vegetable oil and cover with plastic wrap. Refrigerate at least 2 hours. Dough should double in size. Bake in a preheated 350-degree oven for 35 minutes.

Jeanene Nehren
Aurora, Colorado

Yield: 2 loaves

Two-Hour French Bread

 6 cups unsifted flour
 2 packages yeast
 3 tablespoons sugar
 1 tablespoon salt
 1/4 cup plus 2 tablespoons vegetable shortening
 2 1/2 cups warm water
  garlic powder or sesame seeds

Combine all ingredients in a large bowl; stir vigorously and let rest in a warm place for 10 minutes, covered. Stir by hand 75 strokes. Repeat this resting and stirring five times.

Turn out onto a floured board and divide into two pieces. With your hand, pat out the first piece to about 1/2-inch thickness. Cut into three strips, leaving the dough at the top uncut. Braid, being careful not to stretch the dough. Place in a greased 9x13x2-inch pan. Repeat with the other piece and put it in the same pan. Let rise, covered, in a warm place until doubled in size.

Brush with milk and sprinkle with garlic powder or sesame seeds. Bake in a preheated 400-degree oven for 25 to 30 minutes until golden brown.

Nancy Orth
Kiowa, Colorado

Yield: 2 loaves

Pretzels

　　1　package dry yeast
1 1/2　cups lukewarm water
　　1　teaspoon salt
　　2　teaspoons sugar
　　2　tablespoons vegetable oil
　　4　cups flour
　　1　egg, beaten
　　　　coarse salt

Dissolve yeast in water. Stir in salt, sugar, and vegetable oil. Gradually mix in flour. Knead dough until smooth, about 5 minutes. Cover and let rise in a warm place until doubled in bulk, 40 to 50 minutes. Punch dough down and cut into 12 equal pieces. Roll dough between hands into 20-inch ropes. Arrange ropes into pretzel shapes and place on a greased cookie sheet. Brush pretzels with beaten egg. Sprinkle coarse salt on pretzels. Cover and let rise in a warm place until doubled in bulk, 40 to 50 minutes. Bake in a preheated 425-degree oven until browned, about 20 minutes. Best when served warm.

Notes:
When covering dough to rise or let chill, spray a non-stick cooking spray on the plastic wrap before placing it over the container holding the dough. This will make it easy to remove the plastic wrap after the dough has risen.

Toni Fitzwater
Pine, Colorado

Yield: 12 pretzels

Whole Wheat Bread

   1/4 cup blackstrap molasses
   1/4 cup honey
     1 cup hot water
     2 cups warm milk
     2 tablespoons granular yeast
1/2 to 3/4 cup mashed potatoes
   1/4 cup vegetable oil
     2 eggs
     2 teaspoons salt
     2 cups bread flour
     2 cups soy flour
3 to 4 cups whole wheat flour
1 to 2 cups white or unbleached all-purpose flour

In a small saucepan, heat molasses, honey, water, and milk. Pour into a large mixer bowl, allow to cool to lukewarm.

Stir in yeast. Allow to stand about 10 minutes or until mixture foams well. If no foam appears, throw it out and start over.

Warm mashed potatoes and vegetable oil slightly in microwave oven. Add to yeast mixture with eggs and salt. Mix well.

Sift bread flour into mixture. Add soy flour. Stir, then beat thoroughly for 3 to 4 minutes until very smooth.

Beat in whole wheat flour, 1 cup at a time, until dough is too stiff for mixer to handle. Switch to dough kneading hook or turn out on floured board and begin kneading by hand.

Continue to knead well, adding all-purpose flour as needed to control stickiness. Knead until you can't knead in any more flour.

Turn dough into a large oiled bowl. Cover loosely with a large sheet of oiled aluminum foil. Let rise in a warm place for about 1 hour or until at least doubled in size.

(continued)

Whole Wheat Bread
(continued)

Turn out on floured board and knead well. Let rest, covered with foil, for 5 to 10 minutes. Grease three 9x5x3-inch loaf pans. Divide dough evenly among the pans. Shape into nice loaves; grease the tops well. Cover loosely with foil and let rise for about 30 minutes. Do not allow to over rise.

Bake uncovered in a preheated 350 degree oven for 15 minutes.

Due to the sweetness of the dough, tops will be very brown at this point. Cover loosely with the foil and continue baking for another 15 minutes.

Remove from oven. Allow to set for 5 minutes. Turn out onto a cooling rack. Try not to cut for at least 15 minutes (hah!). Allow to cool completely before wrapping in plastic.

Martha Thompson
Lakewood, Colorado

Yield: 3 medium loaves

Refrigerator Rolls

2	cups lukewarm water or potato water
1	package dry yeast
1/2	cup sugar
1/2	cup vegetable shortening
1 1/2	teaspoons salt
2	eggs, beaten
6 to 6 1/2	cups flour, divided

Dissolve yeast in water. Combine all other ingredients, using only 2 to 3 cups of flour and beat 6 to 8 minutes with mixer. This cuts down on kneading time. Knead, gradually adding remaining flour. Put into greased bowl. Cover and let rise until doubled in bulk. Make into crescent rolls, cinnamon rolls, buns, or even raised doughnuts. Let rise again. Bake in a preheated 375-degree oven for 12 or more minutes, until brown.

Notes:
Remaining dough can be refrigerated for a couple of days, allowing you to make fresh rolls for dinner another night.

If you make crescent rolls, spread with butter prior to cutting into shape. All who have used this recipe claim it is great.

Ruth Rupert
Denver, Colorado

Soups, Salads, Vegetables, Side Dishes

Special Notes:

Fired-Up Chili

- 4 slices bacon
- 2 pounds sirloin steak, cut into small pieces
- 2 medium onions, diced
- 1 clove garlic, finely chopped
- 2 14½-ounce cans stewed tomatoes
- 1 8-ounce can tomato sauce
- 1 7-ounce can diced green chilies
- 1 12-ounce can beer
- ½ teaspoon red cayenne
- 1 teaspoon crushed dried red pepper
- 1 tablespoon chili powder
- ½ teaspoon thyme
- salt and pepper, to taste
- 1 teaspoon ground oregano
- 1 30-ounce can pinto beans

Dice bacon. Place in a soup pot or Dutch oven and brown. Place cooked bacon on a paper towel. In bacon drippings, brown sirloin steak, onions, and garlic. Add tomatoes, tomato sauce, green chilies, beer, cayenne, dried red pepper, chili powder, thyme, salt, pepper, oregano, and pinto beans. Heat to medium, stirring often. Then lower heat and simmer for 2 hours, stirring occasionally.

Notes:
This recipe cooks itself while you quilt! Stir occasionally and — voilá!—lunch is ready.

Diane Schlagel
Strasberg, Colorado

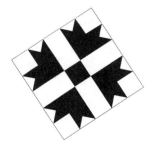

Big D's Famous Chili

- 3 tablespoons butter or margarine
- 3 tablespoons olive oil
- 1 cup chopped celery
- 2 large onions, chopped
- 1 tablespoon crushed garlic
- 1 28-ounce can crushed tomatoes
- 1 teaspoon salt
- 1 tablespoon plus 1 teaspoon chili powder
- 2 large bay leaves
- 6 whole allspice
- 1 teaspoon oregano
- 1/2 teaspoon coarse ground pepper
- 1/4 teaspoon powdered cumin
- 1 30-ounce can pinto beans with juice
- 1 30-ounce can kidney beans with juice
- 1 4-ounce can chopped chili peppers
- rice, prepared according to package directions
- grated cheese

In a heavy deep pan, heat butter and olive oil together. Sauté celery, onions, and garlic. When the onions are translucent, add the tomatoes and spices. Stir thoroughly. Add remaining ingredients. Bring to boil. Simmer uncovered for 1 to 1 1/2 hours. Stir frequently. Serve over rice and top with grated cheese.

Notes:
My husband gave this name to my chili concoction shortly after we were married. It is a real crowd pleaser.

Delia Molloy da Cunha
Boulder, Colorado

New Mexico Chile Verde
(Green Chili)

2	tablespoons olive oil or vegetable oil
¼ to ½	small onion, chopped
1	large garlic clove, chopped
2	tablespoons flour
¼	teaspoon ground cumin
¼	teaspoon black pepper
1½	cups chicken broth
1	8-ounce can green chilies, chopped
¼	teaspoon oregano
½	teaspoon salt
2	teaspoons or more chopped jalapeños for added heat (optional)

Heat the olive oil in a 1- to 2-quart saucepan over medium heat. Add the onion and garlic. Cover and cook over low heat for 5 minutes to wilt the onions. Do not brown. Raise the heat to medium and stir in the flour, cumin, and pepper. Cook, stirring, for 2 minutes. If the onions ball up, don't worry. As the onion mixture begins to color, remove pan from heat and gradually pour in the stock. Stir to prevent lumps. I use a wire whisk.

Add all the remaining ingredients. Put pan back on the heat and bring to the boiling point, but do not boil. Reduce heat to low, cover pan, and simmer for 30 minutes. Stir occasionally. Use at once or can be put in the refrigerator for up to 1 week.

Notes:
I use the Chile Verde for any meal of the day. It is great over eggs for breakfast or to use in your favorite Mexican recipe.

Jan DeBellis
Woodland Park, Colorado

Chicken Chili

Chili:
- vegetable oil
- 1 double boneless chicken breast, cubed
- 1/2 medium onion, chopped
- 1 14 1/2-ounce can chicken broth
- 1 4-ounce can diced green chilies
- 1 teaspoon garlic powder
- 1 teaspoon ground cumin
- 1/2 teaspoon crushed oregano leaves
- 1/2 teaspoon cilantro (optional)
- 1 19-ounce can white kidney beans (cannellini)
- 1 15-ounce can white corn (optional)

Garnishes:
- shredded Monterey Jack cheese
- diced green onion

In a non-stick pan, pour a small amount of vegetable oil. Sauté cubed chicken breast and onion until lightly browned—5 minutes. Add chicken broth, green chilies, garlic powder, cumin, oregano, and cilantro. Simmer 20 minutes. Add white kidney beans and corn. Simmer 10 minutes. Serve with Monterey Jack cheese and onions as garnishes.

June Staab
Longmont, Colorado

White Chili

1	pound dried great northern white beans
3 to 4	chicken breasts (to yield 4 cups cubed cooked chicken)
1	tablespoon olive oil
2	medium onions, chopped
4	garlic cloves, minced
2	4-ounce cans chopped green chilies
2	teaspoons ground cumin
1 1/2	teaspoons dried oregano, crumbled
1/4	teaspoon cayenne pepper
6	cups chicken stock
3	cups grated Monterey Jack cheese, divided
	salt and pepper
	sour cream

Place rinsed beans in a large heavy pot. Add enough cold water to cover beans by at least 3 inches and soak overnight. Place uncooked chicken breasts in another saucepan. Add cold water to cover and bring to simmer. Cook until just tender—about 15 minutes. Drain and cool. Remove skin. Cut into cubes.

Drain beans and reserve in another container. Heat olive oil in same pot over medium-high heat. Add onions and sauté until translucent—about 10 minutes. Stir in garlic, chilies, cumin, oregano, and cayenne. Sauté 2 minutes. Add beans and stock and bring to a boil. Reduce heat, simmer uncovered until beans are very tender, stirring occasionally, about 2 hours. Add chicken and 1 cup cheese to chili and stir until cheese melts. Season to taste with salt and pepper. Ladle chili into bowls. Serve with remaining cheese and sour cream on top.

Sharon Hoffman
Charlotte, North Carolina

New England Clam Chowder

- 8 medium to large potatoes, peeled and cut into cubes
- 2 tablespoons lemon juice
- 4 tablespoons butter or margarine
- 4 tablespoons olive oil
- 1 large onion, halved and thinly sliced
- 1 teaspoon crushed garlic
- 4 tablespoons flour
- 2 cups cream
- 1 10-ounce can baby clams with juice
- 1 8-ounce bottle clam juice (optional)
- 1 8-ounce can mushrooms
- 1 1/2 teaspoons salt
- 1/4 teaspoon fresh ground pepper
- 1/2 teaspoon crushed thyme
- 1/2 teaspoon crushed basil
- 1/2 teaspoon crushed marjoram
- 1/2 teaspoon crushed dried parsley
- 1/2 teaspoon crushed oregano

In a large pot, boil potatoes with lemon juice in water. Melt butter and olive oil together in a Dutch oven. Sauté onion and garlic until translucent. Slowly add flour, mix thoroughly and allow mixture to boil gently for a few minutes. Slowly add cream, stirring until smooth with each addition. Add clams with juice, optional additional clam juice, mushrooms, and spices. **Reduce heat; do not let this boil.** Add potatoes with their liquid. Heat just until potatoes are warm.

Notes:
This soup has been called "divine" by needle workers stitching in its aroma. Enjoy!

Delia Molloy da Cunha
Boulder, Colorado

Harvest Corn Chowder

- 1 medium onion, chopped
- 1 tablespoon margarine
- 2 14$^{1}/_{2}$-ounce cans cream-style corn
- 4 cups whole-kernel corn
- 1 10$^{3}/_{4}$-ounce can cream of mushroom soup
- 1 6-ounce jar sliced mushrooms, drained
- 4 cups diced peeled potatoes
- 3 cups milk
- $^{1}/_{2}$ medium green sweet pepper, chopped
- $^{1}/_{2}$ to 1 medium red sweet pepper, chopped
- pepper, to taste
- $^{1}/_{2}$ pound bacon, cooked and crumbled

Sauté onion in butter until tender. Add cream-style corn, corn kernels, soup, mushrooms, and potatoes. Stir in milk. Add green sweet and red sweet peppers. Season with pepper. Simmer 30 minutes or until vegetables are tender. Garnish with bacon.

Notes:
I do not peel the potatoes; just scrub them and then dice them. Skim milk works well in this recipe.

Gail Tibbetts
Denver, Colorado

Yield: 3$^{1}/_{2}$ Quarts—12 servings

Bear's Paw Black Bean Soup

- 1/2 pound black beans
- 4 tablespoons extra-virgin olive oil
- 1/3 cup chopped red onion, divided
- 1 jalapeño pepper, seeded and chopped
- 2 cloves garlic, chopped
- 2 tablespoons minced fresh coriander, divided
- 1/2 tablespoon ground cumin
- 8 ounces medium to dark beer
- 2 quarts chicken stock or water (approximately)
- salt and freshly ground pepper
- 2 tablespoons diced fresh tomato for garnish
- 2 tablespoons diced avocado for garnish
- 2 tablespoons fresh corn kernels for garnish
- 3 tablespoons creme fraiche or sour cream

Soak beans in water for 2 hours. In a heavy 4- to 5-quart soup pot, heat the olive oil. Sauté 1/4 cup onion, jalapeño pepper, and garlic for 1 minute. Add 1 tablespoon coriander and the cumin, sauté 30 seconds longer, then add the beer and stock. Drain the beans and add them to the onion mixture. Bring to a slow boil and cook for 45 minutes to 1 hour, until the beans are tender. Drain the beans, reserving the liquid. Return the liquid to the soup pot. Purée the beans in a food processor, then force through a sieve, or purée the beans in a food mill. Season to taste with salt and pepper. Return the pureed beans to the soup pot and stir into the liquid. Reheat. Serve garnished with remaining chopped red onion and coriander, tomato, avocado, corn, and creme fraiche.

Teresa Mensch
Evergreen, Colorado

Yield: 6 to 8 servings

Cuban Style Black Bean Soup

      1 pound dried black beans
6 to 8 cups hot water
      1 pound bacon, fried crisp and crumbled
      2 ham hocks or a ham bone
      1 large onion, diced
    1/2 teaspoon bottled hot pepper sauce
    3/4 teaspoon cayenne pepper
    1/4 teaspoon black pepper
      1 teaspoon salt

Rinse and sort beans carefully. Soak beans overnight; drain. Place beans in a large pot with hot water, bacon, ham hocks or bone, onion, hot pepper sauce, cayenne pepper, black pepper, and salt. Boil gently with lid tilted until beans are tender—2 to 3 hours. Add water if needed. Remove from heat, break ham into small pieces, and remove bones. Put half of the bean/meat mixture into a blender and purée. Return purée to remaining mixture. Stir and heat a few minutes and enjoy.

Variations:
For Cajun Style Black Bean Soup, double the onion, hot pepper sauce, cayenne pepper, and black pepper. Very spicy!

Notes:
Reheats well. Can be frozen.

Gwen Lark
Arvada, Colorado

White Bean and Roasted Tomato Soup

- 1/2 cup dried small white beans, such as Great Northern
- 3 cups defatted reduced-sodium chicken stock
- 1 1/2 teaspoons chopped fresh thyme or 1/2 teaspoon dried thyme leaves
- 2 pounds plum tomatoes (about 12 to 15), halved and seeded
- 5 cloves garlic, minced
- 1 1/2 tablespoons olive oil
- 1/4 cup dry vermouth
- 1 tablespoon chopped fresh sage or 1 teaspoon dried rubbed sage
- 1/2 teaspoon sugar
- salt and freshly ground black pepper to taste

Place beans in a medium-sized saucepan with water to cover by 1 inch. Bring to a simmer over high heat. Reduce heat to low and cook for 2 minutes. Cover, remove from heat, and let stand for 1 hour. Drain, return beans to the saucepan, add chicken stock and thyme, and bring to a simmer. Reduce heat to low, cover, and cook until the beans are tender, 30 to 40 minutes.

Arrange tomato halves in a single layer, cut side up in a 9x13x2-inch baking dish. Scatter garlic over the top and drizzle with olive oil.

Bake the tomatoes in a preheated 325-degree oven for 1 1/4 to 1 1/2 hours, brushing them with pan juices occasionally, until the tomatoes are shriveled and beginning to brown. Let cool 10 minutes. Slip off and discard skins. Dice six of the tomato halves and reserve.

Place the remaining tomatoes in a food processor or blender. With a slotted spoon, remove 3/4 cup of the beans and add them to the processor or

(continued)

White Bean and Roasted Tomato Soup
(continued)

blender along with a little of the bean cooking liquid. Purée until smooth. Transfer the purée to the saucepan with the beans and add the reserved diced tomatoes, vermouth, sage, and sugar. Bring to a simmer and cook for 3 minutes. Season with salt and pepper to taste.

Notes:
The soup can be made up to 2 days ahead and stored, covered, in the refrigerator.

Teresa Mensch
Evergreen, Colorado

Yield: 4 servings (about 4$^{1}/_{2}$ cups)

Broccoli Cream Soup

  1 10-ounce package frozen chopped broccoli
1/2 cup frozen chopped onions
  1 cup condensed chicken broth
  2 tablespoons butter or margarine
  2 tablespoons flour
  2 cups half and half
  1 teaspoon salt
1/2 teaspoon finely crumbled basil
1/8 teaspoon white pepper
     sliced almonds

In a saucepan, combine broccoli, onions, and chicken broth. Heat to boiling. Reduce heat and simmer for 5 minutes. Turn into blender jar and blend until smooth. Melt margarine and stir in flour until smooth. Add broccoli mixture, half and half, salt, basil, and pepper to melted margarine mixture. Heat slowly—just to boiling. Reduce heat immediately and simmer 1 minute, stirring constantly. Top each serving with a sprinkling of sliced almonds.

Variations:
For fewer fat grams, use 2 cups evaporated skim milk in place of half and half.

Notes:
This is an elegant soup. Great as a beginning to a meal or a light main course.

Fran von Hagel
Longmont, Colorado

Yield: 4 1/3 cups—4 servings

Broccoli Cheese Soup

- 6 slices bacon
- 1/4 cup chopped onion
- 1/2 cup chopped celery
- 3 cups chicken broth
- 1 cup thinly sliced carrots
- 1 1/2 cups chopped broccoli
- 3 cups milk
- 3/4 cup sliced mushrooms
- 1/2 teaspoon salt
- 1/4 teaspoon pepper
- 8 ounces shredded Cheddar cheese

Fry bacon until crisp; remove from pan and crumble; set aside. Drain fat, leaving 2 tablespoons. Add onion and celery; sauté until soft.

In large pot combine onion, celery, and chicken broth. Add carrots and broccoli. Cover and simmer 15 minutes or until vegetables are tender. Add milk, mushrooms, salt, pepper, and cheese. Cook over medium heat until hot, stirring occasionally. Add crumbled bacon and serve.

Notes:
This is one of my family's favorite soup recipes.

Verna Mullet
Fort Lupton, Colorado

Yield: 6 servings

Baked Potato Soup

Soup:
- 1 cup (2 sticks) butter or margarine
- 2 tablespoons bacon grease
- 2 onions, diced
- 1/2 cup flour
- 3 cups chicken broth
- 8 oven-baked potatoes, peeled and diced (can leave the skins on)
- 1 pound processed cheese
- 1 pint whipping cream

Garnishes:
- grated Cheddar
- green onions, cut up in small pieces
- crumbled cooked bacon
- sour cream

In a large pot, melt the butter and bacon grease. Cook the onion in the butter mixture until the onion is soft. Mix flour and enough broth to make a paste. Then add paste and broth to onions and cook until thickened. Then add the potatoes, cheese, and whipping cream. Heat to serving temperature.

Notes:
The soup can be garnished with Cheddar cheese, green onions, crumbled bacon, and a dollop of sour cream in individual serving bowls.

Sue Peters
Montrose, Colorado

Zucchini Soup

- 5 medium zucchini, cut in 1-inch pieces
- 1 large yellow onion, chopped
- 2 tablespoons butter or margarine
- 6 cups water
- 9 chicken bouillon cubes
- 1/2 cup milk
- 1 teaspoon soy sauce
- freshly ground pepper

Sauté zucchini and onion in butter in a large soup pan. Add water and bouillon cubes. Cook 20 minutes. Purée in blender with milk. Add soy sauce and season with ground pepper.

Notes:
We love this with quiche or a fresh salad and homemade bread.

Charlotte Seaton
Fort Lupton, Colorado

Yield: 8 servings

Hamburger Vegetable Soup

   2 tablespoons butter or margarine
   1 onion, chopped
   1 pound ground beef
1 1/2 teaspoons salt
   1 cup diced carrots
 1/2 cup chopped celery
   1 cup diced potatoes
   2 cups tomato juice
   2 cups milk
 1/4 cup flour

Brown meat and onion in butter. Add remaining ingredients except milk and flour and cook until vegetables are tender. Combine milk and flour and stir until smooth. Add to soup and cook until thickened.

Sherry Barber
Lafayette, Colorado

Yield: 4 to 6 servings

Portuguese Sausage Soup

- 1 pound spicy Italian sausage
- 1 pound mild Italian sausage
- 1 cup sliced zucchini
- 1 cup chopped onion
- 1 cup sliced celery
- 1 cup ripe olive wedges
- 3 large potatoes, cut into ½-inch cubes
- 1 18-ounce can whole peeled tomatoes, undrained
- 1 15½-ounce can kidney beans, undrained
- 5 cups water
- 2 teaspoons minced garlic
- 1 teaspoon anise seed
- ½ teaspoon pepper

Remove casings from sausages. Crumble meat into heated Dutch oven. Cook over moderate heat until done. Drain off fat. Add remaining ingredients. Bring to a boil, reduce heat, and simmer, covered, 30 minutes or until vegetables are tender.

Notes:
This is a winter-time favorite meal with pull-apart herb bread and a salad.

Madelyn Gibbs
Wheat Ridge, Colorado

Yield: 8 servings, 2 cups each

Polish Potato Sausage Soup

- 2 tablespoons margarine
- 1 pound kielbasa (Polish) sausage, sliced
- 1 large onion, chopped
- 4 stalks celery, halved lengthwise, then thinly sliced
- 1 medium head green cabbage, shredded
- 4 carrots, peeled and sliced
- 1 bay leaf
- 1/2 teaspoon dried thyme (optional)
- 2 tablespoons vinegar
- salt to taste
- 1 1/2 cups beef bouillon
- 5 cups water
- 3 cups peeled, cubed potatoes

In a large, heavy pot, melt margarine. Add kielbasa, onion, and celery. Sauté until vegetables are tender. Add cabbage, carrots, bay leaf, thyme, vinegar, salt, bouillon, and water. Cover and cook on medium-low heat for 1 1/2 hours. Add potatoes, cover, and cook 20 minutes. Remove bay leaf and serve hot with pumpernickel or rye bread.

Cathy Maurer
Woodland Park, Colorado

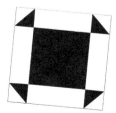

Mexican Hominy Soup

- 1 14-ounce can chicken broth
- 1 28-ounce can diced tomatoes
- 2 cups dried hominy
- 2 cups diced chicken or turkey (raw or cooked)
    small serrano or jalapeño peppers, according to your taste

Include the following spices according to your choice and taste:
- garlic
- ground cumin
- chili powder
- bottled hot pepper sauce
- cilantro
- green onions
- oregano

Place all ingredients in a slow cooker on low setting and cook for 8 to 9 hours.

Notes:
This soup is delicious served with toppings such as chopped onion, cilantro, grated Cheddar cheese, and shredded lettuce.

Jean and Marilyn
Piecemakers Country Store
Ridgeway, Colorado

Scrap Soup

- 1 pound boned chicken breasts
- 1 onion, chopped
- 7 to 8 cups chicken broth
- 8 ounces pasta
- 1 7-ounce can chopped mild green chilies
- "scraps" of your favorite "veggies" (fresh, canned, or frozen)
- 1 bay leaf
- 1/4 teaspoon black pepper
- 1/2 teaspoon celery seeds
- salt to taste

Combine chicken breasts, onion, and broth in a large saucepan. Bring to a boil and simmer for 30 minutes. Remove chicken and cut into chunks. In the large saucepan (or a slow cooker), combine chicken and broth; add spices. Add any "scraps" of the following: celery, carrots, peas, corn, broccoli, tomatoes, cauliflower. The more "scraps," the better! Simmer gently for up to 5 hours. Add water if needed. Twenty minutes before serving, bring 4 quarts of water to a boil. Add pasta. Simmer for 10 minutes; drain. Add cooked pasta to soup and serve.

Variations:
Recipe also works well with turkey breasts, ground beef, ground turkey, or lean sausage.

Notes:
This simmering "scrap soup" provides several hours of stitching time!

Nancy Smith
Denver, Colorado

Oven Soup

- 1 1/2 pounds lean beef stew meat
- 1 cup coarsely chopped onions
- 1 teaspoon minced garlic
- 1 teaspoon salt
- 1/4 teaspoon pepper
- 2 tablespoons olive oil
- 3 10 1/2-ounce cans beef broth
- 2 2/3 cups water
- 1 1/2 teaspoons Italian seasoning
- 1 1-pound can tomatoes, undrained
- 1 15 1/4-ounce can kidney beans, undrained
- 1 1/4 cups pitted canned ripe olives, reserve liquid (can be sliced in half)
- 1 cup liquid from ripe olives
- 1 1/2 cups thinly sliced carrots
- 1 cup small seashell macaroni, uncooked
- 2 cups sliced zucchini
- grated Parmesan cheese for garnish

Preheat oven to 400 degrees. Cut beef into 1 1/4-inch cubes. In an oven-proof Dutch oven mix together beef, onion, garlic, salt, and pepper. Add olive oil and stir to coat meat evenly. Brown meat, uncovered, in preheated oven for about 40 minutes, stirring a couple of times. (Can be browned on top of stove to save time.) Reduce oven heat to 350 degrees and add broth, water, and Italian seasoning. Cover and cook for 1 hour or until meat is almost tender. Remove from oven and stir in tomatoes, beans, olives, olive liquid, and carrots. Add the macaroni and zucchini and cook until macaroni is tender—about 40 to 45 minutes. Serve with grated Parmesan cheese, thick slices of French bread, and a tray of sliced fresh fruit.

Variations:
Cook macaroni and zucchini separately and add when carrots are done.

Marie Stumpf
Denver, Colorado

Yield: 3 1/2 quarts

"Quilt All Day" Stew

- 1 10¾-ounce can tomato soup
- 1 cup red wine
- ¼ cup flour
- 2 pounds stew beef, cut into 1-inch cubes
- 4 large carrots, cut into 1-inch slices
- 1 large white onion, cut into 1-inch chunks
- 6 medium potatoes, cut into 1-inch chunks
- 1 celery stalk, cut into 1-inch slices
- ½ pound fresh, whole mushrooms
- 2 beef bouillon cubes
- 1 teaspoon oregano
- 1 teaspoon thyme
- 1 teaspoon rosemary
- 1 bay leaf
- ½ teaspoon fresh ground black pepper

Preheat oven to 275 degrees. With whisk, blend soup, wine, and flour in a 5-quart casserole. Mix in remaining ingredients. Bake covered for 5 to 6 hours, stirring about once an hour.

Notes:
Since browning the stew beef is unnecessary, preparation time is minimal. This makes an easy, hearty meal served with a green salad and crusty bread.

Sharon Paradis-Sharp
Bailey, Colorado

Yield: 8 servings

Aunt Margaret's French Stew

- 2 pounds beef stew meat, cut in 1-inch cubes
- 1 tablespoon brown sugar
- 1 cup small frozen white onions
- 4 large carrots, cut in 1-inch chunks
- 2½ cups undrained, canned tomatoes
- ½ cup prepared bread crumbs (optional)
- salt and pepper to taste
- 3 large potatoes, cut in 1-inch cubes
- 1 10-ounce package frozen peas
- ½ cup red or white wine
- 1 14½-ounce can beef broth
- 4 tablespoons instant tapioca
- 1 large onion, coarsely chopped
- 1 bay leaf

Preheat oven to 250 degrees. Mix all ingredients in an oven-proof dish. Cover and bake for 6 to 8 hours. Stew may be cooked for a shorter time at a higher temperature (i.e., 4 hours at 300 to 325 degrees). In any case, check for overcooking and stir occasionally.

Notes:
This is the ideal quilter's recipe. Just dump everything in a dish and forget about it. The toughest part is remembering to put it in the oven early enough in the day so you can eat dinner at a decent hour! I was not terribly precise with the measurements. For example, I bought bags of frozen peas and frozen onions and dumped about half a bag in the dish. I did not peel the potatoes or carrots, just scrubbed them well.

Teresa Mensch
Evergreen, Colorado

Yield: 6 to 8 servings

Easy Oven Stew

- 1 pound beef stew meat, cubed
- 1 14$\frac{1}{2}$-ounce can whole potatoes (or 2 to 3 fresh potatoes cut into chunks)
- 1 medium onion, cut into chunks
- 3 carrots, cut into chunks
- 2 stalks celery, cut into chunks
- 1 8-ounce can tomato sauce
- $\frac{1}{4}$ cup beef broth
- 1$\frac{1}{2}$ teaspoons sugar
- $\frac{1}{2}$ teaspoon Italian seasoning
- $\frac{1}{2}$ teaspoon salt
- $\frac{1}{2}$ teaspoon pepper

Preheat oven to 300 degrees. In an oven-proof Dutch oven combine meat, potatoes, onion, carrots, and celery. In a separate container mix together tomato sauce, beef broth, sugar, Italian seasoning, salt, and pepper. Pour over meat and vegetables. Cover and bake for 2$\frac{1}{2}$ to 3 hours or until meat is tender.

Chris Mooney
Longmont, Colorado

Yield: 4 servings

Barley and Black Bean Salad

- 3 cups pearl barley, cooked without salt or fat
- 2 cups drained canned black beans
- 1 1/2 cups frozen whole kernel corn, thawed
- 1 1/2 cups diced tomato
- 1 cup frozen green peas, thawed
- 1 cup peeled, chopped ripe avocado
- 1/4 cup chopped fresh cilantro
- 1/2 teaspoon salt
- 1/4 teaspoon pepper
- 1/2 cup water
- 2 tablespoons fresh lemon juice
- 1 tablespoon grated fresh onion
- 1 tablespoon vegetable oil
- 2 cloves garlic, minced
-   Romaine lettuce leaves
- 18 1/4-inch-thick slices peeled ripe avocado
- 18 1/4-inch-thick slices unpeeled tomato (about 1 medium tomato)

Combine barley, black beans, corn, diced tomato, peas, avocado, cilantro, salt, and pepper; toss gently. Combine water, lemon juice, grated onion, minced garlic, and vegetable oil in a jar. Cover tightly, and shake vigorously. Pour over barley mixture; toss gently. Using a slotted spoon, arrange salad on lettuce-lined plates. Garnish each plate with two avocado slices and two tomato wedges. Serve warm or at room temperature.

Notes:
This is a low-fat recipe. Very tasty. Try adding a squeeze of fresh lemon juice right before serving.

Claudia Kniffin
Littleton, Colorado

Yield: 9 servings

Three-Bean Salad

- 1 teaspoon lime juice
- 3/4 cup thick and chunky salsa
- 1/3 cup vegetable oil
- 1 1/2 teaspoon chili powder
- 2 cups cooked black beans, drained
- 2 cups cooked small red beans, drained
- 2 cups cooked garbanzo beans, drained
- 2 stalks celery, sliced
- 1 medium red onion, sliced or chopped
- 1 medium tomato, diced

One hour before serving or early in the day: In a large bowl, combine lime juice, salsa, vegetable oil, and chili powder. Add beans, celery, onion, and tomato. Toss to mix. Serve at room temperature or cover and chill to serve later.

Bernice Barney
Loveland, Colorado

Yield: 10 servings

Black Bean Salad

- 1 pound dry black beans, sorted and rinsed
- 1/2 teaspoon cayenne, divided
- 2 quarts water
- 1 small red sweet pepper, stemmed, seeded, and finely chopped
- 1/2 cup diagonally sliced green onions
- 2 tablespoons balsamic vinegar
- 1 tablespoon lemon juice
- 1 tablespoon very thinly sliced lemon peel, yellow part only
- 1/2 cup firmly packed cilantro sprigs, chopped
- salt to taste

Combine beans and 1/4 teaspoon of the cayenne and water in a 4- to 5-quart pan. Bring to a boil over high heat. Reduce heat to simmer, cover, and cook until beans are tender, at least 45 minutes. Pour beans into colander, discarding any liquid. Rinse under cold water until water runs clear. Drain well.

Mix remaining 1/4 teaspoon cayenne, red sweet pepper, onions, vinegar, lemon juice, lemon peel, and cilantro with the beans. Add salt to taste. Serve, or cover and refrigerate. Lasts several days.

Variations:
Can substitute red wine vinegar for balsamic vinegar.

Maj-Britt Cawthon
Lakewood, Colorado

Cabbage Salad

Salad:
- ½ head cabbage, shredded
- 3 green onions, chopped (optional)
- 1 package Oriental noodles (Oriental flavor)
- sesame seeds
- slivered almonds

Dressing:
- ½ teaspoon salt
- 3 tablespoons white vinegar
- 2 tablespoons sugar
- ¼ cup vegetable oil
- flavoring packet from Oriental noodle package

Crush dried Oriental noodles and combine with shredded cabbage and onions. Place all dressing ingredients in a jar; cover and shake well. Pour over cabbage mixture and toss salad. Sprinkle sesame seeds and slivered almonds over salad.

Notes:
Serve immediately; it gets soggy if held over.

Libby Lindauer
Littleton, Colorado

Chinese Coleslaw

Salad:
- 1 head of cabbage, shredded
- 1 onion, chopped
- 1 package ramen noodles, uncooked

Dressing:
- 4 tablespoons sugar
- 1 teaspoon salt
- 3/4 cup vegetable oil
- 1 teaspoon pepper
- 5 tablespoons rice vinegar

Place cabbage and onions in a bowl. For dressing, combine all ingredients in a tightly sealed container and shake well. Ten minutes before serving, add dressing and stir well. Just prior to serving, crush ramen noodles (omit flavor packet) and add to cabbage and dressing.

Notes:
Great for a potluck.

Mary Baughn
Fort Collins, Colorado

For your Q-Snap floor frame, use 2 inches of velcro tape. Place the loop side of the velcro on the frame and use long strips of the soft velcro to hold up your excess quilt. Works great!

Sweet and Sour Red Cabbage

- 1 small head red cabbage, thinly sliced
- 1 to 2 tart apples, cored and coarsely chopped
- 1/4 cup cider vinegar
- 1 cup strawberry jam
- 1/4 cup water

Place all ingredients in a large saucepan or slow cooker. Cover and simmer over low heat until the cabbage is tender, about 1 hour, stirring occasionally. May be served hot or cold.

Variations:
Instead of tart apples, use 1/2 cup dried apple slices, cut into 1/2-inch pieces, soaked in water, and then drained.

Can substitute sugar-free jam for regular jam.

Notes:
This is a colorful cold salad to take to a potluck luncheon or picnic. Try using raspberry jam for a slightly different sweet flavor. This keeps well in the refrigerator

Julie Callahan
Buena Vista, Colorado

Take as much time as you need to do it right. If you don't have enough time to do it right the first time, where are you going to find the time to rip it out and do it over?

Spaghetti Salad

      8 ounces spaghetti
          chopped cucumbers
          chopped tomatoes
          chopped broccoli
          chopped cauliflower
          chopped black olives
          small pieces Cheddar cheese
          chopped onion
          chopped mushrooms
$1/2$ to 1 cup Italian dressing

Cook spaghetti and allow to cool. Add vegetables of your choice, selecting the amount to suit your taste. Stir in dressing until mixture is moist and well coated.

Deborah Smith
Greeley, Colorado

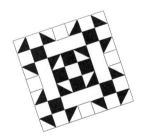

Potsticker Salad

Dressing:
- 1/4 cup sesame oil
- 1/4 cup black soy sauce
- 2 tablespoons sugar
- 1 tablespoon hot chili oil (more if you like it HOT)
- 2 tablespoons balsamic vinegar or black vinegar

Salad:
- 1 1/2 pounds meat-filled ravioli, fresh or frozen
- 2 cups broccoli flowerets
- 1 carrot, peeled, julienned
- 1 large stalk celery, julienned
- 1/2 large red sweet pepper, julienned
- 1/4 cup toasted sesame seeds
- 1/4 cup toasted pine nuts or slivered almonds

Topping:
- 1/4 cup thinly sliced (on the diagonal) green onions
- additional pine nuts or almonds

In a large bowl mix together sesame oil, soy sauce, sugar, chili oil, and vinegar. Cook ravioli until tender; drain well. Toss with dressing and allow to cool to room temperature. You can do this up to a day ahead and hold in refrigerator.

Blanche broccoli in boiling water for 30 to 40 seconds. Drain well and plunge into ice water. When ravioli has cooled, toss with carrot, celery, red sweet pepper, sesame seeds, and nuts. Place in a shallow bowl. Thoroughly drain broccoli and arrange around the edge of bowl or down middle or both. Scatter green onions and additional nuts on top. Serve at room temperature.

Catherine Ilkka
Louisville, Colorado

Yield: 8 to 9 cups

Patchwork Quilt Salad

- 2 cups broccoli flowerets
- 2 cups cauliflower flowerets
- 1 16-ounce package colored spiral noodles
- 3 carrots, sliced into "coins"
- 1/2 6-ounce can small black olives, sliced
- 1 small yellow or zucchini squash, sliced into "coins"
- 1/2 to 1 cup Italian dressing

Microwave broccoli and cauliflower just enough to soften them. The broccoli should be a bright green. Rinse in cold water until broccoli and cauliflower are cool. Chill. Cook noodles according to package directions. Place carrots, black olives, and squash into a bowl. Add cooked noodles and chilled broccoli and cauliflower. Toss with Italian dressing. Chill.

Variations:
Other ingredients you can add are cashews or artichoke hearts.

Debbie Dilley
Gilcrest, Colorado

Fresh Broccoli-Mandarin Salad

- 1 egg, plus 1 egg yolk, lightly beaten
- 1/2 cup sugar
- 1 1/2 teaspoons cornstarch
- 1 teaspoon dry mustard
- 1/4 cup tarragon wine vinegar
- 1/4 cup water
- 3 tablespoons butter or margarine
- 1/2 cup mayonnaise (light is okay)
- 4 cups fresh broccoli flowerets
- 1/2 cup raisins
- 6 slices bacon, cooked and crumbled
- 2 cups sliced fresh mushrooms
- 1/2 cup slivered toasted almonds
- 1 11-ounce can mandarin oranges, drained
- 1/2 red onion, sliced

In top of a double boiler, whisk together eggs, sugar, cornstarch, and mustard. Combine vinegar and water. Slowly pour into egg mixture, whisking constantly. Place over hot water and cook, stirring constantly, until mixture thickens. Remove from heat and stir in butter and mayonnaise. Chill. Toss dressing with remaining ingredients in a bowl.

Notes:
Dressing can be made 2 to 3 days ahead.

Catherine Ilkka
Louisville, Colorado

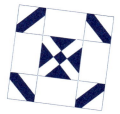

Cauliflower Salad

  1 head lettuce
      cauliflower flowerets
 1/2 purple onion, sliced
  1 cup mayonnaise
  1 teaspoon dijon mustard
  1 2-ounce jar real bacon bits (optional)
 1/4 cup Parmesan cheese

In a straight-sided bowl, tear lettuce into bite-sized pieces. Top with cauliflower flowerets cut into bite-sized pieces. Place sliced purple onion on top of cauliflower. Combine mayonnaise and mustard, mixing well. Spread mixture over onions. Top with bacon bits and Parmesan cheese. Place in refrigerator overnight or for several hours. Before serving, toss until well mixed.

Joyce Smiley
Boulder, Colorado

Wheat Berry Salad Primavera with Dijon Dressing

Salad:
- 1 cup uncooked wheat berries or whole-grain wheat
- 3 cups water
- 1/2 teaspoon salt
- Dijon Dressing (below)
- 1/2 cup frozen green peas, thawed
- 2 tablespoons finely chopped onion
- 1/2 small red sweet pepper, coarsely chopped
- 1 2.5-ounce jar sliced mushrooms, drained

Dressing:
- 1/3 cup vegetable oil
- 2 tablespoons red wine vinegar
- 1 tablespoon Dijon mustard
- 1/4 teaspoon salt
- 1/8 teaspoon red pepper sauce
- 1 clove garlic, crushed

For salad, rinse wheat berries. Heat water and salt to boiling in 3-quart saucepan. Add wheat berries. Heat to boiling, stirring once or twice; reduce heat. Cover and simmer 50 to 60 minutes or until liquid is absorbed and wheat is tender; remove from heat. Let stand 10 minutes.

Prepare Dijon Dressing by combining all ingredients and shaking in a tightly covered container. Mix dressing, wheat berries, and remaining ingredients. Serve warm, or cover and refrigerate about 4 hours or until chilled.

Bernice Barney
Loveland, Colorado

Yield: 6 servings

Quinoa-Almond Salad with Balsamic Vinaigrette

Salad:
- 1 cup uncooked quinoa
- 2 cups water
- 1/2 teaspoon salt
- Balsamic Vinaigrette (below)
- 1/2 cup coarsely shredded carrot (about 1 small)
- 1/4 cup sliced almonds, toasted
- 1/4 cup dried cherries

Vinaigrette:
- 1/4 cup olive or vegetable oil
- 2 tablespoons chopped fresh parsley
- 2 tablespoons balsamic vinegar
- 1/2 teaspoon salt
- dash of pepper

For salad, rinse quinoa. Heat quinoa, water, and salt to boiling in 2-quart saucepan, stirring once or twice; reduce heat. Cover and simmer 12 to 15 minutes; remove from heat. Let stand 5 minutes. Fluff quinoa with fork. Cool 15 minutes.

Prepare Balsamic Vinaigrette by combining all ingredients and shaking in a tightly covered container. Mix vinaigrette, quinoa, and remaining ingredients. Serve warm, or cover and refrigerate about 4 hours or until chilled.

Notes:
Quinoa (pronounced keen-WAH) is a complete protein grain with more protein than any other grain.

Bernice Barney
Loveland, Colorado

Yield: 6 servings

McCarthy's Caesar Salad

- 2 heads crisp romaine lettuce
- 1 1/2 cups croutons, made from French bread
- 1 cup bacon bits, do not use the imitation bacon bits
- 3 cloves (medium-large) fresh garlic
- 3/4 cup olive oil, divided
- 4 anchovy fillets, rolled with capers
- 2 tablespoons worcestershire sauce
- 1/2 teaspoon bottled hot pepper sauce
- 1 teaspoon salt
- 2 teaspoons coarse ground pepper
- 1 teaspoon dry mustard powder
- 1 lemon (medium-large), for juice
- 1 egg
- 1 cup Parmesan cheese

Wash the romaine lettuce and break into small strips. Dry this lettuce very thoroughly (so it will absorb the dressing) and chill in the refrigerator. For the croutons, use French bread, diced large. Fry bacon for bacon bits, reserving the fat. Lightly toast the croutons in the bacon fat. This prevents the croutons from getting soggy.

Mash up the garlic cloves with a little of the olive oil. Add the anchovies (with capers) and mash thoroughly into a paste. This can take a bit of time.* Add worcestershire sauce, hot pepper sauce, salt, pepper, mustard, remainder of the olive oil, juice of the lemon, and egg. Stir thoroughly. When sauce is mixed, add the lettuce, croutons, bacon bits, and Parmesan cheese. Mix thoroughly, making sure the dressing coats the lettuce completely. Serve immediately.

Notes:
It is best to use a wooden bowl for this dressing.
*To save time, mince the anchovies and garlic using a garlic press.
Once the lettuce and dressing are combined, the salad should be served right away. This salad gets soggy quickly.

Jeanne Creighton
Denver, Colorado

Vegetable Salad

- 4 large potatoes, peeled and cut into 1/2-inch cubes
- 2 tablespoons olive oil
- 1/2 teaspoon garlic powder
- 1 teaspoon basil
- 6 medium zucchini, thinly sliced
- 1 pound green beans, cut into 3/4-inch pieces
- 4 large carrots, thinly sliced
- *Piquant Salad Dressing* (page 30)
- Parmesan cheese
- fresh parsley

Simmer potatoes until tender but still firm. Drain and put in a large bowl. Pour olive oil over the potatoes. Sprinkle them with garlic powder and basil. Stir and chill in the refrigerator.

Bring about 1 cup of water to a boil in medium saucepan. Drop zucchini in boiling water all at once. Remove zucchini after 2 minutes. Reserve the hot water. Add zucchini to the potatoes. Chill.

Bring the water to a boil again. Drop green beans in the boiling water. Simmer until just a bit of the crunch remains. Remove green beans. Reserve the hot water. Add green beans to the potatoes and zucchini. Chill.

Bring the water to a boil again. Drop the carrots into the boiling water. Cook until the carrots lose most of their crunch. Remove the carrots. Add to the other vegetables. Chill.

When the mixture is thoroughly chilled, pour about 1/2 cup *Piquant Salad Dressing* over the mixture. Garnish with freshly grated Parmesan cheese and sprigs of fresh parsley.

Delia Molloy da Cunha
Boulder, Colorado

Orange and Romaine Salad

Salad:
- 1/2 cup chopped pecans
- 3 tablespoons sugar
- 1/2 head iceberg lettuce
- 1/2 head romaine lettuce
- 1 cup chopped celery
- 2 green onions, chopped
- 1 11-ounce can mandarin oranges, drained

Dressing:
- 1/2 teaspoon salt
- pepper
- 1/4 cup vegetable oil
- 2 tablespoons sugar
- 2 tablespoons vinegar
- dash of bottled hot pepper sauce

In a small heavy pan over medium heat, cook pecans and sugar, stirring constantly until pecans are coated and sugar dissolved. Cool and store in air-tight container.

For dressing, mix all ingredients and chill.

For salad, break lettuces into bite-sized pieces. Mix lettuces, celery, and onions. Just before serving, add pecans and oranges. Toss with dressing.

Barb Durland
Aurora, Colorado

Yield: 4 to 6 servings

Layered Vegetable Salad with Dressing

Salad:
- 1 head lettuce, broken into bite-sized pieces
- 1 cup diced celery
- 1 cup grated carrots
- 1 10-ounce package frozen peas
- 4 eggs, hard-boiled and chopped
- 8 slices bacon, fried crisp and crumbled
- 1 cup grated cheese

Dressing:
- 1 cup mayonnaise
- 1 cup sour cream
- 2 teaspoons powdered buttermilk salad dressing mix

Layer vegetables in order given. Top with eggs. Toss with dressing. Garnish with bacon and grated cheese. Let stand in refrigerator overnight. Serve with dressing on the side.

To make dressing, combine all ingredients and mix.

Notes:
Be sure to drain the lettuce well.

Pat Rance
Lakewood, Colorado

Yield: 8 servings

Cold Veggie Salad

Salad:
- 1 15-ounce can corn, drained
- 1 15-ounce can peas, drained
- 1 cup chopped celery
- 1 cup chopped red onion
- 1 15-ounce can green beans, drained
- 1 4-ounce can mushrooms, drained
- 1 cup chopped sweet peppers

Dressing:
- 1 teaspoon salt
- 1 cup sugar
- 1/2 teaspoon pepper
- 1/4 cup vinegar
- 1/4 cup vegetable oil

In a large bowl, combine corn, peas, celery, red onion, green beans, mushrooms, and sweet peppers; mix well. For dressing, combine salt, sugar, pepper, vinegar, and vegetable oil in a jar. Put lid tightly on jar and shake well. Pour over vegetables. Marinate in refrigerator overnight.

Notes:
This is an excellent salad to make ahead of time. It keeps well for several days in the refrigerator.

Bev Zabloudil
Buena Vista, Colorado

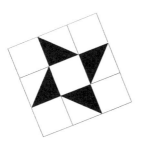

Gazpacho Mold

- 2 tablespoons (2 packets) unflavored gelatin
- 1¼ cups water, divided
- 1 10¾-ounce can tomato soup
- 3 tablespoons olive oil
- 3 tablespoons wine vinegar
- salt, pepper, and bottled hot pepper sauce to taste
- ½ to 1 cup chopped cucumber
- ½ to 1 cup chopped avocado
- ½ to 1 cup chopped tomato
- ½ to 1 cup chopped ripe olives
- ½ to 1 cup chopped green onions

Heat unflavored gelatin with ½ cup water until dissolved. Combine tomato soup, gelatin mixture, remaining ¾ cup of water, olive oil, vinegar, and seasonings. Chill until partially set. Add chopped vegetables and pour into 6- to 8-cup mold. Chill until firmly set.

Variations:
This recipe can be used for a chilled soup by omitting the unflavored gelatin.

Jayne Pritko
Colorado Springs, Colorado

Spinach Salad with Sweet and Sour Dressing

Dressing:
- 3/4 cup sugar
- 1/2 cup vinegar
- 1/2 cup water
- 1 egg, beaten
- 1 teaspoon salt

Salad:
- 1 bunch fresh spinach, cleaned carefully
- 2 eggs, hard boiled, sliced
- 1 red onion, cut into rings
- 1/4 pound bacon, cooked and broken into small pieces
- 1/4 6-ounce box croutons

To make dressing, combine all ingredients and cook 10 minutes, stirring constantly. Cool and refrigerate in a jar overnight.

For salad, tear spinach leaves into bite-sized pieces. Add eggs, onion, bacon, and croutons. Toss and serve.

Marcia Potter
Denver, Colorado

Strawberry Salad with Dressing

Salad:
- 2 bunches fresh spinach
- 1 pint sliced strawberries
- 1 cup chopped walnuts

Dressing:
- 1/2 cup sugar
- 2 tablespoons sesame seeds
- 1 tablespoon poppy seeds
- 1 1/2 tablespoons minced onion
- 1/4 teaspoon worcestershire sauce
- 1/4 teaspoon paprika
- 1/2 cup vegetable oil
- 1/4 cup cider vinegar

Tear spinach into bite-sized pieces. Arrange spinach, strawberries, and walnuts in a bowl. In blender place sugar, sesame seeds, poppy seeds, onion, worcestershire sauce, and paprika. While blender is running, add vegetable oil and vinegar. The dressing will be thick and creamy. Serve salad dressing on the side.

Sue Roushar
Montrose, Colorado

Yield: 6 to 8 servings

No-Fat No-Sugar Lime Salad

- 1 3-ounce package no-fat cream cheese, softened
- 1 3-ounce package sugar-free lime gelatin
- 1 cup boiling water
- 1 cup low fat or skim milk
- 1 15 1/4-ounce can crushed pineapple, drained
  chopped walnuts, to taste
- 1 single-serving packet sugar substitute

Mix cream cheese and gelatin together. Add water, and beat until smooth. Add milk and mix. Add pineapple and walnuts; mix well. Stir in sugar substitute. Let set in refrigerator.

Notes:
Nuts have a fat content, so omit if you want this recipe to be completely fat-free.

Beverly Rhynard
Littleton, Colorado

Fruit Salad

- 1 16-ounce can fruit cocktail, drained (reserve juice)
- 1 16-ounce can sliced peaches, drained (reserve juice), cut into bite-sized pieces
- 1 16-ounce can pineapple chunks, drained, cut into smaller pieces
- 4 to 5 bananas, sliced
- 1 3.4-ounce package vanilla pudding (not instant)

Mix the reserved fruit cocktail and peach juices with the pudding; cook until pudding has thickened. Cool. Add to fruit and mix. Refrigerate.

Variations:
Can substitute sliced strawberries for sliced bananas.

Notes:
Do not use the pineapple juice.

Lois Andis
Denver, Colorado

Apple and Banana Salad

Dressing:
- 3 tablespoons mayonnaise
- 1 tablespoon sugar

Salad:
- 2 medium apples, peeled, cored, and chopped
- 3 bananas, sliced

For dressing, mix mayonnaise and sugar thoroughly.

For salad, add chopped apples and sliced bananas to bowl that dressing is in, mixing thoroughly.

Notes:
Prepare this salad 1 to 2 hours before serving. It needs to have enough time to allow the sugar to dissolve in the mayonnaise, but not so much time that the bananas start turning brown.

Jeanne Creighton
Denver, Colorado

Applesauce Salad

- 1 3-ounce package black raspberry gelatin
- 1½ cups boiling water
- ½ 10½-ounce package cinnamon imperials (known as red hots)
- ½ cup applesauce
- 2 tablespoons lemon juice
- ½ cup chopped nuts

Dissolve gelatin in boiling water. Add cinnamon imperials and stir until dissolved. Let set in refrigerator until gelatin starts to thicken. Add applesauce, lemon juice, and chopped nuts, mixing well. Pour into a gelatin mold. Chill.

Charlotte Seaton
Fort Lupton, Colorado

Blueberry Salad

  2 3-ounce packages raspberry gelatin
3½ cups water, divided
  1 cup half and half
  1 cup sugar
  1 envelope unflavored gelatin
  1 8-ounce package cream cheese, softened
½ cup chopped nuts
  1 teaspoon vanilla
  1 16- to 17-ounce can (2 cups) blueberries with juice
     dash of lemon juice

Dissolve one package raspberry gelatin in 2 cups water in 9x13x2-inch pan. Let set. Heat half and half and sugar until near boiling. Dissolve the unflavored gelatin in ½ cup cold water; add to half and half mixture. Add softened cream cheese; stir until smooth. Add nuts and vanilla. Cool. Pour over gelatin. Let set. Dissolve one package raspberry gelatin in 1 cup boiling water; add blueberries with juice and lemon juice. Cool. Pour over cream cheese mixture. Let set.

Cami Termer
Pueblo, Colorado

Resort Fruit Salad

- 1 20-ounce can pineapple chunks with juice, undrained
- 1 11-ounce can mandarin orange segments, undrained
- 2 bananas, sliced
- 2 cups halved strawberries
- 1 1/2 cups halved green grapes
- 1 cup fresh or frozen blueberries, drained
- 1 3 1/2-ounce package instant vanilla pudding mix
- 1/4 to 1/2 cup granola, pecan halves, or whole almonds (optional)

Drain chunk pineapple and orange segments, reserving liquid in a small bowl. In a large bowl, combine all fruits. Sprinkle pudding mix into reserved liquid; mix until combined and slightly thickened. Fold into fruit until well combined. Garnish with granola, pecan halves, or whole almonds.

Christine Sitzman
Fort Lupton, Colorado

Yield: 16 half-cup servings

Sour Cream Salad

- 2 3-ounce packages strawberry gelatin
- 2 cups boiling water
- 2 bananas, mashed
- 1 20-ounce box frozen strawberries with juice, thawed
- 1 cup crushed pineapple with juice
- 1 8-ounce container sour cream

Dissolve gelatin in hot water. Add bananas, strawberries, and pineapple. Mix well. Pour half of mixture into refrigerator dish (8- or 9-inch square glass cake pan or equivalent). Refrigerate. Leave other half of mixture at room temperature.

When gelatin has set, spread with sour cream. Pour second half of gelatin mixture over the top. Cover and refrigerate until set completely.

Beverly Rhynard
Littleton, Colorado

Strawberry Salad

- 1 6-ounce package strawberry gelatin
- 2 cups boiling water
- 1 20-ounce package frozen strawberries in syrup, partially thawed
- 1 20-ounce can crushed pineapple
- 1/2 cup chopped pecans
- 1 8-ounce container sour cream

Dissolve gelatin in boiling water. Add half-thawed strawberries with syrup. Add crushed pineapple and pecans. Divide into two bowls. Place one bowl of gelatin into the refrigerator to harden and leave the other bowl at room temperature. When gelatin is set, spread sour cream over the top of hardened gelatin. Pour remaining strawberry mixture from second bowl over sour cream. Refrigerate.

Variations:
Can add quartered bananas, too.

Penny Hoopes
Westminster, Colorado

Yield: 10 to 12 servings

Orange Sherbet Salad

   2 3-ounce packages orange gelatin
1 1/2 cups hot water
   1 pint orange sherbet
   1 11-ounce can mandarin oranges, drained
   2 bananas, sliced

Dissolve gelatin in hot water. Immediately add orange sherbet. Stir until well mixed and mixture starts to thicken. Add mandarin oranges and sliced bananas. Refrigerate until firm.

Notes:
Can be set in either a gelatin mold or plain refrigerator dish.

Lucy Ellsworth
Denver, Colorado

White Salad

3 envelopes non-dairy whipped topping mix, prepared
3 ounces cream cheese, softened
1 16-ounce can pineapple tidbits
1 cup grapes
$1/2$ $10 1/2$-ounce bag miniature marshmallows

Prepare whipped topping according to package directions. Blend in cream cheese until smooth. Fold in pineapple tidbits, grapes, and marshmallows. Refrigerate.

Notes:
Increase or decrease pineapple, grapes, and marshamallows according to your taste.

Lois Andis
Denver, Colorado

Broccoli Squares

- 4 tablespoons butter or margarine
- 3 eggs
- 1 cup flour
- 1 cup milk
- 1 2-pound bag frozen cut broccoli
- 1 teaspoon salt
- 1 teaspoon baking powder
- 2 6-ounce packages shredded Monterey Jack cheese

Preheat oven to 350 degrees. In a 9x13x2-inch baking pan, melt butter. Mix together eggs, flour, milk, broccoli, salt, and baking powder. Sprinkle cheese over top. Bake until browned—about 45 minutes. Cut into 2-inch squares and serve hot.

Sue Peters
Montrose, Colorado

Ruby's Broccoli Casserole

1 large onion, chopped
$^1/_2$ cup (1 stick) margarine
1 cup instant rice
1 10$^3/_4$-ounce can cream of chicken soup
6 ounces evaporated milk
8 ounces diced processed cheese
2 10-ounce boxes frozen chopped broccoli, thawed

Preheat oven to 350 degrees. Sauté onion in margarine until transparent. Mix all ingredients in a 2-quart casserole dish and bake for 30 minutes.

Notes:
Great for those quilting potluck dinners.

Ruby Hill Davis
Clifton, Colorado

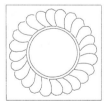

Buttery Grated Carrots

- 2 pounds carrots
- 1 tablespoon vegetable oil
- 1/4 teaspoon finely chopped garlic
- 1/2 teaspoon salt
- 1/8 teaspoon pepper
- 2 tablespoons water
- 1/4 cup margarine

Peel carrots and grate on medium grater. Place in a skillet with a tight-fitting cover. Toss with vegetable oil, garlic, salt, pepper, and water. Cook covered over medium heat, stirring occasionally, for 10 to 15 minutes or until tender. Remove from heat and toss with butter.

Notes:
This recipe always brings raves from guests.

Annabeth Lockhart
Steamboat Springs, Colorado

Yield: 6 servings

Hang a flannel sheet to a curtain rod on a wall in your room. When a quilt block is completed, rub it on the sheet and watch your quilt grow. It's handy to take down, roll up, and take to Show and Tell or to a class.

Baked Corn

- 2 16 1/2-ounce cans cream style corn
- 1 cup soda crackers, crushed
- 2 eggs
   salt and pepper to taste
- 8 strips bacon, raw

Preheat oven to 350 degrees. Mix corn, cracker crumbs, eggs, salt, and pepper together and place in a 2-quart casserole dish. Place raw bacon strips on top of mixture. Bake for 1 hour.

Mary Biesecker
Grand Junction, Colorado

Zucchini Pie

  3 cups diced zucchini
1/2 cup chopped green onions
  1 cup buttermilk baking mix
1/2 cup vegetable oil
  4 eggs
  1 cup cottage cheese
    dash of salt

Preheat oven to 350 degrees. Combine zucchini, green onions, baking mix, vegetable oil, eggs, cottage cheese, and salt. Mix thoroughly. Pour into a greased 8-inch square pan. Bake for 30 to 45 minutes or until golden brown.

Janice White
Colorado Springs, Colorado

Yield: 6 to 8 servings

Onion Casserole

- 2 tablespoons butter or margarine
- 2 large onions*, sliced or chopped
- 8 ounces grated Monterey Jack cheese
- 1 10¾-ounce can cream of chicken soup
- 1 cup milk
- 1 teaspoon soy sauce
- 8 slices French bread

Preheat oven to 350 degrees. Sauté onions in butter until golden. Arrange on bottom of 9x13x2-inch baking dish. Cover with cheese. Combine soup, milk, and soy sauce in saucepan; heat. Mix until smooth. Pour over ingredients in baking dish. Butter bread and lay on top, butter side up. Bake for 30 minutes.

Variations:
Can substitute Swiss or Cheddar cheese for Monterey Jack cheese.

Notes:
*Vidalia, Walla Wallas, or Bermuda onions are best, but any kind will do.

Melba Queener
Leadville, Colorado

Green Chili Potatoes

    instant potatoes, enough for 6 servings
1 cup sour cream
1 cup small-curd, low-fat cottage cheese
1 4-ounce can chopped mild green chilies
1 cup shredded Cheddar cheese
    paprika, to taste

Preheat oven to 350 degrees. Following the directions on the package of instant potatoes, make 6 servings of potatoes. Add sour cream, cottage cheese, chilies, and Cheddar cheese and mix well. Place in a a glass casserole dish and bake for 20 to 25 minutes or until bubbly. Remove from oven and sprinkle with paprika.

Notes:
There will be no leftovers!

Ruth Rupert
Denver, Colorado

Yield: 6 servings

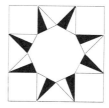

Scalloped Potatoes

  1   32-ounce package frozen shredded hash browns, thawed
  1   10¾-ounce can cream of chicken soup
  1   8-ounce carton sour cream
½ cup grated onion
½ cup (1 stick) melted butter or margarine
1½ cup grated Cheddar cheese, divided
  1   teaspoon salt
½ teaspoon pepper

Preheat oven to 350 degrees. Mix hash browns, cream of chicken soup, sour cream, onion, butter, and 1 cup grated cheese together. Place in a 9x13x2-inch glass casserole dish. Sprinkle remaining ½ cup of cheese on top of mixture. Bake for 45 minutes.

Notes:
This can be mixed the day before and refrigerated. If you do this, you need to allow an additional 10 to 15 minutes baking time.

Sharon Bozman
Center, Colorado

Pot Luck Potatoes

  2 pounds frozen hash brown potatoes with red and green sweet peppers, thawed
10 ounces Cheddar cheese, grated
  1 $10^3/4$-ounce can cream of chicken soup, undiluted
16 ounces (2 cups) sour cream
  1 onion, chopped

Preheat oven to 350 degrees. Mix all ingredients and pour into a 9x13x2-inch pan. Bake, uncovered, for 1 hour.

Mae Jane Keller
Aurora, Colorado

Simply Super Tomatoes

- 6 medium tomatoes, peeled, cut into 1/2-inch slices
- 2/3 cup vegetable oil
- 1/4 cup wine vinegar
- 1/4 cup finely chopped fresh parsley
- 1/4 cup finely chopped green onions
- 1 garlic clove, minced
- 1 teaspoon salt
- 1 teaspoon dried dill weed
- 1 teaspoon dried basil leaves
- 1/4 teaspoon pepper

Arrange tomatoes in serving dish. In a small bowl or jar with lid, combine remaining ingredients; mix well. Pour dressing over tomatoes. Cover and refrigerate for 1 to 2 hours, periodically spooning dressing over tomatoes.

Variations:
Cherry tomatoes can be substituted for tomato slices.

Christine Sitzman
Fort Lupton, Colorado

Yield: 6 servings

Spinach Casserole

- 2 10-ounce packages frozen chopped spinach
- 1 8-ounce package cream cheese, softened
- 1/4 cup margarine, melted
- 1 teaspoon worcestershire sauce
-    dash of bottled hot pepper sauce
- 1/2 16-ounce package stuffing mix
- 1 small onion, grated

Preheat oven to 350 degrees. Barely cook the spinach and drain off most, but not all, of the liquid. Mix the cream cheese into the cooked spinach. Mix in all the remaining ingredients. Reserve a few crumbs of the stuffing and sprinkle on top of the casserole. Bake about 30 minutes.

Notes:
This recipe can be made ahead of time.

Janette Nash
Grand Junction, Colorado

Cheese Pie

- 1 pound Monterey Jack cheese, grated
- 1/2 cup diced green sweet peppers
- 1/2 cup diced red sweet peppers
- 1/2 cup sliced mushrooms
- 1/4 cup chopped onions
- 4 eggs

Preheat oven to 400 degrees. Spray 9-inch pie plate with non-stick cooking spray. Place grated cheese in pie plate. Sprinkle peppers, mushrooms, and onions over the top. Beat eggs. Pour over cheese mixture, making sure it covers all the cheese. Bake until crusty brown. Serve with salad and rolls.

Marybel Schimberg
Morrison, Colorado

Pineapple Puff

- 5 to 6 slices bread
- 1/2 cup (1 stick) butter or margarine, softened
- 3/4 cup sugar
- 3 eggs
- 1 20-ounce can unsweetened crushed pineapple with juice
- dash salt

Preheat oven to 350 degrees. Remove crusts from bread and cut into cubes. Leave cubed bread on counter to harden. Cream butter and sugar; add eggs and beat. Fold in crushed pineapple with juice, cubed hardened bread, and salt. Spread in a lightly greased 1 1/2- to 2-quart casserole dish. Bake, uncovered, for 45 to 50 minutes.

Variations:
If you want, you can mix brown sugar and granulated sugar to add up to 3/4 cup.

Notes:
This casserole is scrumptious. Goes great with ham, pork chops, fowl...or just about anything.

Jo Silkensen
Longmont, Colorado

Yield: 6 to 8 servings

Escalloped Pineapple

- 1/2 cup (1 stick) margarine or butter, softened
- 2 cups sugar
- 2 eggs
- 1 20-ounce can pineapple chunks, drained
- 1 quart fresh white bread cubes (10 slices), crusts removed

Preheat oven to 350 degrees. Cream margarine and sugar. Add eggs and beat well. Add drained pineapple chunks. Stir in bread cubes last. Bake in a buttered 8x12-inch dish for about 45 minutes. Test at 40 minutes with a knife. If the knife comes out clean, the dish is done.

Notes:
This is a good substitute for sweet potatoes at holiday time. The recipe was given to me about 25 years ago by a lady from South America. The quilters on the Western Slope really like this and can't believe the ingredients.

JoAnn Roemer
Grand Junction, Colorado

Yield: 10 servings

Quick serger hint—when threading your serger, place a 4-inch or so object under the front feet so that you are looking at your serger at an angle. You will be surprised at the difference it makes.

Easy Rice Pilaf

- 1 tablespoon vegetable oil
- 1 cup long-grained white rice
- 1 teaspoon salt
- 1/2 teaspoon dehydrated onion
- 1/4 teaspoon oregano
- 2 cups chicken broth (or 2 chicken bouillon cubes dissolved in 2 cups of water)

Heat vegetable oil in skillet and brown rice. Stir in salt, onion, oregano, and chicken broth. Cover and reduce heat to low. Cook 20 minutes or until liquid is absorbed.

Jayne Pritko
Colorado Springs, Colorado

Yield: 4 servings

French Rice

- 1 10³/₄-ounce can onion soup
- ¹/₂ cup (1 stick) margarine, melted
- 1 2.5-ounce jar sliced mushrooms (drain and reserve liquid)
- 1 6-ounce can sliced water chestnuts (drain and reserve liquid)
  water
- 1 cup uncooked regular rice

Preheat oven to 350 degrees. Combine soup and margarine; stir well. Add enough water to mushrooms and water chestnut liquid to equal 1¹/₃ cups. Add mushrooms, water chestnuts, and rice to the liquids. Mix well. Pour into greased 1-quart baking dish. Bake for 1 hour, covered.

Notes:
If you are using this recipe with the *Creamy Baked Chicken* (page 174), place this in the oven 15 minutes before you are ready to put the chicken in oven. That way they will both come out ready to eat at the same time.

Charlotte Hughlett
Longmont, Colorado

Brazilian-Style Rice

    2 tablespoons olive oil
3 to 4 tablespoons chopped onion
  1 1/2 cups long-grain white rice
    3 cups water
        salt to taste

Sauté onion in olive oil. Add rice. Sauté rice until it becomes transparent. Add water and salt. Bring to boil, reduce heat, and simmer until done (about 1 hour).

Delia Molloy da Cunha
Boulder, Colorado

Amish Dressing

- 3 large carrots, diced
- 2 large potatoes, diced
- 1 cup diced celery
- 1/2 cup diced onion
- 1/2 teaspoon dried sage
- 1 teaspoon salt
- dash of pepper
- 1 cup diced cooked chicken
- 1 cup broth
- 2 tablespoons flour
- 6 ounces can evaporated milk
- 1 egg
- 2 to 3 tablespoons vegetable shortening
- 1 loaf bread, toasted and cubed

Preheat oven to 350 degrees. Place carrots, potatoes, celery, onion, sage, salt, pepper, chicken, broth, and bread in a large mixing bowl. In a separate container mix flour, evaporated milk, and egg well. Add milk mixture to vegetable mixture and mix well. In large skillet melt vegetable shortening. Fry dressing mixture in hot vegetable shortening. When dressing turns brown, put in a baking dish and bake for 1 hour.

Connie Wills-Sandstead
Platteville, Colorado

Apricot Pine Nut Pilaf

- 3 tablespoons margarine or butter
- 1/4 cup pine nuts or blanched slivered almonds
- 1 cup uncooked regular rice
- 1 14 1/2-ounce can chicken broth
- 1/2 cup chopped dried apricots
- 1/2 cup thinly sliced green onions

Melt margarine in medium skillet over medium-high heat. Add pine nuts or almonds; cook and stir 2 to 3 minutes or until lightly browned. Remove nuts from skillet with slotted spoon; set aside. Add rice; cook and stir 3 to 5 minutes or until rice is golden brown. Stir in broth; bring to a boil. Reduce heat. Cover; simmer 20 minutes or until rice is tender and liquid is absorbed. Add nuts, apricots, and onions; cook covered over low heat for 5 minutes.

Bernice Barney
Loveland, Colorado

Yield: 7 (1/2 cup) servings

Farofa

- 2 tablespoons butter or margarine
- 1 tablespoon minced onion
- 1 cup unprepared cream of wheat cereal
  butter or margarine

Melt butter in small skillet. Sauté onion in butter until onion is transparent.

Add cream of wheat, about 1 tablespoon or so at a time, stirring well with each addition. Continue adding cream of wheat until the mixture is crumbly. Add butter in $1/2$ teaspoon increments if necessary. The mixture should be very crumbly.

Serve over *Black Beans and Rice (Feijaó)* (page 160).

Notes:
Farofa is traditionally served from a small wooden bowl with a small wooden spoon.

Delia Molloy da Cunha
Boulder, Colorado

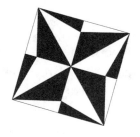

Black Beans and Rice (Feijaó)

- 1 pound dry black beans
- 6 cups water
- 5 tablespoons olive oil, divided
- 1 teaspoon salt
- 1/2 teaspoon cayenne pepper
- 1 bay leaf
- 1 medium to large onion, chopped
- 1 clove garlic, minced
- 1 tablespoon tomato paste

Rinse beans thoroughly. Place in heavy pan with water, 2 tablespoons olive oil, and seasonings. Soak overnight or several hours. After soaking, bring to boil. Reduce heat and simmer until beans are very soft. Add water as necessary.

In a small frying pan, heat 3 tablespoons olive oil. Sauté onion and garlic until onion is transparent. Add tomato paste. Heat, stirring frequently.

Add sauté mixture to beans and continue cooking.

Mash about 1/2 cup of the beans against the side of the pan and stir them into the beans. This helps the liquid thicken properly.

Serve over *Brazilian-Style Rice* (page 156) and top with *Farofa* (page 159).

Variations:
There are as many variations of this recipe as there are cooks who make it. With or without meat it is the national dish of Brazil. No proper Brazilian meal is served without rice and beans.

Delia Molloy da Cunha
Boulder, Colorado

Spicy Refried Beans

1 1/2 cups dried pinto beans
6 cups water
2 tablespoons vegetable oil
1 1/2 medium onions, chopped, divided
3 teaspoons salt, divided
1/4 cup olive oil
3 cloves garlic, minced
1 cup chopped, peeled tomatoes
1 4-ounce can chopped jalapeño peppers
2 tablespoons lemon juice
1/4 teaspoon ground cinnamon
1/8 teaspoon ground cloves
1 tablespoon butter or margarine, softened
1 cup grated Monterey Jack cheese
  sour cream
  salsa
  tortillas

Wash beans and cook with water, vegetable oil, half an onion, and 2 teaspoons salt. Cook for 30 minutes at 15 pounds pressure in pressure cooker or simmer in regular saucepan, covered for 1 1/2 hours. Remove cover and cook until liquid is thickened.

Heat olive oil in skillet. Sauté remaining onion and garlic. Add tomatoes, peppers, and lemon juice. Add remaining 1 teaspoon salt, cinnamon, and ground cloves. Pour beans into seasonings and cook over low heat for about 45 minutes or until mixture is quite thick. Stir in butter and grated cheese.

Serve with sour cream, salsa, and tortillas.

Sally Hershey
Denver, Colorado

Crock Pot Baked Beans

    5 slices bacon, crisply fried and crumbled
    2 16-ounce cans baked beans, drained
    1/2 sweet pepper, chopped
    1/2 medium onion, chopped
    1 1/2 teaspoons prepared mustard
    1/2 cup ketchup
    1/2 cup barbeque sauce
    1/2 cup packed brown sugar

Combine all ingredients in a slow cooker. Cook on low for 8 to 12 hours or on high for 2 to 3 hours.

Notes:
Quick and easy to fix. Goes over well with a crowd—real tasty.

Irene Mable
Buena Vista, Colorado

 When life gives you scraps—make quilts.

Main Dishes & Casseroles

Special Notes:

Golden Dobbin Chicken Casserole

- 1 6- to 8-ounce package seasoned stuffing
- 1/2 cup (1 stick) or less margarine
- 1 cup water
- 2 1/2 cups chicken, cooked and cut in small pieces
- 1/2 cup or less chopped onion
- 1/2 cup chopped celery
- 1/2 cup mayonnaise
- salt (optional)
- 2 eggs
- 1/2 cup milk
- 1 10 3/4-ounce can cream of chicken soup

Preheat oven to 325 degrees. In a medium saucepan, bring water and margarine to a boil. Stir in package of stuffing. In a separate bowl, combine chicken, onion, celery, mayonnaise, and salt. In another bowl, beat eggs; add milk and cream of chicken soup. Grease 9x13x2-inch pan. Spread half of stuffing over bottom of pan. Place the chicken mixture over the stuffing. Spread the remainder of the stuffing on top of chicken mixture. Pour the soup mixture over the top. Bake for 40 minutes.

Variations:
Can use cream of mushroom or cream of celery soup in place of cream of chicken soup.

Mary Christofferson
Littleton, Colorado

Yield: 8 servings

Buttermilk Chicken Potpie

Filling:
- 2½ pounds chicken, cooked and cut in small pieces, reserve chicken broth
- 1 16-ounce can mixed vegetables†, drained
- 1 8-ounce can mixed vegetables†, drained
- 1 10¾-ounce can cream of chicken soup
- 2 cups chicken broth from cooked chicken

Crust:
- 1 cup buttermilk
- ½ cup (1 stick) margarine, melted
- 1 cup flour
- ½ teaspoon pepper
- ½ teaspoon salt
- ¼ teaspoon baking powder
- ½ teaspoon baking soda

Preheat oven to 425 degrees. For filling, in a 9x13x2-inch pan combine the cut-up chicken and drained cans of mixed vegetables. In a separate pan, bring cream of chicken soup and chicken broth to a boil. Pour over chicken mixture. For crust, combine all ingredients and pour over chicken mixture. Spread crust to cover entire pan. Refrigerate* for 1 hour. Bake for 30 to 35 minutes or until golden brown on the top.

Notes:
*Refrigeration is not absolutely necessary, but you will achieve best results by doing so. †I prefer to use Veg-All vegetables. They are very good and do not taste canned. The large can is better because the vegetables are cut larger than they are in the small cans. That is why I mix a large can with a small can.

Kathy Cadwallader
Colorado Springs, Colorado

Yield: 6 servings

Chicken Enchiladas
(Microwave)

Sauce:
- 1/2 cup chicken broth
- 1 10 3/4-ounce can cream of chicken soup
- 1 4-ounce can diced green chilies
- 1 green onion, chopped
- 2 teaspoons chili powder

Filling:
- 2 cups cooked chicken, shredded
- 2 cups sharp Cheddar cheese, grated, divided
- 1/2 cup ripe olives, chopped
- 12 corn or flour tortillas

Topping:
- 1 cup sour cream

Combine sauce ingredients in a 4-cup glass bowl. Microwave on high for 3 minutes; stir as needed to keep ingredients from separating. For filling, combine chicken, 1 cup cheese, olives, and 1 cup sauce.

Fill each tortilla with about 1/3 cup of filling and place seam side down in a 9x12-inch glass casserole dish. Pour remaining sauce over rolled tortillas. Microwave on high for 6 to 8 minutes. Sprinkle with remaining 1 cup cheese; drizzle lines of sour cream over the tortillas. Microwave on high for 1 minute to melt cheese.

Pat Brech
Colorado Springs, Colorado

Yield: 4 to 6 servings

Chicken Casserole

- 16 slices day-old white bread, crusts removed
- 1/2 cup (1 stick) butter or margarine
- 1/4 pound fresh mushrooms, sliced and sautéed in butter
- 2 cups cooked chicken, chopped
- 1/3 cup sliced ripe olives
- 3/4 cup mayonnaise
- 2 tablespoons finely chopped onion
- 1 10 3/4-ounce can cream of chicken soup
- 1 cup sour cream
- 2 tablespoons cooking sherry
- paprika

Preheat oven to 325 degrees. Butter both sides of bread slices. Use remaining butter to sauté mushrooms. Put eight slices of bread in the bottom of a 9x13x2-inch pan. Combine chicken, olives, mayonnaise, and onion. Cover bread slices with this mixture. Top with remaining slices of bread. Mix soup, sour cream, and sherry and spread on top of bread slices. Sprinkle generously with paprika. Bake for 30 to 40 minutes.

Margie Colarelli
Arvada, Colorado

Oriental Chicken Breasts

- 4 chicken breasts
- 1 1/2 cups sugar
- 3 tablespoons cornstarch
- 1/2 teaspoon Accent
- 6 tablespoons ketchup
- 1 teaspoon salt
- 1 teaspoon soy sauce
- 1 cup vinegar
- 1/2 cup pineapple juice
- rice, prepared according to package directions

Preheat oven to 350 degrees. Place chicken breasts in a 9x13x2-inch baking dish. Combine all other ingredients and pour over chicken. Bake for 1 1/2 hours, basting often. Serve over rice.

Nancy Cole
Longmont, Colorado

Curry of Chicken

Chicken:
- 2 tablespoons butter or margarine
- 1 1/2 cups peeled and chopped apples
- 1/2 cup chopped onion
- 1 clove garlic, minced
- 2 tablespoons flour
- 2 to 3 teaspoons curry powder
- 1 teaspoon salt
- 2 cups milk
- 2 cups chicken, cooked and cubed
- rice, prepared according to package directions

Toppings: (to taste)
- chopped peanuts
- raisins
- chutney
- chopped tomatoes
- chopped onions

Melt butter; add apples, onion, and garlic. Cook 5 minutes. Stir in flour, curry powder, and salt. Slowly blend in milk; cook and stir until thick. Add chicken and heat. Serve over cooked rice, with chopped peanuts, raisins, chutney, tomatoes, and/or onions.

Shirley Dunkirk
Boulder, Colorado

If you prick your finger while quilting and get blood on the quilt, use your own saliva to remove the blood. It will come out immediately.

Mexican Noodles

- 2 small or 1 large chicken, approximately 3$^1/_2$ pounds
- 1 10$^3/_4$-can tomato soup
- 1 soup can of water
- 2 large sweet peppers, diced
- 2 cups chopped celery
- 2 cups chopped onion
- 1 2-ounce jar diced pimento
- 3 bay leaves
- 2 cloves garlic, chopped
- 1 tablespoon worcestershire sauce
- 1 tablespoon chili powder
- dash of bottled hot pepper sauce
- 1 tablespoon chopped parsley
- 1 6-ounce jar button mushrooms
- 1 2$^1/_4$-ounce can sliced ripe olives
- 1$^1/_2$ pounds wide ribbon noodles

Cook, bone, and cut chicken into bite-sized pieces. Strain broth left from cooking chicken to cook noodles in. Set aside. In a large saucepan or Dutch oven, combine soup, water, peppers, celery, onion, pimento, bay leaves, garlic, worcestershire sauce, chili powder, hot pepper sauce, and parsley. Simmer 5 to 10 minutes. Add mushrooms and sliced olives to saucepan and mix well. Cook ribbon noodles according to directions on package, using reserved chicken broth instead of water. Stir cut-up chicken into soup mixture in saucepan. Add cooked noodles and mix well. Let mixture stand overnight or at least 2 hours in refrigerator to marinate. Reheat and serve.

June Howard
Northglenn, Colorado

Chicken-with-Dressing Casserole

Chicken:
- 1 3 to 4 pound roasting hen, cut up
- 1 stalk celery, chopped
- 1½ teaspoons salt
- ¼ teaspoon pepper
- 1 tablespoon dry onion soup mix (stir soup mix thoroughly before measuring)
- 1 chicken bouillon cube

Stuffing:
- 1½ quarts dry bread cubes
- ¼ cup minced onions
- ⅓ cup butter or margarine, softened
- ⅛ teaspoon pepper
- ½ teaspoon salt
- ½ teaspoon poultry seasoning

Gravy:
- ½ cup chicken fat
- ¾ cup flour
- 4 cups chicken broth
- 2 egg yolks, well beaten

In a large pot, combine cut up chicken, celery, salt, pepper, onion soup mix, and bouillon cube. Cover with water and cook until chicken is tender. Let chicken cool in broth. Remove chicken from broth, pour broth through sieve, and refrigerate until fat rises to the top and hardens. Remove fat and measure out ½ cup of fat to save for gravy. Remove chicken from bones and cut into bite-sized pieces. Arrange in a 9x13x2-inch baking dish or pan.

For stuffing, in a skillet melt butter and sauté minced onion, pepper, salt, and poultry seasoning. Mix into dry bread cubes and combine thoroughly. Spoon over chicken in casserole.

(continued)

Chicken-with-Dressing Casserole
(continued)

For gravy, melt chicken fat in large skillet and add flour. Blend in chicken broth. In a separate container, add a small amount of gravy to the beaten egg yolks and mix well. Pour this mixture into the gravy and stir well. Pour gravy over chicken and stuffing and bake in a 375-degree preheated oven for 30 to 35 minutes.

Notes:
It takes only 15 to 20 minutes to cook the chicken if you use a pressure cooker.

Rita Hildred
Laporte, Colorado

Creamy Baked Chicken

- 8 chicken breasts, halved and boned
- 8 slices Swiss cheese
- 1 10¾-ounce can cream of chicken soup, undiluted
- ½ cup dry white wine
- 1 cup herb-seasoned stuffing mix or croutons
- ⅓ cup melted margarine

Preheat oven to 350 degrees. Arrange chicken in 9x13x2-inch baking pan. Put cheese over top of each piece. In a bowl mix wine and soup together, then stir in stuffing mix, combining thoroughly. Pour over chicken. Drizzle with margarine. Bake for 40 to 45 minutes. Serve with *French Rice* (page 155).

Charlotte Hughlett
Longmont, Colorado

Minestrone Chicken Dinner

    2   19-ounce cans chunky minestrone soup
    1   tablespoon vinegar
    1   teaspoon sugar
5 to 6   skinless chicken breasts, boned
           rice, prepared according to package directions

Mix minestrone soup, vinegar, and sugar together. Put aside. Place chicken breasts into a slow cooker. Pour soup mixture over chicken. Heat on high until boiling, then turn to low. Continue cooking for at least 4 hours or until chicken is done. Serve over hot rice.

Tesse Kramer
Broomfield, Colorado

Yield: 4 servings

Chicken Glop

4 skinless, boneless chicken breasts
1 10¾-ounce can cream of chicken soup, undiluted
1 10¾-ounce can cream of mushroom soup, undiluted
1 16-ounce container sour cream
1 8-ounce package dressing mix (any flavor)

Preheat oven to 350 degrees. Boil chicken breasts until cooked. Drain and cool. Cut into bite-sized cubes. Mix together soups and sour cream. Add cubed chicken. Prepare dressing per instructions on package. Place soup and sour cream mixture into a 9x11-inch glass cake pan. Top with dressing. Bake for approximately 30 minutes or until lightly browned.

Diane Lindsay
Englewood, Colorado

Kung Pao Chicken

- 1¼ pounds boneless chicken breasts, cut in 1-inch cubes
- 4 tablespoons vegetable oil, divided

Marinade:
- 2 tablespoons soy sauce
- 1½ tablespoons cold water
- ¼ teaspoon garlic powder

Sauce:
- 4 tablespoons soy sauce
- 2 tablespoons sherry
- 2 tablespoons sugar
- 2 teaspoons cornstarch
- 1 teaspoon sesame oil

Vegetables:
- 4 to 7 dried red chilies, tips removed, cut in 1-inch pieces
- 1 teaspoon minced fresh ginger root
- 1 sweet pepper, cut in 1-inch pieces
- 1 8-ounce can bamboo shoots
- 4 green onions, cut in 2-inch pieces
- ½ cup dry-roasted cashews

For marinade, combine soy sauce, cold water, and garlic powder. Combine chicken with marinade and let stand 30 minutes. Heat 2 tablespoons vegetable oil in wok. Add chicken and stir fry for 4 minutes. Remove from wok and add remaining 2 tablespoons vegetable oil.

For sauce, combine soy sauce, sherry, sugar, cornstarch, and sesame oil in a separate bowl and set aside.

For vegetables, stir fry chilies until they turn black. Add ginger root, sweet pepper, bamboo shoots, and green onions. Stir fry for 2 minutes. Add chicken and sauce, stirring until thick. Add cashews.

Teresa Mensch
Evergreen, Colorado

Yield: 4 servings

Chicken in Wine Sauce

4 to 6	chicken breasts or a mixture of thighs and breasts
1/4	teaspoon rosemary
1/4	teaspoon basil
1	10 3/4-ounce can cream of mushroom soup
1/2	cup white wine

Preheat oven to 400 degrees. Place chicken parts in a 9x13x2-inch pan, skin side down, and bake uncovered for 20 minutes. Turn chicken parts over to skin side up and sprinkle with rosemary and basil. Bake another 20 minutes. Combine mushroom soup and wine. Pour over chicken and continue to bake for 20 minutes. Serve with *Rice Pilaf* (page 154).

Notes:
If skinned chicken is used, I recommend covering the pan during the first two 20-minute cooking sessions to retain moisture. After soup/wine mixture is added, continue to cook uncovered.

Jayne Pritko
Colorado Springs, Colorado

Yield: 4 servings

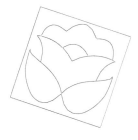

Bailey's Chicken

- 4 thin slices baked ham, cut in half
- 4 whole chicken breasts, split and boned
- 1 $10^{3}/_{4}$-ounce can cream of mushroom soup
- 1 cup sour cream
- $1/_2$ cup Bailey's Irish Cream liqueur
- 1 cup ($1/_4$ pound) sliced fresh mushrooms

Preheat oven to 300 degrees. In an 8x12-inch baking dish, arrange slices of ham with a chicken breast on each slice—skin side up. Mix remaining ingredients and spoon over chicken, covering completely. Bake for $1^1/_2$ hours.

Kristine Scerbo
Fort Collins, Colorado

Yield: 6 to 8 servings

Chicken Divan

- 8 boneless chicken breasts
- 2 cups water
- 1/2 cup chopped celery
- 1 bay leaf
- 1/2 cup chopped onion
- 1 2-pound package frozen broccoli
- 1 10 3/4-ounce can cream of mushroom soup
- 1/4 cup milk
- 3/4 teaspoon curry
- 1/4 cup Italian seasoned bread crumbs
  butter or margarine
- 1/2 cup shredded Cheddar cheese

Preheat oven to 350 degrees. Simmer boneless chicken breasts for 40 minutes with celery, bay leaf, and onion in water. Cook broccoli for 6 minutes. Place broccoli on bottom of a 9x13x2-inch baking dish. Place drained chicken and vegetables (remove bay leaf) on top of broccoli. Mix soup with milk and curry. Pour over chicken. Top with bread crumbs and Cheddar cheese. Dot with pats of butter. Bake 30 minutes.

Charlotte Seaton
Fort Lupton, Colorado

Yield: 6 servings

Chicken and Black Bean Tamale Pie

Filling:
- 1 tablespoon vegetable oil or olive oil
- 1/2 to 1 pound boneless, skinless chicken breasts
- salt and pepper, to taste
- 1/2 onion, chopped
- 1/2 pound mushrooms, washed and quartered
- 1 14 1/2-ounce can salsa with cilantro
- 1/2 cup water
- 1/4 cup (2 ounces) diced green chilies or 2 tablespoons (1 ounce) chopped jalapeño (optional)
- 1 14-ounce can regular black beans, drained and rinsed, or 1 14-ounce can Southwest-style black beans
- 3 to 5 ounces goat cheese (Gjetost is good)

Topping:
- 1/2 cup yellow cornmeal
- 1/2 cup flour
- 2 teaspoons baking powder
- 1/4 teaspoon salt
- 1/2 cup milk
- 2 tablespoons butter or margarine
- 1 egg

Preheat oven to 350 degrees. Heat vegetable oil in skillet. Cut chicken breasts into 1/2-inch pieces and toss with salt and pepper. Brown chicken in hot vegetable oil just until no longer pink on the outside. Remove chicken and set aside. Add onions and mushrooms to hot skillet. Cook until softened, about 4 minutes. Add salsa, water, and chilies. Simmer for about 4 minutes. Add chicken and black beans. Return to simmering. Add goat cheese and swirl to melt. Pour mixture into an ungreased 8x12-inch glass casserole dish.

To prepare topping, melt butter in a medium bowl in microwave. Allow to cool slightly while measuring flour, salt, and baking powder into sifter. Add milk and egg to melted butter and beat. Add cornmeal. Sift flour mixture in and stir just enough to combine all ingredients. Spread batter evenly over top of casserole.

Martha Thompson
Lakewood, Colorado

Chicken and Sausage Jambalaya

Seasoning Mix:
- 4 bay leaves
- 1 teaspoon salt
- 1 teaspoon white pepper
- 1 teaspoon dry mustard
- 1 1/2 teaspoons cayenne pepper
- 1/2 teaspoon ground cumin
- 1/2 teaspoon black pepper
- 1/2 teaspoon dried thyme leaves

Jambalaya:
- 4 tablespoons olive oil
- 1/2 pound smoked sausage
- 1 pound chicken breasts
- 1 cup chopped onions
- 1 cup chopped celery
- 1 cup chopped sweet pepper
- 1 teaspoon minced garlic
- 1 28-ounce can diced tomatoes
- 2 1/2 cups uncooked converted rice
- 1 14 1/2-ounce can chicken broth
- 3/4 cup water

Thoroughly combine the ingredients in the seasoning mix and set aside. In a large heavy pot, heat the olive oil over medium heat. Add the meat and cook for 5 minutes, stirring occasionally. Stir in the seasoning mix, onions, celery, sweet pepper, and garlic. Cook about 10 to 12 minutes until browned, stirring occasionally and scraping the bottom of the pot. Add the tomatoes and cook for 5 minutes. Stir in the rice and cook for 5 more minutes, continuing to stir and scrape the bottom occasionally. Add the broth, stirring well, and bring the mixture to a boil. Reduce heat and simmer for about 20 minutes until the rice is tender but still a bit crunchy. Remove bay leaves and serve immediately.

Teresa Mensch
Evergreen, Colorado

Chicken Cordon Bleu

- 4 skinless, boneless chicken breasts
- 4 1x3-inch slices Monterey Jack or Swiss cheese
- 4 slices cooked ham
- 1 egg, well beaten
  - Italian bread crumbs
  - butter or margarine
  - parsley flakes

Preheat oven to 325 degrees. Wash chicken and drain. Pound chicken breasts flat between two pieces of waxed paper. On one-half of the chicken place slice of cheese and ham. Fold chicken in half with cheese and ham inside. Dip in beaten egg and then in bread crumbs. Place chicken in 8x8-inch baking dish and top with a pat of butter. Sprinkle with parsley flakes. Bake for 40 minutes, uncovered.

Notes:
Delicious served with scalloped potatoes.

Charlotte Seaton
Fort Lupton, Colorado

Yield: 4 servings

Lynda's Chicken Enchiladas

- 1 small chicken (1 1/2 pounds)
- 1 large onion, chopped
- 2 10 3/4-ounce cans cream of chicken soup
- 2 cups milk
- 1 7-ounce can whole green chilies, chopped
- 12 ounces Cheddar cheese, shredded, divided
- 12 ounces Monterey Jack cheese, shredded, divided
- 10 8-inch flour tortillas

Boil chicken with chopped onion until chicken is tender. Drain, reserving broth and chopped onions. Allow chicken to cool. Pick chicken from bones, breaking into bite-sized pieces.

Mix soup, milk, and reserved chopped onion. Stir until smooth. Add chicken pieces and green chilies to mixture. Combine the two cheeses. Reserve 3/4 cup of combined shredded cheese. Put the remaining cheese into the soup mixture and stir well.

Coat a 9x13x2-inch pan with non-stick cooking spray. Place 1/2 cup reserved chicken broth in bottom of pan. Tear flour tortillas in quarters and place one layer on the bottom of the pan. Spread half of the chicken mixture over the tortillas. Top chicken mixture with another layer of torn tortillas. Top the tortillas with the remaining chicken mixture. Sprinkle the reserved 3/4 cup of cheeses over the top and bake for 30 to 40 minutes in a preheated 350-degree oven until bubbling hot.

Variations:
Can use a light Cheddar cheese, if desired. Other soup options are cream of mushroom or cream of celery.

Lynda Vickers
Aurora, Colorado

Yield: 8 to 12 servings

Herb Chicken Casserole

1/2	cup chopped onion
1	cup chopped celery
1 to 2	tablespoons vegetable oil
1/2	cup chopped almonds
2/3	cup butter or margarine
1 1/2 to 2	cups herb stuffing mix
3-4	pounds chicken or chicken breasts, cooked and chopped
1 1/3	cup evaporated milk
2	10 3/4-ounce cans cream of mushroom soup
2	10 3/4-ounce cans cream of chicken soup
1	5-ounce can chow mein noodles
1	8-ounce can sliced water chestnuts

Preheat oven to 350 degrees. Heat onion and celery in vegetable oil. Sauté almonds in margarine. Add stuffing mix and onions and celery to almonds. Stir well. Combine chicken, evaporated milk, cream of mushroom soup, cream of chicken soup, chow mein noodles, and water chestnuts. Mix well. Put this mixture into an 8x15-inch casserole dish. Spread stuffing mixture on top. Bake for 1 hour.

Notes:
This freezes well, but add 1/2 to 1 cup of water before baking. Great recipe to have for those days when you have been out being creative all day.

Fran von Hagel
Longmont, Colorado

Sweet-Sour Chicken

1 3- to 4-pound whole fryer chicken
1 8-ounce bottle Russian dressing
1 8-ounce jar apricot jam
1 1.25-ounce package dry onion soup mix

Preheat oven to 350 degrees. Skin chicken; cut into serving pieces. Thoroughly mix salad dressing, jam, and onion soup mix. Place chicken in a 9x13x2-inch baking pan. Cover with the dressing mixture. Bake, covered, for 1 hour. Remove cover and bake for an additional 30 minutes.

Katy Westerman
Alamosa, Colorado

Imperial Chicken

   1 cup bread or cracker crumbs
 1/2 cup Parmesan cheese
 1/4 cup chopped fresh parsley
 1/2 teaspoon garlic powder or 1 teaspoon crushed fresh garlic
   1 teaspoon salt
 1/2 teaspoon pepper
 1/4 cup margarine
   1 3- to 4-pound chicken, cut up

Preheat oven to 350 degrees. Blend crumbs, cheese, parsley, garlic, salt, and pepper. Melt margarine. Dip chicken pieces into melted margarine, then roll into crumb mixture. Arrange chicken in a single layer in a shallow baking dish that has been sprayed with a non-stick cooking spray. Make sure pieces of chicken do not touch. Bake uncovered for 1 hour. Turn chicken over and continue baking for another 30 minutes.

Sissi Williams
Westminster, Colorado

Yield: 4 to 8 servings

Turn your ironing board "backwards" so the iron rests on the narrow end; great to press blocks.

Vince's Low-Fat Oven-Fried Chicken

- 1   3- to 4-pound whole fryer chicken
- 1   tablespoon olive oil or canola oil
- 1   cup white or whole wheat flour
- 1   teaspoon savory salt
- 1/2 teaspoon pepper
- 1 1/2 teaspoons onion powder
- 1   teaspoon ground sage
- 1 1/2 teaspoons garlic powder

Preheat oven to 375 degrees. Cut wings off the chicken and set aside in a large bowl. Skin remaining chicken; cut into serving pieces. Place all chicken into large bowl with wings; add olive oil. In another bowl, place flour, salt, pepper, onion powder, sage, and garlic powder. Mix thoroughly. Cover cookie sheet with foil. Place cooking rack on top of cookie sheet. Turn chicken in olive oil so chicken is completely covered with olive oil. Dredge chicken in flour and spice mix, and place on cooking rack. Bake for 45 minutes. Remove chicken from oven, turn over, and continue baking for 35 minutes. Remove from oven and allow to cool for a few minutes. Serve.

Katy Westerman
Alamosa, Colorado

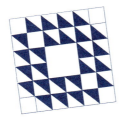

Turkey Enchiladas

3 to 4	cups cooked turkey, chopped
2	10¾-ounce cans cream of chicken soup
2	4-ounce cans diced mild green chilies
1	cup sour cream
2	cups shredded Cheddar cheese, divided
1	cup diced onion
10 to 12	flour tortillas

Preheat oven to 350 degrees. In a saucepan mix chopped turkey, cream of chicken soup, green chilies, sour cream, 1 cup shredded Cheddar cheese, and onion together. Heat until cheese melts to blend flavors. Divide mixture among flour tortillas, roll up, and place in a pan. Spread extra mixture on top. Cover with remaining shredded Cheddar cheese. Bake for 15 to 20 minutes until heated through and cheese is melted.

Notes:
These enchiladas freeze well and can be reheated in the oven or microwave quickly.

Bev Zabloudil
Buena Vista, Colorado

Yield: 10 to 12 enchiladas

Tangy Grilled Turkey Tenderloins

- 1 tablespoon low-sodium soy sauce
- 1 tablespoon dijon mustard
- 1 teaspoon lemon juice
- 1/2 teaspoon tarragon
- 1/8 teaspoon garlic powder
- 1 pound turkey tenderloins

Coat a grill rack with non-stick cooking spray. Fire up the grill and allow it to heat until hot. Place the rack on the grill.

In a medium bowl, combine the soy sauce, mustard, lemon juice, tarragon, and garlic powder. Add the tenderloins, turning them several times to coat with the marinade.

Place the tenderloins on the rack and grill them until cooked through, 5 to 7 minutes on each side. Remove tenderloins from the heat and let stand for 1 to 2 minutes. Cut the tenderloins into 1-inch diagonal slices.

Variations:
Substitute chicken breasts for the turkey tenderloins.

Notes:
This is a no-fail recipe that takes very little time to make. The turkey comes out tender and moist each time.

Gail Tibbetts
Denver, Colorado

Yield: 4 servings

Turkey Taco Filling

6 to 8   toasted taco shells

Filling:
- 1 tablespoon olive oil
- 1/2 large onion, finely chopped
- 1 teaspoon minced garlic
- 1 pound ground turkey
- 1 tablespoon plus 1 teaspoon chili powder
- 2 teaspoons paprika
- 2 teaspoons crushed oregano
- 1 teaspoon ground cumin
- 1/4 teaspoon ground red pepper
- 3/4 cup water

Toppings: (to taste)
- grated cheese
- chopped tomatoes
- black or green olives, sliced
- shredded lettuce

Sauté onion in olive oil until transparent. Add garlic and turkey. Sauté and crumble turkey until thoroughly cooked. Pour off any remaining liquid. Add spices and water. Bring to boil. Reduce heat and simmer until all water is boiled off.

Serve in toasted taco shells topped with grated cheese, chopped tomatoes, black or green olives, and lettuce.

Delia Molloy da Cunha
Boulder, Colorado

Yield: 6 to 8 tacos

Country Potpie

- 2 cups cubed, cooked turkey
- 1 17-ounce can cream-style corn
- 3/4 cup frozen peas
- 2 carrots, finely chopped
- 3 tablespoons minced onion
- 3 diced potatoes
- 2 cups diced Monterey Jack cheese
- 2 tablespoons chopped fresh parsley
- 1/4 teaspoon garlic powder
- 1/4 teaspoon salt
- black pepper
- 1 1/2 cups milk
- 1 tablespoon worcestershire sauce

enough pie dough to cover top of 9x13x2-inch pan (use your favorite recipe)

Preheat oven to 375 degrees. Mix all the ingredients together and turn into a buttered 9x13x2-inch baking dish. Cover filling with your favorite pastry, sealing edges of pan. Bake for 1 hour. Cover top with foil if crust is browning too much.

Linda Holst
Wheatland, Wyoming

Use a fabric softener sheet to lay over pins on top of applique. This will help to keep thread from catching on pins and also keep thread from knotting as you stitch.

Oriental Turkey Bake

- 1   10³/₄-ounce can cream of celery soup
- ¹/₃ cup water
- 2   tablespoons soy sauce
- 2   medium green onions, sliced
- 1   15-ounce can mixed vegetables, drained, or 16-ounce bag of frozen mixed vegetables
- 2   cups cooked cubed turkey
- 2   cups cooked rice (instant is okay)
- ¹/₂ cup canned French-fried onions

Preheat oven to 350 degrees. In a 2-quart casserole, mix soup, water, soy sauce, green onions, mixed vegetables, turkey, and rice. Bake, covered, for 25 minutes. Stir. Sprinkle French-fried onions over turkey mix. Bake, uncovered, for 5 minutes or until onions are golden brown.

Notes:
Great with leftover turkey. I prefer Veg-All canned mixed vegetables.

Melba Queener
Leadville, Colorado

Yield: 4 servings

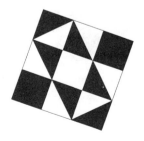

Beef Samovar

- 2 tablespoons margarine
- 1 pound round steak, cut into $1/2$-inch cubes
- 1 small onion, chopped
- $1/2$ clove garlic, minced
- 1 tablespoon flour
- $1/2$ cup chopped mushrooms, with juice from jar/can
- $1/4$ cup chopped celery
- 1 8-ounce can tomato sauce
- $1/2$ teaspoon salt
- pepper to taste
- 1 teaspoon worcestershire sauce
- $1/2$ cup sour cream
- rice, prepared according to package directions

Preheat oven to 325 degrees. In a skillet, melt margarine. Add cubed round steak and brown lightly. Add onion and garlic and brown lightly. Add flour, mushrooms with juice, celery, tomato sauce, salt, pepper, worcestershire sauce, and sour cream. Mix well. Place into casserole dish. Bake, uncovered, for $1 1/2$ hours. Serve over rice.

Penny Hoopes
Westminster, Colorado

Yield: 6 to 8 servings

Swiss Steak

- 2 pounds round steak
- 1/2 cup flour
- 1/4 cup vegetable oil
- 1/2 pound sliced mushrooms (optional)
- 1/2 sweet pepper, diced in large pieces
- 1 tablespoon A-1 sauce
- 1 1.25-ounce package dry onion soup mix
- 1 16-ounce can tomatoes

Preheat oven to 350 degrees. Remove bone and fat from steak. Cut steak into serving size pieces. Pound meat with mallet to tenderize. Dredge thoroughly with flour. Brown in vegetable oil in large skillet. Stack on side of skillet while you sauté mushrooms. Mix remaining ingredients with meat drippings in pan. Bury steak pieces in sauce. Simmer on stove top or bake in oven for 2 hours. Add small amounts of water during cooking if necessary.

Notes:
The sauce makes an excellent gravy. Serve with mashed potatoes.

Rose McCullough
Pueblo, Colorado

Barbeque Beef Sandwiches

1 to 2 pounds cooked beef (leftover pot roast works best)
1 15-ounce can tomato sauce
3/4 cup chopped onion
1/4 cup chopped sweet pepper
2 tablespoons brown sugar
2 tablespoons worcestershire sauce
1 tablespoon dry mustard
 dash of bottled hot pepper sauce
1 tablespoon pickling spice
 ground cinnamon, to taste
 ground cloves, to taste
 ground nutmeg, to taste
 dash of liquid smoke
1/2 cup barbeque sauce
 hamburger buns

In a large pot (or slow cooker), combine beef, tomato sauce, onion, sweet pepper, brown sugar, worcestershire sauce, dry mustard, and hot pepper sauce. Place pickling spice in cheesecloth and add to pot. Simmer (or cook on low if you are using a slow cooker) for 8 to 10 hours.

One hour before serving, add cinnamon, cloves, nutmeg, liquid smoke, and barbeque sauce. Mix well and continue to simmer for 1 hour. Just before serving, remove cheesecloth with pickling spice. Place meat mixture on hamburger buns and serve.

Notes:
There is lots of time to quilt while this mixture simmers.

Ginny Moore
Broomfield, Colorado

Salsa-Garlic Flank Steak

- 1 pound lean flank steak
- 1 teaspoon ground cumin
- 1 teaspoon ground coriander
- 1/2 teaspoon chili powder
- 1 cup medium picante sauce, divided
- 1 1/2 teaspoons minced fresh garlic
- non-stick cooking spray
- 1/4 cup frozen whole kernel corn, thawed

Trim fat from steak. Combine cumin, coriander, and chili powder; rub steak with spice mixture. Combine steak, 1/2 cup picante sauce, and garlic in a zip-top heavy duty plastic bag; seal bag. Marinate in refrigerator at least 8 hours, turning bag occasionally.

Remove steak from bag; discard marinade. Coat grill rack with non-stick cooking spray; place rack on grill over medium-hot coals. Place steak on rack; cook 8 minutes on each side or until desired degree of doneness. Cut diagonally across the grain into thick slices. Combine remaining 1/2 cup picante sauce and corn; stir will. Serve over steak.

Gail Tibbetts
Denver, Colorado

Yield: 4 servings

Flat Brisket of Beef

4 to 7 pounds brisket of beef (not corned beef)
seasoned pepper
1 1.25-ounce package onion soup mix
3/4 cup (6 ounces) beer
1/4 teaspoon garlic powder
ketchup

Preheat oven to 225 degrees. Place brisket in a 9x13x2-inch oven-proof pan. Season brisket by sprinkling with seasoned pepper and onion soup mix. Pour beer and ketchup over top of brisket. Tightly cover pan with foil. Set pan with brisket in a larger pan with water in it. Cook overnight, keeping brisket covered tightly. When done, allow brisket to set in juices for a while. Remove brisket from pan and pour off juices, then set juices aside so fat can congeal. Skim off fat. Save remaining juices for gravy or pour over sliced brisket and reheat at 350 degrees for 45 minutes, uncovered. (Slice meat against the grain when brisket is cooled.)

Notes:
Make this and everyone will want your recipe.

Ann Moss
Grand Junction, Colorado

Wax your own thread...it is better! Heat paraffin in a small can set in a larger pan of water. Lower spool of thread into melted wax. Roll gently until tiny bubbles stop rising from thread. Remove and place on a rack to cool.

All Day Chuck Roast

- 1 1.25-ounce package onion soup mix
- 2 10¾-ounce cans golden mushroom soup (do not dilute)
- 1 chuck roast (enough for however many people you are serving)
- 2 medium white onions per person, cut into fourths
- 1 16-ounce package small carrots
- 1 russet potato per person, cut into fourths

Preheat oven to 400 degrees. With enough foil to make an envelope that can be sealed tight, line a large glass or metal pan. Mix onion soup mix and mushroom soup together. Pour a small amount of the soup mixture into the bottom of the foil-lined pan. Place meat in center of the pan. Place vegetables around and on top of the meat. Pour remaining soup mixture on top of the meat and vegetables. Seal foil tightly across top and at each end. Cook for 1 hour. Reduce heat to 250 to 225 degrees and cook all day.

Notes:
This is a great recipe to prepare before heading out for a day in the mountains or to a quilt meeting. Serve with tossed salad and crusty crunchy bread.

L. Elaine Penkava
Loveland, Colorado

I cut templates for a pattern, put them in a zip-top plastic bag, and staple to the back cover of the pattern book with the pattern name inside.

Barbequed Spareribs

10 pounds spare ribs

Pete and Winkie's barbeque sauce:
- 1 cup catsup
- 1/3 cup worcestershire sauce
- 1/4 teaspoon bottled hot pepper sauce
- 1 teaspoon chili powder
- 1 teaspoon salt
- 2 cups water*

Place ribs into a pan of boiling water. Continue to boil ribs, keeping them completely covered in water for 40 minutes or until the meat starts coming away from the bone. Have the barbeque coals ready.

Combine all ingredients for the sauce thoroughly.

Brush the ribs with sauce; turn and brush again. Grill; continue brushing and turning ribs for about 20 minutes. Let the ribs get brown, but not black. They can be kept warm in the oven, but do not let them dry out. Serve with remaining sauce on the side.

Notes:
*For the water in the barbeque sauce, you can use 2 cups of the water that the ribs were boiled in.

Jeanne Creighton
Denver, Colorado

Yield: 8 servings

Grilled Island Teriyaki

1 1/2 to 2 pounds sirloin steak

Marinade:
- 1/2 cup soy sauce
- 1/4 cup packed brown sugar
- 2 tablespoons vegetable oil
- 1 teaspoon dry ginger
- 1/4 teaspoon cracked pepper
- 1 clove garlic, minced

Cut steak into 1/4x1-inch strips.

To make marinade, mix soy sauce, brown sugar, vegetable oil, ginger, pepper, and cloves. Add meat and stir to coat. Marinate for at least 2 hours. Lace meat accordion style on skewers. Grill meat over hot coals for 10 minutes. Turn often and baste with marinade.

Charlotte Seaton
Fort Lupton, Colorado

Enchilada Pie

- 2 pounds ground beef
- 1 medium clove garlic, minced
- 1 medium onion, chopped
- 1 7-ounce can green chilies, drained and diced
- 1 10¾-ounce can cream of mushroom soup
- 1 16-ounce can stewed tomatoes
- ½ teaspoon chili powder
  salt and pepper
  corn chips
- 16 ounces Longhorn cheese, grated

Preheat oven to 350 degrees. Crumble beef into heated skillet. Add garlic and onion. Cook over medium heat, stirring occasionally until meat loses red color. Drain off grease. Combine chilies, soup, and tomatoes. Add to meat mixture with chili powder, salt, and pepper. Mix well. Arrange corn chips in bottom of 9x13x2-inch pan. Spoon half of meat mixture over chips. Sprinkle half of cheese on meat. Repeat layers. Cover loosely with foil. Bake 45 minutes to 1 hour.

Mary Baughn
Fort Collins, Colorado

Mexican Lasagna

- 1½ pounds ground beef
- 1 medium onion, chopped
- 1 clove garlic, minced
- 1 16-ounce can of tomatoes
- 1 10-ounce can red chile sauce (or use picante sauce)
- 1 4-ounce can chopped olives
- 1 teaspoon salt
- ¼ teaspoon pepper
- 8 ounces Monterey Jack cheese
- 8 ounces Ricotta cheese
- 1 egg
- ½ cup shredded Cheddar cheese
- tortilla chips

Preheat oven to 350 degrees. Brown ground beef, onion, and garlic. Add tomatoes, chili sauce, olives, salt, and pepper. Simmer 20 minutes or more—until the sauce is cooked down.

Slice the Monterey Jack cheese in thin slices. Mix Ricotta cheese with the egg.

Spread one-third of the meat mixture in a 2-quart casserole dish. Top with half of the Monterey Jack slices, then half of the Ricotta cheese mixture. Add a layer of tortilla chips. Repeat layers. Reserve one-third of the meat sauce for the top. Sprinkle with Cheddar cheese. Bake for 20 minutes or until cheese is melted.

Jo Griffin
Bayfield, Colorado

Zucchini Lasagna

- 1 pound ground beef
- 1 onion, chopped
- 1 tablespoon chopped sweet pepper
- 1 teaspoon salt
- 1/4 teaspoon pepper
- 1 6-ounce can tomato paste
- 1 1/2 cups water
- 1 10 3/4-ounce can tomato soup
- 1/2 teaspoon oregano
- 3 medium zucchini
- 12 ounces small-curd cottage cheese
- 1/2 cup grated Parmesan cheese
- 1 tablespoon parsley flakes
- 2 eggs, beaten
- 1 1/2 teaspoons salt
- 1/2 teaspoon pepper
- 12 ounces Mozzarella cheese, thinly sliced

Preheat oven to 350 degrees. Brown meat; spoon off excess grease. Add onions, sweet peppers, salt, and pepper. Cook until onions are tender. Add tomato paste, water, and soup. Cook slowly for 30 to 45 minutes. Add oregano. Slice zucchini lengthwise so it is like lasagna noodles. Make a layer of zucchini in a 9x13x2-inch pan. Mix together cottage cheese, Parmesan cheese, parsley flakes, eggs, salt, and pepper. Spread half of this mixture over layer of zucchini. Add half of Mozzarella cheese and top with half of meat sauce. Repeat. Bake for 40 to 45 minutes. Let stand for 10 minutes before cutting.

Notes:
Freezes well.

Joan Christopherson
Englewood, Colorado

Dorothy's Sloppy Joes

2 pounds ground round
1 onion, chopped
1 sweet pepper, chopped
1 cup chopped celery
1 8-ounce can tomato sauce
1 cup ketchup
2 tablespoons brown sugar
1 tablespoon worcestershire sauce

Break up and brown ground round. Add chopped onion, sweet pepper, and celery. In a separate bowl, combine tomato sauce, ketchup, brown sugar, and worcestershire sauce. Add to ground beef mixture. Simmer.

Betty Jo Dreith
Longmont, Colorado

Swiss Hamburger Onion Pie

  1 cup plus 2 tablespoons buttermilk baking mix, divided
  1/3 cup light cream or milk
  1 pound ground beef
  2 medium onions, sliced very thin
    salt and pepper to taste
  2 eggs, beaten
  1 12-ounce carton small-curd cottage cheese, slightly beaten
    paprika

Preheat oven to 350 degrees. Mix 1 cup baking mix and cream or milk with fork. Roll out for 9-inch pie crust. Place crust in pie pan and shape edge. In skillet, sauté ground beef, onions, salt, and pepper until meat is browned. Stir in 2 tablespoons baking mix. Spread meat mixture over pie crust. In a separate bowl beat eggs and blend in cottage cheese. Pour over meat mixture. Sprinkle generously with paprika. Bake 30 to 40 minutes or until custard top is firm and crust is a delicate brown.

Notes:
You can cut this pie into wedges to serve for a main dish or cut into narrow pieces as an appetizer. Good hot or cold. Freezes well.

Lucy Ellsworth
Denver, Colorado

Mexican Manicotti

1	pound ground beef or turkey
2 to 3	16-ounce cans refried beans
1	teaspoon ground cumin
1	teaspoon oregano
16	uncooked manicotti shells
2	cups water
2	cups picante sauce
1	cup shredded Cheddar cheese

Preheat oven to 350 degrees. Brown beef or turkey and drain well. Add refried beans and reheat; mixing well. Add cumin and oregano. Stuff uncooked shells. Place in 9x13x2-inch pan. Mix water, picante sauce, and any unused meat/bean mixture. Pour over shells. Sprinkle shredded cheese on top. Cover and bake 20 minutes. Remove cover and bake an additional 5 to 10 minutes. Let stand 5 minutes before serving.

Variations:
May also layer meat/bean mixture with uncooked lasagna noodles. Follow remaining instructions.

Lori Erickson
Denver, Colorado

Hearty Rice Casserole

  1   10¾-ounce can condensed cream of mushroom soup, undiluted
  1   10¾-ounce can condensed creamy onion soup, undiluted
  1   10¾-ounce can condensed cream of chicken soup, undiluted
  1   pound raw lean ground beef
  1   pound raw pork sausage
  1   large onion, chopped
  1   large sweet pepper, chopped
1½   cups uncooked long grain rice

Preheat oven to 350 degrees. Combine all of the ingredients in a greased 4-quart baking dish; mix well. Cover tightly and bake for 60 to 70 minutes or until the rice is tender.

Shirley Franzen
Thornton, Colorado

Yield: 12 to 16 servings

Baked Italian Spaghetti

- 1 medium onion, chopped
- 1 pound ground beef
- 3 8-ounce cans tomato sauce
- 1/4 teaspoon dried oregano
- 1/4 teaspoon dried marjoram
- 1/4 teaspoon dried basil
- dash of garlic salt
- 1 tablespoon sugar
- 1/2 teaspoon salt
- 1/4 teaspoon pepper
- 1/2 pound spaghetti noodles, broken into 6-inch lengths
- 1 cup grated Cheddar cheese, divided

The day before serving, in a large skillet, sauté onion and ground beef until brown. Add tomato sauce, rinsing cans and adding water to sauce. Add oregano, marjoram, basil, garlic salt, and sugar. Simmer, covered, stirring occasionally, for 1 hour. Meanwhile, cook spaghetti as directed on package and drain. Add 1/2 cup grated cheese to the sauce just before mixing sauce with the spaghetti. Put into a greased 3-quart casserole. Refrigerate overnight. About 1 1/2 hours before serving, sprinkle top with remaining 1/2 cup cheese. Bake covered in a preheated 325-degree oven for 45 minutes. Remove cover and bake for 30 more minutes.

Notes:
This is an easy recipe to do ahead of time.

Carolynn Fox
Lakewood, Colorado

Amish "Yum-A-Setta"

- 2 pounds ground beef
- 1/4 cup chopped onion
- salt and pepper, to taste
- 2 tablespoons brown sugar
- 1 10 3/4-ounce can tomato soup
- 1 16-ounce package noodles
- 1 10 3/4-ounce can cream of chicken soup
- 1 8-ounce package processed cheese, cut into small cubes or grated

Preheat oven to 350 degrees. Brown meat with onion, salt, pepper, and brown sugar. Stir in tomato soup. Set aside. Cook and drain noodles. Stir in cream of chicken soup. Layer ground beef mixture and noodle mixture in 2-quart casserole dish. Place cheese on top. Cover with foil. Bake for 30 minutes.

Beverly Giffin
Pueblo West, Colorado

Barbequed Hamburgers

Hamburgers:
- 1 1/2 pounds ground beef
- 3/4 cup rolled oats
- 1 cup milk
- 3 teaspoons minced onion
- 1 1/2 teaspoons salt
- 1/2 teaspoon pepper

Sauce:
- 2 cups ketchup
- 2 tablespoons worcestershire sauce
- 2 teaspoons dry mustard
- 3 tablespoons vinegar
- 1/2 cup packed brown sugar
- 1 cup water
- 6 tablespoons minced onion

Preheat oven to 350 degrees.

For hamburgers, combine all ingredients and form meat mixture into size hamburgers desired. Flour and brown in hot skillet. Arrange in a baking dish.

For sauce, combine all ingredients and heat until warm. Pour over hamburgers and bake for 30 minutes.

Alice Mathews
Loveland, Colorado

Picnic Pizza

1½ pounds ground beef
1 8-ounce can tomato sauce
1 cup chopped black or green olives
   celery salt, to taste
   garlic salt, to taste
   garlic pepper, to taste
   Italian seasoning, to taste
1 cup grated Provolone cheese
   submarine rolls
   American cheese
   oregano, to taste

Preheat oven to 375 degrees. Brown ground beef in frying pan. Add tomato sauce and chopped olives. Add celery salt, garlic salt, garlic pepper, and Italian seasoning to mixture and stir well. Add Provolone cheese and stir constantly until cheese has melted. Remove from heat and spread meat in submarine rolls. Place slices of American cheese on top and sprinkle with oregano. Wrap in aluminum foil and bake for 15 minutes.

Doris Matson
Pueblo, Colorado

Stuffed Peppers

Peppers:
- 6 to 8 sweet peppers
- 1 cup water
- 1 teaspoon margarine
- 1/2 teaspoon salt
- 1/2 cup uncooked rice
- 2 eggs, beaten
- 3/4 cup milk
- 1/2 cup bread crumbs
- 1/2 1.25-ounce package dry onion soup mix
- 1 pound ground beef

Sauce:
- 2 tablespoons margarine
- 1/4 onion, chopped
- 1 5 1/2-ounce can tomato juice
- 1 6-ounce can tomato paste
- 1/4 cup packed brown sugar
- 2 tablespoons worcestershire sauce
- 1 teaspoon salt
- 1/2 teaspoon ground nutmeg

Preheat oven to 350 degrees. Wash the sweet peppers; cut off and reserve the tops; remove seeds; set aside. Bring water to boil; add margarine, salt, and rice. Cook until rice is tender, but not fully cooked. Combine eggs, milk, bread crumbs, and onion soup mix and let stand a few minutes. Add ground beef and rice with its liquid; mix well. Fill peppers and place in a baking dish.

Chop reserved sweet pepper and place in a saucepan with margarine and onions. Cook until tender. Add tomato juice, tomato paste, brown sugar, worcestershire sauce, salt, and nutmeg. Pour over stuffed peppers. Bake in oven for 1 hour or in a slow cooker for 4 to 5 hours.

Ellen McAninch
Littleton, Colorado

Yield: 6 to 8 servings

Chili Pizzeria Bake

- 1 pound ground beef
- 1 small onion, chopped
- 1 16-ounce can beans in chili sauce
- 1 29-ounce can tomatoes
- 1 6-ounce can tomato paste
- 1/4 cup chopped sweet pepper
- 1 teaspoon salt
- 1/2 teaspoon oregano
- 1/4 teaspoon thyme
- 1 teaspoon chili powder
- 1 cup uncooked shell macaroni
- 1/4 cup grated Parmesan cheese
- 1/4 cup grated Mozzarella cheese

Preheat oven to 350 degrees. Brown ground beef and onion. Add beans, tomatoes, tomato paste, sweet pepper, salt, oregano, thyme, chili powder, and macaroni. Mix well. Pour into a 2-quart casserole dish and bake for 45 to 50 minutes, stirring occasionally. Remove from oven; top with Parmesan and Mozzarella cheeses. Return to oven and bake about 15 minutes or until cheeses are bubbly.

Nancy Orth
Kiowa, Colorado

Spaghetti Pie

Crust:
- 6 ounces spaghetti
- 2 tablespoons margarine
- 2 eggs, well beaten
- 1/3 Parmesan cheese

Filling:
- 1/2 pound ground beef
- 1/2 pound Italian sausage
- 1/2 cup chopped onion
- 1/4 cup chopped sweet pepper
- 1 7 1/2-ounce can tomatoes, cut up
- 1 6-ounce can tomato paste
- 1 teaspoon sugar
- 1 teaspoon dried oregano, crushed
- 1/4 teaspoon garlic salt
- 1 cup cream-style cottage cheese
- 1 cup shredded Mozzarella cheese

Preheat oven to 350 degrees. Cook spaghetti according to package directions; drain. You should have about 3 cups cooked spaghetti. Stir margarine into hot spaghetti. Stir in eggs and Parmesan cheese. Press spaghetti mixture into buttered 10-inch pie plate, forming crust.

In a large skillet, cook beef, sausage, onion, and sweet pepper until vegetables are tender and meat is browned. Drain off fat. Stir in undrained tomatoes, tomato paste, sugar, oregano, and garlic salt. Heat through. Spread cottage cheese over bottom of prepared spaghetti crust. Top with meat mixture. Bake, uncovered, for 20 minutes. Sprinkle Mozzarella cheese on top. Bake another 5 minutes until cheese is melted.

Charlotte Seaton
Fort Lupton, Colorado

Yield: 6 servings

Barbequed Meatballs

Meatballs:
- 1 5-ounce can evaporated milk
- 1 1/2 pounds lean ground beef
- 1 cup quick cooking oatmeal
- 1 egg, beaten
- 1/4 cup chopped onions or 1 tablespoon dried onions
- 1 teaspoon salt
- 1/4 teaspoon pepper
- 1 teaspoon chili powder

Sauce:
- 1 cup ketchup
- 3/4 cup packed brown sugar
- 1/4 teaspoon garlic powder
- 1 tablespoon chopped onion or 1 teaspoon dried onion
- 2 teaspoons liquid smoke

Preheat oven to 350 degrees. Mix all ingredients and shape into large balls—use ice cream scoop. Place in a single layer on a flat-bottomed 9x13x2-inch casserole dish.

Combine all ingredients for sauce and mix well. Pour over meatballs. Bake for 1 hour.

Notes:
Can be frozen.

Ruth Rupert
Denver, Colorado

Broccoli-Cheese Stromboli

- 1/2 pound ground meat (lean beef, sausage, or pork)
- 1 medium onion, chopped
- 1 14 1/2-ounce can Italian-style tomatoes
- 1/2 cup chopped broccoli
- 1/2 teaspoon Italian seasoning
- 1/4 teaspoon pepper
- 1/4 cup chopped red or green sweet pepper
- 1/4 cup sliced pitted ripe olives
- 6 mushrooms, chopped
- 1 10-ounce package refrigerated pizza dough
- 1 cup shredded Mozzarella cheese

Preheat oven to 375 degrees. To make filling, in a medium skillet cook meat and onion until meat is no longer pink and onion is tender. Drain fat. Stir in undrained tomatoes, broccoli, Italian seasoning, and pepper. Bring to a boil; reduce heat. Simmer, uncovered, about 15 minutes or until most of the liquid has evaporated, stirring occasionally. Stir in sweet pepper, olives, and mushrooms. Cool slightly.

Spray a 10x15x1-inch baking pan with non-stick cooking spray; set aside. On lightly floured surface, roll pizza dough into a 14x12-inch rectangle. Cut dough into four 7x6-inch rectangles. Down center of each rectangle, spoon one-fourth of the meat mixture. Sprinkle with cheese. Moisten dough edges with milk. Bring long edges together over filling; stretch and pinch to seal. Fold the ends up and over seam; seal. Arrange rolls, seam side down, on baking sheet. Bake uncovered for 25 to 30 minutes or until lightly brown.

Charlotte Seaton
Fort Lupton, Colorado

Yield: 4 servings

Talerini

- 1 pound ground beef
- 2 onions, chopped
- 1 garlic clove, minced
- 1 sweet pepper, chopped
- 1 15-ounce can tomato sauce
- 1 4-ounce can button mushrooms
- 1 tablespoon chili powder
- 1/2 teaspoon cayenne pepper
- salt and pepper, to taste
- 1 8-ounce package egg noodles
- 1 15-ounce can cream-style corn
- 1 pound processed cheese, divided
- 1 6-ounce can pitted olives

Preheat oven to 350 degrees. Brown the ground beef, onions, garlic, and sweet pepper. Add tomato sauce, mushrooms, chili powder, cayenne pepper, salt, and pepper. Cook egg noodles according to package directions. Do not rinse. Cut 1/2 pound cheese into cubes. Add corn, the cheese you just cut up, and olives to the noodles. Stir thoroughly. Combine meat mixture and noodle mixture and place in a large casserole dish. Cut the remaining 1/2 pound cheese into slices. Arrange the slices of cheese over the top of the mixture. Bake, uncovered, for 30 minutes.

Gail Tibbetts
Denver, Colorado

Yield: 6 to 8 servings

Fancy Beans

- 1/2 pound ground beef
- 1/2 pound bacon, diced
- 1 cup chopped onion
- 1/2 cup ketchup
- 1 teaspoon salt
- 3/4 cup packed brown sugar
- 1 teaspoon dry mustard
- 2 teaspoons vinegar
- 1 15-ounce can lima or butter beans
- 1 15-ounce can kidney beans
- 2 16-ounce cans baked beans

Preheat oven to 350 degrees. Brown meat and onions. In a 3-quart casserole dish, combine all ingredients and mix well. Bake for 25 minutes or until hot and bubbly.

Karen Scully
Colorado Springs, Colorado

Jan's Mexican Manicotti

- 1 pound ground beef
- 1 onion, chopped
- 1 clove garlic, minced
- salt and pepper, to taste
- 1 15-ounce can refried beans
- 14 manicotti pasta, uncooked
- 1 16-ounce jar picante sauce
- 2 cups water
- 1 cup shredded Monterey Jack cheese
- sour cream

Preheat oven to 350 degrees. Brown ground beef with onion, garlic, salt, and pepper. Add refried beans. Stuff 14 uncooked manicotti with mixture. Place in a 9x13x2-inch pan. Cover with picante sauce and water. Cover with foil. Bake for 1 hour and 20 minutes. Cover with cheese. Bake until melted. Serve with sour cream.

Jan Shuping
Pueblo, Colorado

Mexican Casserole

- 1 pound ground beef or 2 chicken breasts
- 1 large onion, chopped
- 2 tablespoons vegetable oil
- corn tortillas or tortilla chips
- 1 4-ounce can chopped green chilies
- 1 10¾ can cream of mushroom soup
- ½ cup milk
- 1 pound cheese, shredded, divided

Preheat oven to 325 degrees. If using ground beef, sauté ground beef and onion in vegetable oil until browned. If using chicken, cook, bone, and cut chicken into bite-sized pieces and sauté with onion in vegetable oil.

In a greased 2-quart casserole dish, spread tortillas or chips over the bottom of the dish. Place ground beef with onions over chips. Sprinkle chilies over ground beef. Sprinkle half of cheese over top of ground beef.

In a saucepan heat cream of mushroom soup and milk. Pour over mixture in casserole dish. Top with remaining cheese. Bake for 30 to 40 minutes.

Variations:
Lessen or increase amount of shredded cheese to your liking.

Notes:
I got this recipe from a quilting group at the Voyager RV Resort in Tucson, Arizona.

Roberta Grandpre'
Colorado Springs, Colorado

Yield: 6 servings

French Bread Surprise

1 pound ground beef
1 onion, chopped
1 10^{3}/$_{4}$-ounce can tomato soup
1 10^{3}/$_{4}$-ounce can cheese soup or 1^{1}/$_{3}$ cups grated Cheddar cheese
1 loaf French bread

Preheat oven to 350 degrees. Fry ground beef and onion together until browned and onions are translucent. Drain grease. Add tomato soup and cheese soup (or grated cheese). Cut loaf of bread in half lengthwise. Take middle out of both halves of bread. Break the bread you remove into pieces and put into ground beef and soup mixture. Fill hollowed-out bread with mixture. Put top on bread and wrap in foil. Bake for 15 minutes. Cut into slices and serve with a salad.

Jan Shuping
Pueblo, Colorado

Meat and Potato Puff Casserole

2 pounds ground beef, browned and drained
2 10¾-ounce cans cream of mushroom soup
1 16- to 20-ounce package frozen potato puffs

Preheat oven to 350 degrees. Place ground beef in the bottom of a 9x12-inch pan. Cover with undiluted soup. Distribute potato puffs to cover surface completely. Squeeze in as many as possible. Bake 1 hour.

Variations:
Can substitute ground turkey for the ground beef.

Jo Silkensen
Longmont, Colorado

Yield: 6 to 8 servings

Salsburg Steak
(Poor Man's Steak)

Meatloaf:
- 3 pounds ground beef
- 1 cup water
- 1 cup cracker crumbs
- dash of salt

Gravy:
- 8 ounces processed cheese, sliced
- 1 10¾-ounce can cream of mushroom soup
- water (enough to make soup gravy consistency)

Combine ground beef, water, cracker crumbs, and salt thoroughly. Mix and press into 9x5x3-inch loaf pan. Let set in refrigerator overnight. Cut into 1-inch-thick slices and pan fry until browned. Put slices in roaster pan.

For gravy, combine cream of mushroom soup and water, mixing thoroughly. Pour gravy over meat slices.

Place slices of processed cheese on top of each meat slice. Preheat oven to 350 degrees and bake for 1 hour.

Connie Wills-Sandstead
Platteville, Colorado

Cabbage Bread

- 1 pound ground beef
- 1 pound hot pork sausage
- 2 1.25-ounce envelopes onion soup mix
- 1½ cups water
- 1 head cabbage, chopped
- ½ teaspoon celery seed
- salt and pepper, to taste
- frozen prepared white bread dough, enough for two 1-pound loaves, thawed

Brown meats together in large skillet. Add both packets of onion soup mix, water, chopped cabbage, celery seeds, salt, and pepper. Simmer covered until cabbage is tender—20 to 30 minutes. Cool. Let bread dough rise for 1 hour. Roll half of dough at a time onto lightly floured board to a 12x18-inch rectangle. Cut into nine 4x6-inch sections. Fill each section with cabbage mixture and seal. Shape each into a long and narrow loaf. Place seam side down on greased baking sheet. Bake in 400-degree preheated oven for about 20 minutes or until browned.

Notes:
Leftovers can be refrigerated or frozen and reheated later.

Leann Woertman
Denver, Colorado

Yield: 18 loaves—1 serving each

Hero Burger

- 1 1/2 pounds ground beef
- 1 10 3/4-ounce can tomato soup
- 1/3 cup finely chopped onion
- 1 tablespoon prepared mustard
- 1 tablespoon worcestershire sauce
- 1 teaspoon prepared horseradish
- 1 teaspoon salt
- 1 loaf French bread or 6 hotdog buns
  sliced tomatoes
  sliced cheese

Mix ground beef, tomato soup, chopped onion, mustard, worcestershire sauce, horseradish, and salt together. Split (lengthwise) and toast French bread or hotdog buns. Spread mixture evenly over bread, covering completely. Broil 4 inches from heat for 12 minutes. Top with sliced tomatoes and cheese. Place under broiler until cheese melts.

Notes:
A real quick meal for a few or for many.

Bev Zabloudil
Buena Vista, Colorado

Yield: 6 servings

Spicy Bratwurst and Onions

  2 cups sliced onions
1/4 cup chili sauce
  1 tablespoon worcestershire sauce
1/4 cup ketchup
  2 tablespoons cider vinegar
  2 tablespoons brown sugar
1/2 teaspoon paprika
  1 pound bratwurst
  6 ounces beer

Cook bratwurst on grill until golden brown. Place all ingredients in 3-quart Dutch oven. Simmer, covered, 15 minutes until onions are tender. To serve, divide sauce, onions, and bratwurst evenly among four plates.

Notes:
This cooks up nicely in a slow cooker.

Shirley Franzen
Thornton, Colorado

Yield: 4 servings

Sausage Vegetable Dinner

- 1 pound bratwurst
- 4 medium baking potatoes, peeled and sliced
- 1 medium-sized sweet pepper, cut in strips
- 4 medium carrots, sliced $1/4$-inch thick
- 1 16-ounce can French-cut green beans
- 1 medium onion, quartered
- 1 medium head cabbage, cored and quartered
- salt and pepper, to taste
- 1 cup water

Layer bratwurst, potatoes, sweet pepper, carrots, green beans, onion, and cabbage in Dutch oven, seasoning each layer with salt and pepper, according to taste. Add water. Bring to a boil. Cover. Reduce heat and simmer 45 minutes or until vegetables are tender.

Charlotte Seaton
Fort Lupton, Colorado

Yield: 6 servings

Pork Chops Supreme

6 pork chops
3/4 cup ketchup
1/2 cup packed brown sugar
6 lemon slices

Preheat oven to 350 degrees. Lay pork chops in an ungreased baking dish. In a small bowl mix ketchup and brown sugar together. Spread mixture over pork chops. Lay a slice of lemon on each chop. Bake for 1 hour.

Notes:
I like to put potatoes in the oven to bake about 30 minutes before I put the chops in. Start the potatoes at 400 degrees, then turn the oven down when the chops go in. The pork chops are pretty for a company dish.

Marie Gifford
Aurora, Colorado

Sweet and Sour Pork

- 1½ pounds pork tenderloin, cut in 2x½-inch strips
- 2 tablespoons vegetable shortening
- ¼ cup thinly sliced onion
- ¼ cup water
- 1 tomato, sliced
- 1 20-ounce can pineapple chunks
- ¼ cup packed brown sugar
- 2 tablespoons cornstarch
- ¼ cup vinegar
- 1 tablespoon soy sauce
- 1 tablespoon molasses
- ½ teaspoon salt
- 2 carrots, sliced and cooked
- 1 sweet pepper, cut in strips
  rice, prepared according to package directions or chow mein noodles

Brown pork slowly in hot vegetable shortening. Add onion and cook slowly for 5 minutes. Add water; cover and simmer until tender, about ½ hour. Add tomato and cook 10 minutes more.

Drain pineapple, reserving syrup. Combine brown sugar and cornstarch; add pineapple syrup, vinegar, soy sauce, molasses, and salt. Pour over hot, cooked pork; stir over low heat until thick.

Add pineapple, cooked carrots, and sweet pepper. Cook 3 minutes. Serve over rice or chow mein noodles.

Variations:
Works well with chicken or other meat.

Roberta Niquette
Clifton, Colorado

Yield: 6 servings

Pork Chops with Apples and Sauerkraut

   4 pork chops
 1/2 cup chopped onions
   1 14-ounce can sauerkraut, drained
   1 large tart apple, pared, cored, and thinly sliced
 1/2 cup apple juice
 1/4 teaspoon ground sage
   1 tablespoon brown sugar
 1/8 teaspoon pepper

Preheat oven to 350 degrees. Brown chops and onion in cast iron skillet or oven-proof Dutch oven for about 4 minutes per side. Add sauerkraut, apple slices, apple juice, sage, brown sugar, and pepper. Cover tightly and bake for 1 hour.

Mae Jane Keller
Aurora, Colorado

Pork Chops and Amber Rice

   6 pork chops
2²/₃ cups instant rice
   2 cups orange juice
   1 10¾-ounce can chicken and rice soup

Preheat oven to 350 degrees. In a skillet, brown pork chops, seasoning to taste. Place instant rice and orange juice in a 9x13x2-inch baking dish and mix well. Place browned pork chops on top of rice. Pour chicken and rice soup over pork chops. Bake for 45 minutes, covered. Remove cover and continue to bake for another 10 minutes.

Tesse Kramer
Broomfield, Colorado

Yield: 6 servings

Tijuana Train Wreck

- 3 to 5 pounds pork loin roast
- 1 pound dried pinto beans
- 7 to 12 cups water
- 1/2 large onion, chopped
- 2 large garlic cloves, minced
- 1 tablespoon salt
- 2 tablespoons chili powder
- 1 8-ounce can chopped mild green chilies
- 1 tablespoon ground cumin
- 1 tablespoon oregano
- 1 16-ounce bag corn chips

Garnishes:
- shredded Cheddar cheese
- shredded Monterey Jack cheese
- chopped green onions
- more green chilies
- chopped tomatoes
- sour cream
- shredded lettuce
- guacamole
- black olives
- chopped celery

Soak beans overnight. Place all ingredients in a deep roasting pan and bake in a preheated 350-degree oven, covered, for 5 hours. Can remove lid during last half hour of baking. Check contents periodically. As needed, add more water and stir. Meat will be well cooked and falling apart. Mixture should be a little thick.

Place corn chips on plate, then add your Train Wreck and all the other garnishes.

Notes:
Caution: smaller plates are best because guests stack the toppings and cannot eat it all. Beans/pork mixture can be frozen for another crowd of guests.

Ruth Rupert
Denver, Colorado

Deanna's Sweet and Sour Pork

- 1 1/2 pounds lean pork
- 2 tablespoons vegetable oil
- 1/2 cup water
- 1 20-ounce can pineapple chunks
- 1/2 cup packed brown sugar
- 2 tablespoons cornstarch
- 2 to 3 tablespoons soy sauce
- 1/4 cup vinegar
- 1/2 teaspoon salt
- 1 small sweet pepper, cut fine
- 1/4 cup chopped onion
- rice, prepared according to package directions

Cut pork into bite-sized pieces and brown in hot vegetable oil. Add water, cover, and simmer (do not boil) until tender, approximately 1 hour. Drain pineapple, reserving syrup. Combine brown sugar, cornstarch, soy sauce, pineapple syrup, vinegar, and salt. Drain water from pork and then add sauce. Cook and stir until sauce thickens. Add pineapple, sweet pepper, and onion. Cook 2 to 3 minutes or until vegetables are tender. Serve over hot fluffy rice and pass the soy sauce.

Deanna Naumann
Aurora, Colorado

Ham Shredded Wheat Casserole

Crust:
- 2 teaspoons prepared mustard
- 2 cups milk
- 4 shredded wheat biscuits

Filling:
- 1 3-ounce can sliced mushrooms
- 4 tablespoons butter
- 4 tablespoons flour
- 1½ cups cooked ham, diced
- ½ teaspoon salt
- ⅛ teaspoon pepper
- ½ teaspoon onion salt
- ½ cup grated Cheddar cheese

Preheat oven to 425 degrees. Add mustard to milk. Quickly dip shredded wheat biscuits into milk and drain immediately. Reserve milk for filling. With point of small knife, separate biscuits into halves. Place halves in a greased 9-inch baking dish. Bake 10 minutes. Remove from oven.

For filling, drain mushrooms reserving liquid. Melt butter in saucepan. Add flour and cook until bubbly. Add milk mixture and stir until thickened. Add reserved mushroom liquid if it is too thick. Add mushrooms and ham to sauce; stir in seasonings. Spoon ham mixture over shredded wheat biscuits; top with cheese. Bake 15 minutes or until cheese is golden.

Variations:
Try dried Shiitake mushrooms in place of regular mushrooms.

Notes:
Although this recipe sounds weird, it is wonderful. The shredded wheat makes a kind of crust. This is our family's absolute favorite.

Peggy Melfi
Aurora, Colorado

Yield: 4 servings

Premium Glazed Ham

- 1¼ cups crushed saltine crackers
- 2 tablespoons finely chopped onion
- 3 eggs, slightly beaten
- ¼ cup milk
- 1½ pounds cooked ham, finely ground
- 1 teaspoon pepper
- 1 tablespoon prepared yellow mustard
- 1 teaspoon worcestershire sauce
- 1 cup lightly packed brown sugar

Preheat oven to 325 degrees. Combine cracker crumbs, onion, eggs, milk, ham, pepper, mustard, and worcestershire sauce. Mix well. Pat into a 9x5x3-inch loaf pan. Pat brown sugar evenly on top. Cover pan with foil. Bake for 2 hours. Place piece of foil on rack beneath pan in case of runover. After 90 minutes, remove top foil and bake for 30 minutes uncovered. Let cool 10 minutes before turning out onto serving plate.

Notes:
After ham loaf is prepared, you will have 2 hours to quilt. Goes great with a salad and au gratin potatoes. (You know—those "quick" ones!)

Diane Schlagel
Strasburg, Colorado

Yield: 8 servings

Ham-Potato Au Gratin

- 1/4 cup chopped onion
- 1/4 cup chopped sweet pepper
- 2 tablespoons butter or margarine
- 1 tablespoon flour
- dash of pepper
- 1 cup milk
- 1 cup (4 ounces) shredded sharp American cheese
- 1/4 cup mayonnaise
- 2 cups (3 medium) cooked and diced potatoes
- 2 cups (1 pound) diced cook ham

Preheat oven to 350 degrees. Sauté onion and sweet pepper in butter until tender. Stir in flour and pepper. Add milk and bring to a boil, stirring constantly. Reduce heat. Add cheese and mayonnaise; stir until cheese melts. Combine potatoes and ham with sauce. Bake in a 10x6x1 1/2-inch baking dish for 35 to 40 minutes.

Variations:
When potatoes are done, sprinkle with dry bread crumbs.

Pattie Timmerwilke
Palisade, Colorado

Yield: 6 servings

Tuna Fish Casserole

- 1 6-ounce can tuna fish in water, drained
- 1 10¾-ounce can cream of mushroom soup
- ½ teaspoon salt
- ¼ teaspoon pepper
- ½ cup evaporated milk
- ⅔ cup Cheddar cheese, grated, divided
- ¼ cup chopped onion
- 1 8-ounce package noodles, cooked

Preheat oven to 400 degrees. Mix tuna, soup, salt, pepper, evaporated milk, ⅓ cup cheese, and onion together. Add noodles and stir so noodles are covered with mixture. Pour into a 2-quart casserole dish and sprinkle with the remaining ⅓ cup of cheese. Bake for 20 minutes.

Mary Biesecker
Grand Junction, Colorado

Impossible Tuna Pie

- 1 9-ounce can tuna fish, drained
- 1/3 cup chopped celery
- 2 cups shredded cheese
- 1 1/2 cups milk
- 4 eggs
- 1 cup buttermilk baking mix
- 1/4 teaspoon salt
- 1/2 teaspoon pepper
- 1/2 teaspoon grated lemon rind
- 1 tablespoon lemon juice
- 1/2 teaspoon crushed garlic

Preheat oven to 350 degrees. Combine tuna fish, celery, and cheese. Spread in the bottom of a 9-inch pie pan. In a blender combine milk, eggs, buttermilk baking mix, salt, pepper, grated lemon rind, lemon juice, and garlic. Blend for 1 minute and pour over tuna mixture. Bake for 55 to 60 minutes.

Variations:
Can also add chopped black olives, peas, or mushrooms to mixture if you like.

Margy Miller
Englewood, Colorado

Orange Roughy

- 3 tablespoons olive oil
- 1/2 cup sliced onion
- 2 cups thinly sliced zucchini
- 1 teaspoon dried oregano
- 1 tomato, chopped
- 1 pound orange roughy, cut into serving-sized pieces
  salt and pepper to taste
- 1/2 cup grated Provolone cheese

Heat olive oil in large skillet. Add onion, zucchini, and oregano. Sauté over medium-high heat, stirring often, for about 4 minutes. Place tomato and fish over vegetables in skillet. Sprinkle fish with salt and pepper.

Cover skillet, reduce heat, and simmer until fish is opaque and flakes easily with a fork—about 1 1/2 minutes. Serve immediately. Top with grated cheese just before serving.

Sharon Hoffman
Charlotte, North Carolina

Yield: 4 servings

Shrimp Boats

- 1 cup finely chopped onion
- 1 cup finely chopped celery
- 2 teaspoons minced garlic
- 1/3 cup margarine
- 1 teaspoon dill
- salt and pepper, to taste
- 1 loaf French bread, sliced in half lengthwise
- 1 pound medium shrimp, cooked, peeled, sliced in half lengthwise
- 10 ounces Monterey Jack cheese, grated

Preheat oven to 350 degrees. Sauté onion, celery, and garlic in margarine until translucent. Add dill, salt, and pepper to taste. Spread onion mixture evenly over bread halves. Top each with shrimp. Follow with a generous layer of cheese. Bake 15 to 20 minutes until cheese is melted and bread is heated through.

Slice each "boat" in half for four generous servings or into 1 1/2 to 2-inch sections for hot hors d'oeuvres.

Sharon Paradis-Sharp
Bailey, Colorado

Yield: 4 servings, or cut smaller for appetizer

Shrimp Creole

- 3 tablespoons butter or margarine
- 1 cup chopped onion
- 3/4 cup chopped sweet pepper
- 1/2 cup diced celery
- 1 clove garlic, minced
- 1/4 teaspoon pepper
- 1 teaspoon salt
- pinch of rosemary
- pinch of thyme
- 1 small bay leaf
- 1/4 teaspoon crushed red pepper
- 2 to 4 cups canned tomatoes
- 1 pound large shrimp, peeled and deveined
- rice, prepared according to package directions

Melt butter in large frying pan. Sauté onion, sweet pepper, celery, and garlic until the onion is transparent. Add seasonings and tomatoes. Bring to boil. Reduce heat and simmer 15 to 20 minutes. Arrange shrimp on top of sauce. Cover and reduce heat; cook 10 to 15 minutes more. Serve over rice.

Delia Molloy da Cunha
Boulder, Colorado

Seafood Fettucini

- 2 tablespoons butter or margarine
- 4 teaspoons flour
- 1 1/2 cups evaporated skim milk
- 1/4 cup grated fresh Parmesan cheese
- 1 teaspoon Old Bay Seasoning or to taste
- 1 6-ounce package imitation crab, flake style
- 6 ounces fettucini Florentine, cooked
- 1 tablespoon parsley, chopped

Melt the butter and stir in the flour. Gradually add the evaporated skim milk; cook and stir until thickened. Add Parmesan cheese and Old Bay Seasoning and cook until smooth. Fold in the crab and heat for 3 minutes, stirring occasionally. Toss the cooked fettucini with the sauce and sprinkle with the parsley. Serve immediately.

Mae Jane Keller
Aurora, Colorado

Semolina Pizza Dough and Sauce

Dough:
- 1/4 teaspoon sugar or 1 teaspoon honey
- 1 tablespoon olive oil, preferably extra virgin, plus a little extra oil for oiling the bowl and pizza pan
- 2 1/2 teaspoons salt
- 2 cups semolina flour
- 2 1/3 to 2 2/3 cups all purpose white flour

Sauce:
- 1/2 cup finely chopped onion
- 1 8-ounce can tomato sauce
- 1/4 teaspoon salt
- 1/8 teaspoon garlic powder
- 1/8 teaspoon black pepper
- 2 teaspoons dry oregano

Preheat oven to 500 degrees.

For dough, mix all ingredients together. Roll out dough and put into two large pizza pans that have been oiled, or make eight 6-inch crusts.

For sauce, mix all ingredients and then spread on top of the pizza dough. Add your choice of toppings and choice of cheese. Bake for 10 to 15 minutes.

Variations:
For a different flavor of pizza dough you may add 1 tablespoon garlic powder, 1 to 3 tablespoons basil, 1 to 3 tablespoons oregano, or all three.

Bernice Barney
Loveland, Colorado

Pizza Burgers

- 1 pound hot Italian sausage
- 1 pound lean ground beef
- ¼ teaspoon garlic powder
- 1 teaspoon oregano
- 1 15-ounce can tomato sauce
- 1 3.9-ounce jar sliced mushrooms, drained
- 5 to 6 toasted English muffins (10 to 12 halves)
- 10 to 12 slices Mozzarella cheese

Preheat oven to 400 degrees. In a skillet brown Italian sausage and ground beef. Add garlic powder, oregano, tomato sauce, and mushrooms. Mix well. Place on top of toasted English muffin halves on a cookie sheet. Place one slice of Mozzarella cheese on top of each muffin. Bake for 8 to 10 minutes.

Janine Hultquist
Aurora, Colorado

When fingers become very sore from quilting, dab with rubbing alcohol. They will heal overnight.

Deep-Dish Cheese/Sausage Pizza

Crust:
- 1 package dry yeast
- 1 cup warm water
- 1 tablespoon sugar
- 1 1/2 teaspoons salt
- 1 tablespoon vegetable oil
- 2 3/4 cups flour
- cornmeal

Topping:
- 12 ounces Mozzarella cheese, grated
- 1 pound Italian sausage, browned and drained
- 1 28-ounce can pear tomatoes, drained and cut up
- 2 teaspoons oregano
- 1 teaspoon fennel seed
- 1/2 cup Parmesan cheese
- 1/2 teaspoon salt

Dissolve yeast in water. Add sugar, salt, and vegetable oil. Stir in flour to make soft dough. Knead until elastic. Put in greased bowl. Cover and let rise 1 hour. Punch dough down. Brush 14-inch pizza pan with oil; sprinkle with cornmeal. Press dough on bottom and sides of pan. Let rise, covered, for 20 minutes.

For topping, sprinkle Mozzarella cheese on dough. Arrange sausage on top. Sprinkle with seasonings. Top with Parmesan cheese. Place pizza in preheated 500-degree oven. Reduce heat to 425 degrees and bake for 25 minutes or until cheeses are melted and set.

Variations:
Extras for topping: mushrooms, sweet peppers, and onion.

Beverly Rhynard
Littleton, Colorado

Oat Burgers

- 4 1/2 cups water
- 1/2 cup soy sauce
- 4 1/2 cups rolled oats
- 1/3 cup vegetable oil
- 1 onion, diced
- 1 teaspoon garlic salt or powder
- 1/4 teaspoon Italian seasoning
- 1/4 teaspoon sage
- 1/4 cup brewers yeast
- 1 tablespoon hickory smoked dried tourla yeast

Preheat oven to 350 degrees. Bring water and soy sauce to a boil. Turn down heat and add rolled oats. Cook approximately 5 minutes. Set aside to cool. In a separate pan, sauté onions in vegetable oil. Add sautéed onions, garlic salt, Italian seasoning, sage, and yeasts to oat mixture. Form patties and bake until nicely browned, turning patties periodically so they are evenly browned on both sides.

Notes:
The 100% hickory smoked dried tourla yeast has a taste similar to bacon. You can get the tourla yeast and the brewers yeast at health food stores.

Bernice Barney
Loveland, Colorado

Vegetable Lasagna Supreme

8	ounces lasagna noodles
16	ounces fat-free cottage cheese
15	ounces fat-free Ricotta cheese
1	teaspoon salt
1	teaspoon pepper
1	tablespoon whole basil
1	tablespoon whole oregano
2	egg whites
40	ounces fat-free pasta sauce (marinara)
2	pounds mixed frozen vegetables, Florentine style, thawed
6 to 8	ounces low-fat Mozzarella cheese, shredded

Preheat oven to 400 degrees. Cook noodles and drain. Mix cottage cheese, Ricotta cheese, spices, and egg whites. In a 9x13x2-inch pan, spread 1 cup pasta sauce. Add one layer of noodles (three noodles), one-third of cheese mixture, one-third of vegetables, one third of shredded cheese, and then one-third of pasta sauce. Make three layers, ending with shredded cheese. Bake for 1 hour.

Variations:
One pound of vegetables may be replaced with one 10-ounce package frozen spinach, thawed, in cheese mixture.

Notes:
Freezes well. Approximately 5 grams of fat per serving.

Naomi Bennett
Aurora, Colorado

Yield: 8 to 10 servings

Macaroni and Cheese

Macaroni:
- water
- salt
- olive oil
- 3 1/2 cups macaroni

Sauce:
- 3 tablespoons olive oil
- 1 cup minced onion
- 3 tablespoons flour
- 3 cups milk, warmed
- 1 bay leaf
- 1/2 teaspoon salt
- 1/2 teaspoon crushed thyme
- 1/4 teaspoon white pepper
- 1/4 teaspoon ground nutmeg
- 1/2 pound Fontina cheese, coarsely grated
- 1/4 pound Monterey Jack cheese, coarsely grated
- 1/2 cup finely grated Parmesan cheese
- fresh ground pepper

Preheat oven to 375 degrees. In a large pot bring water with salt and olive oil to a boil. Add macaroni. Cook until *al dente* (firm to the bite, chewy). Drain in colander and shake out excess water.

While the macaroni is cooking, prepare the sauce. Heat the olive oil in a medium saucepan. Sauté the onion until translucent. Add the flour, 1 tablespoon at a time. Stir smooth with each addition. Add more olive oil if mixture becomes too dry. Reduce heat and begin adding the warm milk 1/2 cup at a time. Stir each addition smooth before continuing. Add spices and reduce heat so that the milk does not scald. Stir frequently. In a 13-inch round, 3-inch deep baking dish place half of the macaroni; top with half of the cheeses and half of the sauce. Grind desired amount of pepper on this layer. Repeat with remaining ingredients. Bake for 30 to 40 minutes.

Delia Molloy da Cunha
Boulder, Colorado

Super Easy Super Shells

- 1 12-ounce box jumbo pasta shells
- 1 32-ounce box American cheese*
- 1 24-ounce container cottage cheese
- 1 26-ounce jar spaghetti sauce†

Preheat oven to 350 to 375 degrees. Cook shells as directed on package. While shells are cooking, grate two-thirds of box of American cheese. Mix grated cheese with cottage cheese until well blended. When shells are done, drain and rinse with cold water. Fill each shell with cheese mixture. Place in baking dish(es). Pour sauce over filled shells. Cover with foil. Bake for 25 minutes or until centers of shells are warm and cheese is melted.

Notes:
*Make sure cheese is American cheese. Processed cheese makes the filling too runny.

†I recommend Ragu Old World Style spaghetti sauce.

Micki Elworthy
Windsor, Colorado

Chilies Rellenos Jose

6 to 8	green chilies, charred, skinned, and seeded
1/2	pound Monterey Jack cheese, sliced
1/4	pound Cheddar Cheese, grated
3	large eggs
1/4	cup flour
1/4	teaspoon salt
	pepper to taste
3/4	cup milk
	paprika

Preheat oven to 350 degrees. Put slice of Monterey Jack cheese into each pepper. Place in single layer in greased 8- or 9-inch square baking dish. Beat eggs, flour, milk, salt, and pepper. Pour over peppers. Sprinkle grated Cheddar on top. Sprinkle with paprika. Bake uncovered for about 45 minutes.

Chris Mooney
Longmont, Colorado

Yield: 6 to 8 servings

No-Meat Enchiladas

8 corn tortillas

Sauce:
- 3 tablespoons vegetable oil
- 1 1/2 tablespoons chili powder
- 1 1/2 tablespoons flour
- 1 1/2 cups water
- 1 teaspoon vinegar
- 1/2 teaspoon onion powder
- 1/2 teaspoon salt
- 1/4 teaspoon dried oregano

Filling:
- 3/4 cup refried beans
- 4 ounces Monterey Jack or Cheddar cheese, shredded
- 1/2 cup cottage cheese
- 1 tablespoon finely chopped onions
- 1/2 cup chopped black olives

Preheat oven to 350 degrees. For sauce, in a small saucepan heat vegetable oil, chili powder, and flour. Add water and stir until smooth. Stir in vinegar, onion powder, salt, and oregano. Simmer for 3 minutes.

Place 1 tablespoon each of refried beans, cheese, cottage cheese, onions, and olives in the center of each tortilla. Roll up. Place seam side down in a shallow baking dish. Pour sauce over enchiladas. Sprinkle with a little cheese. Bake for 20 minutes or until bubbly.

Opal Frey
Arvada, Colorado

Quickie Lunch

    instant rice
1   10¾-ounce can cream of chicken soup
    chopped onion (optional)
    parsley flakes (optional)

Prepare instant rice for one or two servings according to package directions. Set aside. Heat soup using just enough water to make the soup the consistency of gravy. Place mound of rice on plate. Cover with soup and sprinkle with onion and parsley flakes.

Notes:
Real quick to make. Uses ingredients commonly found in a kitchen.

Nella Jennings
Denver, Colorado

Yield: 1 or 2 servings

Navajo Tacos

- 1 loaf frozen white bread dough
- 1 15-ounce can chili with beans
- 1 tablespoon vegetable oil
  - shredded lettuce
  - chopped tomatoes
  - grated cheese
  - salsa

Place frozen bread loaf in the refrigerator to thaw. It will take 8 hours (or less) to thaw. Do not let dough thaw on counter top; you do not want it to rise, just thaw.

Heat chili on medium heat. Split bread loaf in half; on a floured surface, roll dough to the size of a large frying pan. In a non-stick frying pan, heat vegetable oil over medium heat. Add bread dough. Cook on one side until it turns a medium-brown color. Turn over and repeat. Keep bread warm in oven (low heat). Roll out second half of bread dough on floured surface and cook as above. Place cooked loaves on plates; top with chili, lettuce, tomato, cheese, and salsa.

Notes:
You can split dough into fourths and make four small tacos.

Diane Lindsay
Englewood, Colorado

Yield: two large tacos or four small tacos

Vegetable Tamale Pie

Vegetable Filling:
- 1 14-ounce can cooked pinto beans, drained
- 2 cups chopped canned low-sodium tomatoes, drained
- 1 cup chopped onion
- 6 ounces grated sharp Cheddar cheese
- 1/2 cup cubed red sweet pepper
- 1/2 cup cubed green sweet pepper
- 1 to 2 pickled or fresh jalapeño peppers, seeded and finely chopped
- 8 pitted ripe olives, sliced
- 3/4 teaspoon ground cumin
- 3/4 teaspoon garlic powder
- 3/4 teaspoon chili powder

Tamale Topping:
- 1/2 cup plus 1 tablespoon all-purpose flour
- 1/2 cup yellow cornmeal
- 1 1/2 teaspoons baking powder
- 1/2 teaspoon baking soda
- 1/8 teaspoon salt
- 1/2 cup plain yogurt
- 1 large egg at room temperature
- 2 teaspoons margarine, melted and cooled
- 1 tablespoon cut chives for garnish (optional)

Preheat oven to 375 degrees. To prepare filling, in a 9-inch-square baking pan or a 2-quart baking pan, place all filling ingredients. Toss until well mixed; set aside. To prepare tamale topping, in medium bowl place flour, cornmeal, baking powder, baking soda, and salt; stir until evenly mixed. In a small bowl, beat yogurt, egg, and margarine. Add to dry ingredients and stir just until dry ingredients are moistened. Spoon mixture evenly on top of vegetable filling. If desired, sprinkle evenly with chives. Bake 35 to 45 minutes until filling is hot and bubbly, topping is lightly browned, and a toothpick inserted in center of topping comes out clean.

Teresa Mensch
Evergreen, Colorado

Yield: 4 servings

Ruth's Chilies Rellenos Jose

- 1 7-ounce can whole mild green chilies
- 1 pound Monterey Jack cheese cut into 1x3x1-inch strips
- 1/2 pound Cheddar cheese, grated, divided
- 5 large eggs, beaten
- 1 1/4 cups milk
- 1/4 cup flour
- 1/2 teaspoon salt
- pepper or bottled hot pepper sauce to taste
- paprika, to taste
- salsa and bottled hot pepper sauce for garnishes

Preheat oven to 350 degrees. Rinse chilies, remove seeds, and dry on paper towels. Roll the cheese strips into the chilies. Lay the chilies in a greased 7x13-inch baking dish. Sprinkle half the grated Cheddar cheese on top. To make the custard, in a separate container, mix eggs, milk, flour, salt, and pepper. Cover with plastic wrap, leaving area open for venting. Cook in microwave on low for 10 minutes. Pour over chilies. Sprinkle with paprika. Bake for 45 minutes or until knife comes out clean. Let sit a few minutes prior to serving. Serve with hot pepper sauce and salsa as garnishes.

Variations:
I omit the whole chilies and use one 4-ounce can of chopped green mild chilies, juice and all. It is faster, but for guests, be elegant and use whole chilies.

Ruth Rupert
Denver, Colorado

Red Beans and Rice

- 1/2 pound dry kidney beans, rinsed
- 1/2 pound dry pinto beans, rinsed
- 4 cups water
- 4 cups chicken broth
- 2 garlic cloves, minced
- 2 bay leaves
- 1 14 1/2-ounce can tomatoes, chopped, with liquid
- 1 large green sweet pepper, chopped
- 1 large red sweet pepper, chopped
- 1 large onion, chopped
- 1 cup chopped celery
- 1 4-ounce can diced green chilies
- 1/4 cup snipped fresh parsley
- 1/4 to 1/2 teaspoon crushed red pepper flakes
- 1/4 to 1/2 teaspoon ground cumin
- 1/4 to 1/2 teaspoon hot pepper sauce
- 1 teaspoon paprika
- 1 teaspoon salt
- 1 tablespoon vinegar
- rice, prepared according to package directions

Place beans in Dutch oven with water. Bring to boil; simmer 2 minutes. Remove from heat. Cover and let stand 1 hour. Drain and rinse beans. Return to Dutch oven with broth, garlic, and bay leaves; bring to a boil. Reduce heat; cover and simmer for 1 1/4 hours. Stir in all remaining ingredients. Cover and simmer for 1 hour or until beans and vegetables are tender and gravy is thick. Remove bay leaves. Serve over rice or with cornbread.

Notes:
Can also be made in the slow cooker.

Charlotte Seaton
Fort Lupton, Colorado

Yield: 12 servings

Lynda's Patchwork Crock Pot Rice

- 3/4 onion, chopped
- 1 1/2 pounds zucchini, thinly sliced
- 3 tablespoons margarine
- 1 16-ounce can tomatoes
- 1 16-ounce can whole kernel corn, drained
- 1/2 teaspoon ground coriander
- 1/4 teaspoon dried oregano
- 3 cups cooked rice (do not use instant rice)
- salt and pepper, to taste (optional)

Sauté onions and zucchini in margarine until tender. Place in 3 1/2-quart slow cooker. Add remaining ingredients to slow cooker. Cook on high for 3 hours.

Variations:
May add cumin and chili powder to make it a Mexican dish. Will taste great with any spice combination you desire.

Notes:
Ready for that one-pot lunch at a quilting bee. Delicious too. I prepare this the night before, place it in refrigerator sealed tight so zucchini won't brown, and take it with me to my quilting bees.

Lynda Vickers
Aurora, Colorado

When traveling, carry a 100-watt light bulb to replace the dim one in the motel room. Makes for better stitching.

Cakes, Cookies, Brownies & Other Bars

Special Notes:

Pound Cake

- 1½ cups (3 sticks) butter or margarine, softened
- 3 cups sugar
- 5 large eggs
- 3 cups flour, sifted
- ½ teaspoon lemon extract
- 1 teaspoon vanilla extract
- ½ teaspoon almond extract
- ⅞ cup ginger ale or similar soda

Preheat oven to 275 degrees. Cream margarine until light. Cream in sugar and beat until fluffy. Beat in eggs, one at a time. Beat in 1 cup flour, then add extracts and a little ginger ale. Continue adding flour, alternating with ginger ale, until all ingredients are used. Beating can be done by hand or mixer until smooth. Pour batter into two greased and floured loaf pans or one tube or bundt pan. Bake for 1 hour and 45 minutes. Let cool in pan.

Notes:
This stuff freezes great. High altitude adjustments: use 2⅔ cups sugar and just shy of 9 ounces of soda.

Karen Scully
Colorado Springs, Colorado

When your sewing machine has to take a car trip to get to class or a retreat, set it in the seat of the car and strap it in with the shoulder safety belt. This will keep it from taking tumbles along the way.

German Biscuit

- 4 eggs, separated
- 1 cup sugar
- 2 teaspoons vanilla
- 4 tablespoons water
- 1 1/4 cup flour
- 1 teaspoon baking powder

Preheat oven to 350 degrees. Separate eggs; beat whites until very stiff. In a separate bowl combine egg yolks, sugar, vanilla, water, flour, and baking powder. Mix well. Fold in egg whites and blend thoroughly. Pour batter into a 9x5x3-inch loaf pan that has been greased well with margarine. Bake for 30 to 40 minutes or until light brown. Remove from pan while still warm. Store in a sealed container.

Notes:
This is similar to a pound cake. Great with fruits or coffee.

Toni Fitzwater
Pine, Colorado

Yield: 1 loaf

White Russian Chocolate Pound Cake

Cake:
- 1 18 1/2-ounce package chocolate cake mix (do not use a mix that has pudding in it)
- 1 4-ounce package instant chocolate pudding
- 1/2 cup vegetable oil
- 4 eggs
- 3/4 cup coffee-flavored liqueur
- 1/2 cup half and half
- 1/4 cup water

Glaze:
- 1 cup powdered sugar
- 1 tablespoon liqueur
- 1 tablespoon water

Preheat oven to 350 degrees. Beat all ingredients in a large bowl at medium speed of electric mixer for 2 minutes. Bake in greased and floured 12-cup bundt pan for 55 minutes. Cool 10 minutes and remove from pan. Allow cake to cool completely then dust with powdered sugar or combine all ingredients in glaze recipe above and drizzle over cake.

Naomi Bennett
Aurora, Colorado

Pumpkin Jelly Roll

Cake:
- 3 eggs
- 3/4 cup sugar
- 2/3 cup canned pumpkin
- 3/4 cup flour
- 2 teaspoons ground cinnamon
- 1/2 teaspoon baking powder
- 1/2 teaspoon ground ginger
- 1/2 teaspoon ground cloves
- 1/2 teaspoon ground nutmeg

Filling:
- 1 cup powdered sugar
- 1 8-ounce package cream cheese, softened
- 4 tablespoons butter or margarine, softened
- 1/2 teaspoon vanilla

Preheat oven to 375 degrees. Beat eggs, then add remaining cake ingredients, mixing well. Pour onto a greased cookie sheet. Bake for 17 minutes. While hot, invert thin cake onto a tea towel that has been dusted with powdered sugar. Roll up the towel with cake inside and refrigerate the roll shape for 30 minutes. Remove roll carefully from towel. Mix filling and spread on top of unrolled cake. Once filling has been spread on the cake, roll cake back up. Wrap in plastic or foil wrap. Refrigerate or freeze.

Lori Anderson
Wellington, Colorado

Jello Lightning Cake

Cake:
- 3 cups packaged buttermilk baking mix
- 1/2 cup sugar
- 1 3-ounce package lemon gelatin
- 4 eggs, beaten
- 1/2 cup milk
- 1/3 cup vegetable oil

Glaze:
- 1 1/2 cups sifted powdered sugar
- 1/2 cup orange juice

Preheat oven to 350 degrees. Mix baking mix, sugar, and dry gelatin. In a separate bowl, combine eggs, milk and vegetable oil. Stir this mixture into the dry ingredients until moistened. Beat by hand 1 minute or until smooth. Pour into greased and floured 9x13x2-inch pan. Bake 25 to 30 minutes or until done. Cool 5 minutes. Using a long tined fork, poke holes all over the top of cake. Continue to allow cake to cool completely. Prepare glaze by mixing powdered sugar and orange juice together. Pour glaze over top of cooled cake. Serve with ice cream.

Naomi Bennett
Aurora, Colorado

Aunt Sukey's Choice Cake

- 1 18½-ounce package yellow cake mix
- 1 cup orange juice
- ¾ cup salad dressing
- 3 eggs
- ¼ cup poppy seeds

Preheat oven to 350 degrees. Mix all ingredients with an electric mixer at medium speed for 2 minutes. Pour into greased and floured 10-inch tube pan or 12-inch fluted tube pan. Bake 35 to 40 minutes or until toothpick inserted near center comes out clean. Let stand 10 minutes. Remove from pan.

Notes:
This recipe works with regular or light salad dressing.

Janet Corray
Buena Vista, Colorado

Yield: 12 servings

Oatmeal Cake with Broiled Frosting

Cake:
- 1 1/4 cups boiling water
- 1 cup uncooked oatmeal
- 1/2 cup (1 stick) margarine, softened
- 1 cup granulated sugar
- 1 cup packed brown sugar
- 1 teaspoon vanilla
- 2 eggs
- 1 1/2 cups flour
- 1 teaspoon baking soda
- 1/2 teaspoon salt
- 1/4 teaspoon ground nutmeg
- 3/4 teaspoon ground cinnamon

Frosting:
- 1/2 cup (1 stick) margarine, melted
- 1 cup packed brown sugar
- 6 tablespoons half and half
- 1/2 cup walnuts, chopped
- 1 cup coconut

Preheat oven to 325 degrees.

For cake, mix boiling water and oatmeal together. Let stand 15 minutes. Cream margarine, granulated sugar, and brown sugar until smooth. Mix in the vanilla and eggs. Add the oatmeal to this mixture. Add in the flour, baking soda, salt, nutmeg, and cinnamon. Mix well. Bake for 25 to 35 minutes.

For frosting, mix all ingredients and carefully spread frosting on top of baked cake. Broil for just a few minutes—don't let it burn.

Mary Christofferson
Littleton, Colorado

Lemonade Cake

Cake:
- 1 18½-ounce package white cake mix with pudding
- 1 3½-ounce package instant vanilla pudding mix
- 4 eggs
- 1 cup plus 2 tablespoons water
- ½ cup vegetable oil

Topping:
- 2 cups powdered sugar, sifted
- 1 6-ounce can frozen lemonade, thawed

Preheat oven to 350 degrees. Mix cake mix, vanilla pudding, eggs, water, and vegetable oil per instructions on box and pour into a greased and floured 9x13x2-inch pan. Bake for 35 to 40 minutes. While cake is baking combine topping ingredients. Remove cake from oven and poke hot cake with fork. Pour topping mixture over the cake and bake for an additional 5 minutes.

Mae Jane Keller
Aurora, Colorado

Poppy Seed Sherry Cake

- 1 18½-ounce package yellow cake mix
- 1 3.4-ounce package instant vanilla pudding
- ⅓ cup poppy seeds
- 1 cup sour cream
- 4 eggs
- ½ cup vegetable oil
- ½ cup sherry

Preheat oven to 350 degrees. Grease bundt pan well. Combine all ingredients and mix well. Pour into bundt pan and allow to rest for 10 minutes. Bake for 45 to 50 minutes. Cool about 15 minutes until cake can be easily removed from bundt pan. Sprinkle with powdered sugar, if desired.

Variations:
Can use egg substitute instead of eggs.

Notes:
I prefer Duncan Hines yellow cake mix.

Beverly Rhynard
Littleton, Colorado

Moon Cake

Crust:
- ½ cup (1 stick) margarine
- 1 cup boiling water
- 1 cup flour
- ¼ teaspoon salt
- 4 eggs

Pudding:
- 2 3-ounce packages instant vanilla pudding mix, prepared
- 1 8-ounce package cream cheese, softened
- 1 8-ounce container frozen non-dairy whipped topping, thawed chocolate curls or chocolate syrup

Preheat oven to 400 degrees. To make crust, put margarine into boiling water. Add flour and salt. Stir until mixture forms a ball. Place into mixing bowl, beat, and cool. Add eggs, one at a time. Spread mixture on ungreased jelly roll pan. Bake 23 minutes. The cream puff crust will have air bubbles and look like the moon. Let cool and top with pudding mixture.

To make pudding, to prepared pudding mixes, add softened cream cheese and beat. Spread over crust. Spread non-dairy whipped topping on top and decorate with chocolate curls or syrup. Chill and serve.

Barbara Shie
Colorado Springs, Colorado

Turtle Cake

- 1   18½-ounce package chocolate cake mix
- 1   14-ounce bag caramels
- ½   cup evaporated milk
- ½   cup (1 stick) butter or margarine
- 1   cup chocolate chips
- 1   cup pecans, chopped, divided

Preheat oven to 375 degrees. Prepare cake mix according to directions on package. Pour half of the batter into a greased 9x13x2-inch baking pan. Bake for 15 minutes. Unwrap caramels and melt with butter and milk in microwave or double boiler. Pour this melted mixture over the half-baked cake. Top melted caramel with nuts and chocolate chips. Pour remaining cake batter over top. Continue baking for 25 minutes.

Wendy Wade
Parker, Colorado

Italian Cream Cake

Cake:
- 1/2 cup (1 stick) margarine, softened
- 1/2 cup vegetable shortening
- 2 cups sugar
- 5 eggs
- 1 cup buttermilk
- 1 teaspoon vanilla
- 2 cups flour
- 1 teaspoon baking soda
- 1/2 teaspoon salt
- 1 cup chopped pecans
- 1 cup coconut

Frosting:
- 1 8-ounce package cream cheese, softened
- 1 16-ounce box powdered sugar (or more)
- 1 teaspoon vanilla
- 1/4 cup margarine, softened
- 1 cup coconut

Preheat oven to 375 degrees. Cream margarine, vegetable shortening, and sugar together until smooth. Add eggs, buttermilk, and vanilla. Mix well. Combine flour, baking soda, and salt. Add to creamed mixture and mix thoroughly. Fold in pecans and coconut. Pour into three greased and floured 9-inch round cake pans. Bake for 35 minutes. Cool.

Prepare frosting by combining cream cheese, powdered sugar, vanilla, and margarine. Mix until smooth. Stir in coconut. Spread on cooled cakes.

Sissi Williams
Westminster, Colorado

Rum Cake Jubilee

Cake:
- 1 18 1/2-ounce package yellow cake mix with pudding
- 1 cup sour cream
- 1/3 cup vegetable oil
- 1/4 cup rum
- 3 eggs

Sauce:
- 1 21-ounce can cherry pie filling
- 1 16-ounce can whole cranberry sauce
- 1/2 cup rum

Preheat oven to 375 degrees. For cake, combine all ingredients. Beat at low speed of electric mixer until moistened. Beat 2 minutes at high speed. Pour into two greased and floured 8- or 9-inch round cake pans. Bake 25 to 30 minutes. Allow cake to cool to room temperature.

For sauce, just before serving, heat pie filling and cranberry sauce in skillet until mixture comes to boil. Pour rum over hot fruit. DO NOT STIR. Ignite and ladle over cake wedges.

Variations:
For cake, at high altitudes over 3500 feet, add 3 tablespoons flour to cake mix.

For sauce, if desired, heat fruit and stir in 1/4 cup rum. Spoon over cake wedges without igniting.

Naomi Bennett
Aurora, Colorado

Yield: 16 servings (2 Cakes)

Rum Cake and Sauce

Cake:
- 1 cup chopped pecans
- 1 18 1/2-ounce package yellow cake mix
- 1 3.4-ounce package French vanilla instant pudding
- 1/2 cup flour (at high altitudes)†
- 1/2 cup water
- 1/2 cup vegetable oil
- 1/2 cup rum
- 5 eggs

Sauce:
- 1 cup sugar
- 1/2 cup (1 stick) butter or margarine
- 1/4 cup water
- 1/4 cup rum

Preheat oven to 325 degrees. Sprinkle nuts on bottom of a greased and floured bundt or tube pan. Mix together cake mix, pudding, flour, water, vegetable oil, and rum. Beat in eggs, one at a time. Beat well. Pour batter into the baking pan and bake for 1 hour. Let cake cool in pan for 30 minutes, then pour rum sauce over top of cake in pan. Let cake cool completely before turning over on cake plate to remove.

To make rum sauce, combine all ingredients in a saucepan and boil until sugar is dissolved. Pour over cake while cake is still in the pan.

Notes:

Sometimes I use 6 eggs and sliced almonds instead of pecans. This cake freezes well.

†I live in Leadville at 10000+ feet altitude, so I add 1/2 cup flour to compensate for this.

Melba Queener
Leadville, Colorado

Carrot Cake with Cream Cheese Frosting

Cake:
- 4 eggs, beaten
- 2 teaspoons baking soda
- 1 teaspoon salt
- 1 teaspoon ground cinnamon
- 2 cups sugar
- 1 1/2 cups vegetable oil
- 2 6-ounce jars junior baby food carrots
- 1 1/2 cups flour
- 1/2 cup chopped walnuts

Frosting:
- 1 8-ounce package cream cheese, softened
- 3 1/2 cups powdered sugar
- 1/2 cup (1 stick) margarine, softened
- 1 teaspoon vanilla

Preheat oven to 350 degrees. In a large bowl beat eggs well. Add the baking soda, salt, cinnamon, sugar, vegetable oil, and baby food. Mix well. Add the flour and mix until smooth. Fold in walnuts. Place in a greased 9x13x2-inch pan and bake for 50 to 60 minutes. Cool completely.

For frosting, mix cream cheese, powdered sugar, margarine, and vanilla until well blended. Spread on cooled cake.

Toni Fitzwater
Pine, Colorado

Pineapple Carrot Cake

Cake:
- 3 large eggs
- 1/2 cup (1 stick) butter or margarine, softened
- 1 cup unsweetened pineapple juice
- 2 1/2 cups unbleached white flour
- 1 teaspoon baking soda
- 2 teaspoons baking powder
- 1 teaspoon ground nutmeg
- 1 teaspoon ground cinnamon
- 3 cups grated fresh carrots

Topping:
- 1 cup crushed pineapple, well drained
- 1 teaspoon ground cinnamon

Preheat oven to 350 degrees. Beat together eggs, butter, and pineapple juice. Add flour, baking soda, baking powder, nutmeg, and cinnamon. Beat well. Stir in grated carrots and mix well. Spread batter evenly in a greased and floured 9x13x2-inch baking pan. Toss topping ingredients together and sprinkle over batter. Bake for 25 to 30 minutes or until browned. Cool on a wire rack.

Jeanne Arnoldy
Littleton, Colorado

Yield: 8 to 10 servings

Spicy Bean Cake

- 1/4 cup margarine, softened
- 2 eggs
- 2 cups pinto beans, cooked and mashed
- 1 cup flour
- 1 teaspoon ground cinnamon
- 1/4 teaspoon ground nutmeg
- 1/2 teaspoon ground cloves
- 1 teaspoon baking soda
- 4 tablespoons cocoa
- 1 cup sugar
- 3/4 cup raisins
- 2 cups apples, diced
- 1/4 cup nuts, chopped
- 1 1/2 teaspoons vanilla

Preheat oven to 375 degrees. Cream margarine; add eggs, one at a time. Beat well after each addition. Stir in beans. Add dry ingredients; beat well. Fold in apples, raisins, nuts, and vanilla. Pour into a greased 9x13x2-inch cake pan. Bake for 45 to 50 minutes

Variations:
Frost with maple icing.

Bernice Barney
Loveland, Colorado

Banana Zucchini Cake

- 4 eggs, at room temperature
- 2 cups sugar
- 1 cup vegetable oil
- 2 medium-sized ripe bananas, mashed
- 2 cups shredded zucchini
- 3 cups flour
- 1½ teaspoon baking soda
- 1½ teaspoon baking powder
- 2½ to 3 teaspoons ground cinnamon
- 1 teaspoon salt
- 1 cup chopped nuts
- 1 cup raisins

Preheat oven to 350 degrees. Beat eggs; blend in sugar and vegetable oil. Beat 1 minute. Add bananas and zucchini. Mix well. Sift dry ingredients together and fold into banana mixture. Stir in nuts and raisins. Pour into greased and floured bundt pan. Bake 1 hour. Cool 15 minutes, remove from pan, and continue cooling.

Naomi Bennett
Aurora, Colorado

Apple Bundt Cake

- 2 cups sugar
- 2 eggs
- 1 cup vegetable oil
- 1/3 cup buttermilk
- 2 cups flour
- 1 teaspoon salt
- 1 teaspoon baking soda
- 1 teaspoon ground cinnamon
- 1 teaspoon ground nutmeg
- 1 teaspoon fresh lemon juice
- 1 teaspoon vanilla
- 2 apples, peeled, cored, and chopped
- 1/2 cup pecans

Preheat oven to 350 degrees. Combine sugar, eggs, vegetable oil, and buttermilk. Sift flour, salt, baking soda, cinnamon, and nutmeg. Add to egg mixture. In a separate bowl, mix together lemon juice and vanilla, then add to mixture. Add apples and pecans. Pour into greased and floured bundt pan. Bake for 1 hour and 10 minutes.

Variations:
You can substitute walnuts for pecans.

Joan Christopherson
Englewood, Colorado

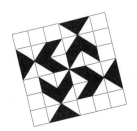

Applesauce Cake

- ½ cup (1 stick) butter or margarine, softened
- 1 cup sugar
- 1 egg, well beaten
- 1 cup chopped dates
- 1½ cups applesauce
- 1 cup nuts, chopped
- 1 cup raisins
- ½ teaspoon ground cloves
- ½ teaspoon ground cinnamon
- 1 teaspoon or more vanilla (to taste)
- 2 teaspoons baking soda
- 2 cups flour

Preheat oven to 350 degrees. Cream butter and sugar. Add egg and mix well. Stir in dates, applesauce, nuts, raisins, cloves, cinnamon, and vanilla. Add baking soda and flour and mix thoroughly. Place in a greased and floured 9x13x2-inch pan and bake for 30 minutes. Cool and top with your favorite frosting.

Lucy Ellsworth
Denver, Colorado

Rhubarb Cake

Cake:
- 1/2 cup vegetable shortening
- 1 1/2 cups sugar
- 1/2 teaspoon salt
- 1 egg
- 1 teaspoon baking soda
- 1 cup sour milk
- 2 cups plus 1 tablespoon flour
- 3 cups chopped rhubarb
- 1/4 cup colored candy sprinkles

Topping:
- 1/3 cup sugar
- 1/3 cup chopped nuts
- 1 teaspoon ground cinnamon

Preheat oven to 350 degrees. Cream vegetable shortening and sugar. Add salt and egg; mix well. In a separate container, mix baking soda with sour milk. Alternately add this milk mixture and flour to batter. Add rhubarb and sprinkles. Pour batter into a greased 9x13x2-inch pan. Combine all ingredients for topping and sprinkle over batter. Bake for 45 minutes.

Shirley Franzen
Thornton, Colorado

Fresh Rhubarb Cake

Cake:
- 1/2 cup vegetable shortening
- 1 1/2 cups packed brown sugar
- 1 egg
- 1 cup buttermilk
- 1 teaspoon vanilla
- 2 cups flour
- 1 teaspoon baking soda
- 1/2 teaspoon salt
- 2 cups cut up rhubarb

Topping:
- 1/4 cup sugar
- 1 teaspoon ground cinnamon

Preheat oven to 350 degrees. Cream vegetable shortening, sugar, and eggs. Add buttermilk and vanilla. Sift together flour, baking soda, and salt. Add rhubarb to flour to coat. Then stir flour and rhubarb into creamed mixture. Pour into a greased and floured 9x13x2-inch pan. Mix topping ingredients and sprinkle over top of batter. Bake for 45 minutes.

Rita Hildred
Laporte, Colorado

Pineapple Paradise Cake

Cake:
- 1 18½-ounce package yellow cake mix with pudding
- 4 eggs
- ⅓ cup vegetable oil
- 1 15¼-ounce can crushed pineapple

Frosting:
- 1 12-ounce container frozen non-dairy whipped topping, thawed
- 1 3¾-ounce package instant coconut cream pudding
- 1 15¼-ounce can crushed pineapple
- ¼ cup macadamia nuts, chopped (optional)

Preheat oven to 350 degrees. For cake, mix the cake mix, eggs, vegetable oil, and crushed pineapple until moistened, then beat for 2 minutes on high speed. Pour into greased and floured 9x13x2-inch pan. Bake for 30 minutes. Let cool. For frosting, mix the whipped topping and the instant coconut cream pudding until smooth. Add the crushed pineapple and mix until well blended. Frost the cooled cake and top with chopped macadamia nuts if desired. Refrigerate any leftovers.

Mae Jane Keller
Aurora, Colorado

Yield: 12 servings

Fruit Cocktail Cake and Frosting

Cake:
- 1/4 cup packed brown sugar
- 1/2 cup chopped nuts
- 1 1/2 cups granulated sugar
- 2 cups flour
- 2 teaspoons baking soda
- 1 teaspoon salt
- 1 16-ounce can (2 cups) fruit cocktail with juice
- 2 eggs, well beaten

Frosting:
- 1/2 cup evaporated milk
- 3/4 cup granulated sugar
- 1/2 cup (1 stick) margarine
- 1 cup grated coconut

Preheat oven to 350 degrees. Mix together brown sugar and nuts. Set aside. Mix granulated sugar, flour, baking soda, salt, and fruit cocktail. Pour into a greased and floured 9x13x2-inch pan. Sprinkle brown sugar mixture over top of batter. Bake for approximately 30 minutes.

For frosting, place evaporated milk, granulated sugar, and margarine in a saucepan. Bring to a boil, and allow to boil for 2 minutes, stirring constantly. Remove from heat and stir in coconut. Pour over cake while frosting is still warm.

Notes:
This cake has no vegetable shortening or butter in it. Cake travels well in disposable lasagna pans to church, quilting group meeting, etc.

Nella Jennings
Denver, Colorado

Apple Dapple Cake

Cake:
- 1½ cups vegetable oil
- 2 cups sugar
- 3 eggs or egg substitute
- 3 cups flour
- 1 teaspoon salt
- 1 teaspoon baking soda
- 2 teaspoons vanilla
- 3 cups chopped apples
- 1½ cups chopped walnuts

Glaze:
- ½ cup (1 stick) margarine
- 1 cup packed brown sugar
- ¼ cup milk

Preheat oven to 350 degrees. In a bowl, mix vegetable oil, sugar, and eggs well. Add flour, salt, and baking soda and mix well. Add vanilla, apples, and walnuts and mix well. Batter will be stiff. Pour into greased and floured angel food cake pan. Bake for 1½ hours. Top will be crusty. When cake is nearly done, mix glaze ingredients in saucepan. Bring to a boil and continue to cook for 2½ minutes, stirring constantly. Cake is done when toothpick inserted in center of cake comes out clean. Poke holes all around cake with meat fork or ice pick. Pour glaze over top and into holes. Cool completely before removing cake from pan.

Beverly Rhynard
Littleton, Colorado

Strawberry Cake

- 1 10.5-ounce bag miniature marshmallows
- 2 10-ounce boxes frozen sliced strawberries, thawed
- 1 3-ounce package strawberry gelatin
- 2¼ cups flour
- 1½ cup sugar
- ½ cup vegetable shortening
- 3 eggs
- 2½ teaspoons baking powder*
- 1 cup milk
- 1 teaspoon vanilla
- dash salt

Preheat oven to 375 degrees. Grease bottom only of a 9x13x2-inch pan. Cover bottom with marshmallows. Mix strawberries and gelatin and set aside.

In a large bowl, combine flour, sugar, vegetable shortening, eggs, baking powder, milk, vanilla, and salt. Mix at low speed until moistened. Do not beat. Pour evenly over marshmallows.

Spoon strawberry gelatin mixture over batter.

Bake for 40 to 45 minutes. Marshmallows will rise to top and strawberries will go to the bottom of pan.

Serve with ice cream, whipped cream, or non-dairy whipped topping.

Notes:
*For low altitudes, use 3 teaspoons baking powder.

Joyce Rorman
Lakewood, Colorado

Mayonnaise Cake

- 1 cup sugar
- 1 cup mayonnaise or salad dressing
- 2 cups flour
- 4 tablespoons cocoa
- 2 teaspoons baking soda
- 1 cup boiling water
- 1 tablespoon vanilla

Preheat oven to 375 degrees. Combine sugar and mayonnaise. Add flour and cocoa. Dissolve soda in boiling water and add to flour mixture. Add vanilla. Mix well. Pour batter into a greased and floured 9x13x2-inch pan. Bake for approximately 30 minutes or until toothpick inserted in center of cake comes out clean. Frost with your favorite frosting.

Notes:
This is a very good, moist cake.

Ruby Williams
Montrose, Colorado

Chocolate Eclair Cake

Crust:
- 1 cup water
- 1/2 cup (1 stick) margarine
- 1 cup flour
- 1/4 teaspoon salt
- 4 eggs, at room temperature

Filling:
- 2 3-ounce packages vanilla instant pudding
- 2 1/2 cups plus 3 to 4 tablespoons cold milk, divided
- 1 8-ounce package cream cheese, softened
- 1 12-ounce container frozen non-dairy whipped topping, thawed
- 3 ounces chocolate chips
- 2 tablespoons margarine
- 1 cup powdered sugar

Preheat oven to 400 degrees. Boil water and margarine until margarine is melted. Add flour and salt all at once; beat until a ball forms. Cool slightly. Add eggs, one at a time, beating well after each addition. Spread in ungreased 10x15x1 1/2-inch pan. Bake for 30 minutes. Remove from oven and push bubbles down with a fork while hot. Cool completely. Mix pudding with 2 1/2 cups milk. Add softened cream cheese and mix well. Spread on crust. Top with non-dairy whipped topping. Melt chocolate chips and margarine. Mix in powdered sugar and 3 to 4 tablespoons milk until a thin glaze forms. Drizzle over non-dairy whipped topping. Chill well before serving.

Peggy Sparks
Glenwood Springs, Colorado

Yield: 12 servings

Janet's Chocolate Chip Cake

1 3/4 cups boiling water
   1 cup uncooked oatmeal
   1 cup lightly packed brown sugar
   1 cup granulated sugar
 1/2 cup (1 stick) butter or margarine, softened
   3 medium eggs
1 3/4 cup sifted flour
   1 teaspoon baking soda
 1/2 teaspoon salt
   1 tablespoon cocoa
  12 ounces (1 1/2 cups) chocolate chips, divided
 3/4 cup chopped walnuts, divided

Preheat oven to 350 degrees. Pour boiling water over oatmeal and let sit for 10 minutes. Add the brown sugar, granulated sugar, and butter. Stir until butter melts. Add eggs and mix well. Add flour, baking soda, salt, and cocoa. Mix well. Add 3/4 cup of chocolate chips and half the nuts and fold into batter. Pour into a greased and floured 9x13x2-inch pan. Sprinkle the remaining chocolate chips and nuts on top of the batter. Bake for 40 minutes.

Janet Kay Skeen
Denver, Colorado

Wonder Cake

- 1³/₄ cups flour
- 1 cup sugar
- ¼ cup cocoa
- 1 teaspoon baking soda
- ½ teaspoon salt
- ⅓ cup vegetable shortening, softened
- 1 tablespoon vinegar
- 1 cup water

Preheat oven to 375 degrees. Sift flour, sugar, cocoa, baking soda, and salt together in a bowl. Add vegetable shortening, vinegar, and water and mix until almost smooth. Bake in a greased and floured 9-inch cake pan for 30 minutes or until toothpick inserted in center of cake comes out clean.

Jan Shuping
Pueblo, Colorado

Better-Than-Sex Cake

- 1   18½-ounce package yellow cake mix
- 1   3½-ounce box instant vanilla pudding
- ½ cup vegetable oil
- ½ cup water
- 4 large eggs
- 1 cup sour cream
- 4 to 6 ounces German chocolate, grated
- 1 6-ounce package chocolate chips (miniatures are great)
- 1 cup chopped pecans
- 1 cup shredded coconut

Preheat oven to 350 degrees. In a mixer bowl, combine cake mix, pudding mix, vegetable oil, and water. Add eggs, one at a time, beating well after each addition. Stir in sour cream, grated chocolate, chocolate chips, pecans, and coconut. Turn batter into a well-greased bundt or tube pan. Bake for 55 to 60 minutes or until a tester inserted in cake comes out clean.

Notes:
I have used this recipe "as is" with no adjustment for altitude and it is great.

Barbara Shie
Colorado Springs, Colorado

Whipped Cream Devil's Cake

   1 cup cream
   2 eggs
   1 cup sugar
1 1/2 cups flour
  1/2 cup hot water
   5 tablespoons cocoa
   1 teaspoon baking soda
   1 teaspoon vanilla

Preheat oven to 375 degrees. Whip cream; add eggs and whip some more. Add sugar and flour and whip some more. In a separate container mix hot water, cocoa, and baking soda; stir until dissolved. Add to whipped mixture and mix well. Stir in vanilla. Bake in a greased 9-inch square pan until cake tests done—30 to 35 minutes.

Notes:
My mother got this recipe from Harper's Weekly in the late 1930s.

Roberta Niquette
Clifton, Colorado

Chocolate Cola Cake with Frosting

Cake:
- 2 cups flour
- 2 cups sugar
- 1 cup (2 sticks) margarine
- 3 tablespoons cocoa
- 1 cup cola beverage
- 1/2 cup buttermilk
- 1 teaspoon baking soda
- 1 teaspoon vanilla
- 2 eggs
- 1 1/2 cups miniature marshmallows

Frosting:
- 1/2 cup (1 stick) margarine
- 6 tablespoons cola beverage
- 3 tablespoons cocoa
- 1 16-ounce box powdered sugar
- 1 teaspoon vanilla
- 1 cup miniature marshmallows
- 1 cup chopped nuts

Preheat oven to 350 degrees. For cake, sift flour and sugar together. Place margarine, cocoa, and cola in a saucepan. Bring to a boil then add to flour mixture. Dissolve baking soda in buttermilk. Add remaining ingredients and buttermilk mixture to flour/sugar mixture and mix well. Batter will be thin with marshmallows floating on top. Pour into a greased 9x13x2-inch pan. Bake for 30 to 35 minutes.

For frosting, bring margarine, cola, and cocoa to a boil. Add remaining ingredients and stir until well mixed. Frost while cake is warm.

Notes:
For high altitudes, add 1 more tablespoon of flour and a little more buttermilk and bake at 375 degrees.

Deanna Naumann
Aurora, Colorado

Alma's Chocolate Cake with Icing

Cake:
- 2½ cups flour
- ½ teaspoon salt
- 2 teaspoons baking soda
- ½ cup cocoa
- 1 cup (2 sticks) butter or margarine, softened
- 2½ cups sugar
- 4 eggs
- 1 cup buttermilk
- 1 cup hot water
- 2 teaspoons vanilla
- 2 teaspoons red food coloring (optional)

Icing:
- ½ cup (1 stick) butter or margarine
- 1 cup milk
- 1 16-ounce box powdered sugar
- 1 to 4 ounces unsweetened chocolate, to taste

Preheat oven to 350 degrees. Mix flour, salt, baking soda, and cocoa together well and set aside. Cream butter and sugar. Add eggs, one at a time, beating well after each addition. Add buttermilk, alternating with flour mixture. Mix well. Add hot water, vanilla, and food coloring. Pour into a 9x13x2-inch cake pan and in an 8-inch square pan. Bake for 25 to 30 minutes. When done, remove from pans and pour icing over warm cake.

For icing, while cake is baking, place butter, milk, powdered sugar, and chocolate in a saucepan and cook over very low heat, stirring occasionally. Pour over warm cake.

Notes:
Will be a very gooey chocolate cake. Great cure for chocolate craving.

Melody Munson
Colorado Springs, Colorado

Chocolate Sheet Cake with Frosting

Cake:
- 2 cups flour
- 2 cups sugar
- 1 cup (2 sticks) margarine
- 4 tablespoons cocoa
- 1 cup water
- 2 eggs, beaten
- 1/2 cup buttermilk or sour cream
- 1 teaspoon baking soda
- 1/4 teaspoon salt
- 1 teaspoon vanilla

Frosting:
- 1/2 cup (1 stick) margarine
- 4 tablespoons cocoa
- 4 tablespoons milk
- 1 to 2 pounds powdered sugar

Preheat oven to 350 degrees. In a large bowl mix flour and sugar well; set aside. Melt margarine, add cocoa and water, and bring to a boil. Add to flour and sugar mixture. Add eggs, buttermilk, baking soda, salt, and vanilla, blending well. Pour into an 11x17-inch greased cookie sheet with sides. Bake for 20 minutes.

For frosting, melt margarine, add cocoa and milk, and bring to a boil. Add powdered sugar as needed. Spread over hot cake as soon as it is removed from the oven.

Verna Mullet
Fort Lupton, Colorado

Chocolate Chip Cake

- 1³/₄ cups boiling water
- 1 cup uncooked oatmeal
- 1 cup lightly packed brown sugar
- 1 cup granulated sugar
- ½ cup (1 stick) margarine, softened
- 2 extra large eggs
- 1³/₄ cups flour
- 1 teaspoon baking soda
- 1 teaspoon salt
- 1 tablespoon cocoa powder
- 1 12-ounce package semi-sweet chocolate chips, divided
- ³/₄ cup chopped walnuts

Preheat oven to 375 degrees. Pour boiling water over oatmeal; let stand at room temperature for 10 minutes. Add brown sugar, granulated sugar, and margarine. Stir until margarine is smoothly blended. Add eggs; mix well. Sift together flour, soda, salt, and cocoa. Add flour mixture to sugar mixture. Stir well. Add half of the package of chocolate chips. Pour into greased and floured 9x13x2-inch pan. Sprinkle with walnuts and remaining chocolate chips, evenly covering the top of the cake. Bake 40 minutes.

Notes:
Very moist. Because there is no icing, this cake travels well.

Terri Lynn Ballard
Denver, Colorado

Grandma's Chocolate Cake and Icing

Cake:
- 2 cups all purpose flour
- 1 teaspoon salt
- 1 teaspoon baking powder
- 2 teaspoons baking soda
- 3/4 cup unsweetened cocoa
- 2 cups sugar
- 1 cup vegetable oil
- 1 cup hot coffee
- 1 cup milk
- 2 eggs
- 1 teaspoon vanilla extract

Favorite Icing:
- 1 cup milk
- 5 tablespoons all-purpose flour
- 1/2 cup (1 stick) butter or margarine, softened
- 1/2 cup vegetable shortening
- 1 cup sugar
- 1 teaspoon vanilla extract

Preheat oven to 325 degrees. Sift together dry ingredients in a mixing bowl. Add vegetable oil, coffee, and milk. Mix at medium speed 2 minutes. Add eggs and vanilla. Beat 2 more minutes. Batter will be thin. Pour into two greased and floured 9-inch round cake pans. Bake for 25 to 30 minutes or until cake tests done. Cool 15 minutes before removing from pan. Continue cooling on wire racks.

To make icing, combine milk and flour in a saucepan. Cook until thick. Cover and refrigerate. In a mixing bowl beat butter, vegetable shortening, sugar, and vanilla until creamy. Add chilled flour/milk mixture and beat 10 minutes. Frost cooled cake.

Ann Moss
Grand Junction, Colorado

Yield: 12 servings

Chocolate Cake
(not from scratch...but enhanced)

1 18 1/2-ounce package devil's food cake mix

Follow preparation and cooking instructions on cake package substituting coffee for the water.

Notes:
Unbelievably reliable and yummy. The coffee adds no coffee flavor, but brings out the chocolate flavor.

Jeanne Creighton
Denver, Colorado

Hurry-Up Chocolate Cake

- 2 cups flour
- 2 cups sugar
- 2 teaspoons baking soda
- 1/2 cup cocoa
- 1/4 teaspoon salt
- 1 cup vegetable oil
- 1 cup buttermilk
- 2 eggs
- 1 cup boiling water

Preheat oven to 350 degrees. Put all ingredients in a bowl, adding boiling water last. Beat about 3 minutes with electric mixer at high speed. Batter will be thin. Grease and flour 9x13x2-inch pan. Pour batter into pan, and bake for 35 minutes. Frost with *Fudge Frosting* (page 302).

Ruby Hill Davis
Golden, Colorado

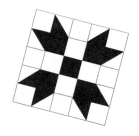

Best-Ever Chocolate Cake

- 2 cups flour
- 2 cups sugar
- 1/2 cup (1 stick) butter or margarine
- 1/2 cup vegetable oil
- 4 tablespoons cocoa
- 1 cup water
- 1/2 cup buttermilk
- 1 teaspoon vanilla
- 1 teaspoon ground cinnamon (optional)
- 1/4 teaspoon salt
- 1 teaspoon baking soda
- 2 eggs, beaten

Preheat oven to 400 degrees. Sift flour and sugar together and set aside. In a saucepan bring butter, vegetable oil, cocoa, and water to a boil. Remove from heat and add buttermilk and mix well. Add flour mix, vanilla, cinnamon, salt, baking soda, and eggs. Stir until thoroughly mixed. Pour batter into a greased and floured 9x13x2-inch pan for 25 to 30 minutes. Do not over bake. Frost cake while it is still warm using *Best Ever Chocolate Cake Frosting* recipe (page 301).

Notes:
For a thinner cake, bake in a greased and floured 9x13x2-inch pan and a 9x5x3-inch loaf pan. Freeze the small cake for one of those days you want to spend quilting.

Ellen McAninch
Littleton, Colorado

Best-Ever Chocolate Cake Frosting

- ½ cup (1 stick) butter or margarine
- 4 tablespoons cocoa
- 5 tablespoons milk
- 1 16-ounce box powdered sugar
- 1 teaspoon vanilla
- 1 cup pecans, chopped

Bring butter, cocoa, and milk to a boil. Remove from heat; add powdered sugar and vanilla. Stir until right consistency to spread. If frosting seems too thick, add a little more milk. Nuts may be stirred into frosting or placed on top.

Ellen McAninch
Littleton, Colorado

Recipe for Treatment of Dry, Over-Worked Quilter's Hands

Place about 1 teaspoon sea salt in palm of hand and moisten with a few drops of almond oil. Rub into hands and cuticles. Rinse and dry.

You won't believe how wonderful your hands feel until you have tried it! Both ingredients are inexpensive and available in health food stores.

Fudge Frosting

- 1 cup sugar
- 1/4 cup milk
- 1/3 cup margarine
- dash salt
- 3 tablespoons cocoa
- 1 teaspoon vanilla
- pecan halves

Place sugar, milk, margarine, salt, and cocoa in a saucepan and boil hard for 1 minute. Remove from heat. Add vanilla. Put pan in cold water and beat until frosting is thick enough to spread. Spread immediately on cake. Decorate with pecan halves.

Notes:
This frosting goes great with *Hurry-Up Chocolate Cake* (page 299).

Ruby Hill Davis
Clifton, Colorado

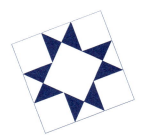

Frosting for Cake and Sugar Cookies

    1 pound powdered sugar
    ½ cup (1 stick) butter or margarine, softened
1 to 3 teaspoons vanilla, to taste
        milk to consistency

Mix sugar, margarine, and vanilla together. If frosting is not the consistency needed for spreading, add a little milk and stir again. Continue adding milk a little at a time until frosting reaches the consistency you desire.

Jeanne Creighton
Denver, Colorado

Chocolate Covered Cherry Cookies

Cookies:
- 1/2 cup (1 stick) butter (no substitutes)
- 1 cup sugar
- 1 egg
- 1 teaspoon vanilla
- 1 1/2 cups flour
- 1/4 teaspoon salt
- 1/2 teaspoon baking soda
- 1/3 cup cocoa
- 1/2 teaspoon baking powder
- 48 maraschino cherries, drained (reserve juice)

Frosting:
- 6 ounces chocolate chips
- 1/2 cup sweetened condensed milk
- 2 to 3 tablespoons reserved cherry juice

Preheat oven to 350 degrees. Cream butter and sugar until fluffy. Add egg and vanilla, mixing well. Combine dry ingredients and gradually add to creamed mixture, mixing well with each addition. Drain juice from maraschino cherries, reserving liquid. Blot the cherries dry. Shape dough into 48 walnut-sized balls. Place dough on ungreased cookie sheet. Push one cherry into each ball. Bake for 10 to 12 minutes. Do not over bake. Allow cookies to cool.

To prepare frosting, place chocolate chips, sweetened condensed milk, and cherry juice in a saucepan. Stirring mixture constantly, melt over very low heat. Pour 1 teaspoon of frosting over each cooled cookie.

Edytha Vickers
Aurora, Colorado

Yield: 48 cookies

Chocolate Marshmallow Cookies

Cookies:
- 2 cups sugar
- 1 cup vegetable shortening
- 2 eggs
- 1 teaspoon vanilla
- 3 1/2 cups flour
- 1 teaspoon baking soda
- 2/3 cup cocoa
- 1 teaspoon salt
- 1 cup milk
- 1 10 1/2-ounce bag miniature marshmallows

Frosting:
- 2 cups powdered sugar
- 1 egg
- 1/4 teaspoon salt
- 2 ounces (2 squares) unsweetened chocolate, melted

Preheat oven to 350 degrees. Cream sugar and vegetable shortening until smooth. Add eggs and mix well. Stir in vanilla. Combine flour, baking soda, cocoa, and salt. Mix well. Alternately add milk and dry ingredients to sugar mixture. Drop dough by teaspoonfuls onto greased cookie sheet. Bake until almost done—8 to 10 minutes. Remove from oven and place 2 or 3 miniature marshmallows on each cookie. Put cookies back in the oven to finish baking—2 to 3 minutes. Allow cookies to cool.

To make frosting, combine powdered sugar, egg, salt, and melted chocolate. Mix until smooth. Spread on cookies.

Judy Veyera
Conifer, Colorado

Monster Cookies

- 12 eggs
- 1 2-pound bag sugar
- 4 cups granulated sugar
- 1 tablespoon corn syrup
- 1 tablespoon vanilla
- 2 cups (4 sticks) margarine
- 8 teaspoons baking soda
- 3 pounds peanut butter
- 18 cups oatmeal
- 1 pound chocolate chips
- 1 pound M&M's chocolate candy

Preheat oven to 350 degrees. In a large pan, mix eggs, brown sugar, granulated sugar, syrup, vanilla, and margarine. Mix until smooth. Add baking soda, peanut butter, oatmeal, chocolate chips, and M&M's, mixing well. Drop by teaspoonfuls onto greased cookie sheets. Bake for 10 minutes. Do not over bake. Let cookies cool on cookie sheets for 5 minutes before removing.

Notes:
Making a half batch is possible. At higher altitudes, you can add 3 to 5 extra cups of oatmeal.

Cami Termer
Pueblo, Colorado

Yield: 200 large cookies

$10,000 Cookies

- 1½ cups light packed brown sugar
- 1 cup granulated sugar
- 1¼ cup butter-flavored vegetable shortening
- 3 large eggs
- 1¼ cups chunky peanut butter
- 4½ cups rolled oats
- 2 teaspoons baking soda
- 1 cup semi-sweet chocolate chips
- 1 cup butterscotch chips
- 1 cup chopped walnuts

Preheat oven to 350 degrees. Cream brown sugar, granulated sugar, and vegetable shortening, scraping sides of bowl frequently. Add eggs and mix well. Add peanut butter, continuing to mix well. Combine rolled oats and baking soda; add to creamed mixture, mixing until well blended. Add chips and nuts. Drop by well-rounded spoonfuls 2 inches apart onto ungreased cookie sheet. Bake for 10 to 11 minutes. Cool on pan for 2 minutes, then remove to cooling rack.

Jeanne Arnoldy
Littleton, Colorado

No-Bake Chocolate Cookies

  2 cups sugar
1/2 cup cocoa
1/2 cup milk
1/2 cup (1 stick) butter or margarine
  3 cups old fashioned oatmeal
1/2 cup peanut butter
1/2 teaspoon vanilla
    pinch of salt

Heat sugar, cocoa, milk, and butter together and boil for 2 minutes. Add oatmeal, peanut butter, vanilla, and salt. Mix well. Drop on buttered cookie sheet and cool.

Beth Sayers
Colorado Springs, Colorado

Chocolate Chipper Champs

- ³/₄ cup butter or margarine, softened
- 1¹/₂ cups packed packed brown sugar
- 2 eggs
- 1 teaspoon vanilla
- 2¹/₄ cups flour
- 1 teaspoon baking soda
- ¹/₂ teaspoon salt
- 1 cup M&M's plain candy
- ¹/₂ cup chopped walnuts

Preheat oven to 350 degrees. Beat butter and brown sugar; add eggs and vanilla and mix well. Add flour, soda, and salt. Stir in M&M's and nuts. Drop by heaping teaspoonfuls onto a greased cookie sheet. Press three to four M&M's on the top of each cookie. Bake for 8 to 10 minutes. Cool on cookie sheet for 3 minutes. Move to rack to continue cooling.

Judy Kiser
Grand Junction, Colorado

Yield: 2 dozen

Fudge Cookies
(no-bake)

- 2 cups sugar
- 1/2 cup milk
- 1/3 cup cocoa
- 1/4 cup margarine
- 1/2 cup peanut butter
- 1 teaspoon vanilla
- 3 cups rolled oats
- handful of coconut (optional)

In a 2-quart saucepan combine sugar, milk, cocoa, and margarine. Boil for 1 minute (hard boil). Remove from heat and immediately add the peanut butter, vanilla, rolled oats, and coconut. Drop by teaspoons on waxed paper. Allow to cool.

Notes:
Since these are a no-bake cookie, they are quick to make. Only takes one pan. Has everyone's favorite ingredients—chocolate and peanut butter.

Marie Gifford
Aurora, Colorado

Cowboy Cookies

- 1 cup granulated sugar
- 1 cup packed brown sugar
- 1 cup vegetable shortening
- 2 eggs
- 2 cups flour
- 1 teaspoon baking soda
- 1/2 teaspoon baking powder
- 2 cups rolled oats
- 1 teaspoon vanilla
- 1 6-ounce package chocolate or butterscotch chips

Preheat oven to 350 to 375 degrees. Cream granulated and brown sugars with vegetable shortening. Add eggs and beat well. Sift together flour, baking soda, and baking powder. Add to dough and mix well. Stir in rolled oats, vanilla, and chocolate or butterscotch chips. Form dough into round balls. Place on a cookie sheet and flatten with a damp fork. Bake for 10 to 15 minutes.

Variations:
Use raisins instead of chocolate or butterscotch chips.

Shirley Franzen
Thornton, Colorado

New England Fruit Cookies

- 1 cup (2 sticks) margarine, softened
- 1 1/2 cups packed brown sugar
- 3 eggs, well beaten
- 1 teaspoon vanilla
- 1 teaspoon baking soda
- 2 tablespoons boiling water
- 3 cups flour, sifted
- 3/4 teaspoon salt
- 1 teaspoon ground cinnamon
- 1/4 teaspoon ground cloves
- 1/4 teaspoon ground allspice
- 1 cup chopped nuts
- 1 8-ounce package chopped dates
- 1 cup raisins

Preheat oven to 300 degrees. Cream margarine and brown sugar together. Add eggs and mix well. Stir in vanilla. Dissolve baking soda in boiling water and add to mixture. In a separate bowl, combine flour, salt, cinnamon, cloves, and allspice and mix. Add to creamed mixture and mix well. Add nuts, dates, and raisins. Fold into batter. Drop by teaspoonfuls onto greased and floured cookie sheet. Bake 12 minutes.

Maxine Tamlin
Fort Collins, Colorado

Cornmeal Cookies

    1 cup vegetable shortening
1½ cups sugar
    2 eggs
    1 teaspoon vanilla
2½ cups flour
    1 cup yellow cornmeal
    ½ teaspoon salt
    1 teaspoon ground nutmeg
    1 teaspoon baking powder
    ½ cup raisins

Preheat oven to 400 degrees. Cream vegetable shortening and sugar together. Add eggs and mix well. Mix in vanilla. In a separate bowl, combine flour, cornmeal, salt, nutmeg, and baking powder and mix well. Add the flour mixture to the creamed mixture, mixing until smooth. Fold in raisins. Drop by teaspoonfuls onto greased cookie sheet and bake for 10 minutes.

Variations:
You can roll the dough into 1½- to 2-inch rolls and refrigerate or freeze. Once chilled, slice roll of dough into ¼-inch-thick slices and bake as directed above. If dough is frozen, it will need to be partially thawed before you will be able to slice it.

Jeanne Simpson
Fort Collins, Colorado

Busy Day Cookies

 2 cups sugar
 1/2 cup (1 stick) butter or margarine, softened
 1/4 teaspoon salt
 1/2 cup milk
 1/2 cup cocoa
 1 teaspoon vanilla
 1/2 cup peanut butter
3 1/2 cups rolled oats

Mix sugar, butter, salt, milk, cocoa, and vanilla together in a saucepan. Stir over medium heat until dissolved. Bring to boil. Remove from heat. Add peanut butter and rolled oats. Mix thoroughly. Drop by heaping teaspoonfuls onto waxed paper. Let cool.

Notes:
My mother would make these cookies for us when I or one of my four sisters needed to bring goodies to a school function. They were always the first to go.

Ren Wright
Littleton, Colorado

Oatmeal Whole Wheat Cookies

- 1 cup granulated or brown sugar or ³/₄ cup honey
- 3 large eggs
- ¹/₂ cup vegetable shortening
- 2 teaspoons baking powder
- ¹/₂ teaspoon salt
- 1 teaspoon baking soda
- 2 cups whole wheat flour
- 2 cups rolled oats or granola or combination of both
- 1 teaspoon vanilla

Preheat oven to 350 degrees. Mix ingredients in order given. Drop by heaping teaspoonfuls onto an ungreased cookie sheet. Bake 7 to 8 minutes.

Variations:
May add chocolate chips, M&M's, raisins, etc.

Kathy Kerrigan
Salida, Colorado

Yield: 4 dozen

Grandmother's Oatmeal Cookies

- 1 cup vegetable shortening
- 1 cup packed brown sugar
- 1 cup granulated sugar
- 3 eggs, well beaten
- 1 teaspoon vanilla
- 2½ cups sifted flour
- 1 teaspoon salt
- 1 teaspoon baking soda
- 2 teaspoons ground cinnamon
- 2 cups uncooked rolled oats
- 1 cup raisins
- ½ cup chopped walnuts

Preheat oven to 350 degrees. In a large mixing bowl, cream vegetable shortening, brown sugar, and granulated sugar together. Add beaten eggs and vanilla; mix well. Sift together flour, salt, baking soda, and cinnamon, then add to the above ingredients. When mixture is beaten smooth, add uncooked rolled oats. Add the raisins and nuts and beat the mixture well. Drop cookies 2 inches apart on a well-greased cookie sheet and bake for 10 to 12 minutes or until lightly browned. Do not over bake.

Variations:
Sometimes I omit the raisins and add a package of butterscotch or chocolate chips and **more nuts**.

Betty Jo Dreith
Longmont, Colorado

Lemon-Frosted Pecan Sandies

Cookies:
- 1 cup (2 sticks) butter or margarine, softened
- 3/4 cup sifted powdered sugar
- 2 tablespoons milk
- 1 1/2 cups sifted flour
- 3/4 cup sifted cornstarch
- 3/4 cup chopped pecans

Frosting:
- 2 1/2 cups sifted powdered sugar
- 1 tablespoon butter or margarine
- 3 tablespoons lemon juice
- few drops of yellow food coloring

Preheat oven to 350 degrees. For cookies, cream butter; add powdered sugar, milk, flour, cornstarch, and chopped pecans. Cream until well blended. Chill. Place small balls 2 inches apart on ungreased cookie sheet. Flatten slightly. Bake for 12 to 15 minutes. Cool.

For frosting, combine all ingredients and spread over cooled cookies.

Variations:
Also excellent unfrosted.

Nancy Cole
Longmont, Colorado

Yield: 4 dozen cookies

Biscochitos
(Cookies)

- 2 cups (4 sticks) margarine, softened
- 1 cup sugar
- 2 teaspoons anise seeds, crushed by rolling in palms of your hands
- 2 teaspoons anise extract
- 2 eggs, beaten
- 4 cups flour
- 3 teaspoons baking powder
- 1/2 teaspoon salt
- 1/4 cup whiskey and orange juice, mixed
- 1 heaping teaspoon ground cinnamon
- 1/2 cup sugar

Preheat oven to 350 degrees. Cream margarine, sugar, anise seeds, and anise extract, beating until smooth. Add beaten eggs. Combine flour, baking powder, and salt. Sift together and add to creamed mixture. Add whiskey and orange juice. On a floured surface, roll dough out to 1/2-inch thickness. Mix cinnamon and sugar together. Using a round cookie cutter, cut out cookies and dip each into cinnamon mixture. Place on greased cookie sheet. Bake 11 to 12 minutes or until lightly browned.

Variations:
May omit whiskey and use 1/4 cup orange juice.

Katy Westerman
Alamosa, Colorado

Slice-and-Bake Almond Cookies

- 2¾ cups all purpose flour
- 2 teaspoons ground cinnamon
- ½ teaspoon ground nutmeg
- ½ teaspoon baking soda
- 1 cup (2 sticks) butter or margarine, softened
- 1 cup firmly packed light brown sugar
- ¼ cup sour cream
- ½ cup finely chopped blanched almonds

Sift together flour, cinnamon, nutmeg, and baking soda. Set aside. In a large bowl, cream butter, brown sugar, sour cream, and chopped almonds together until smooth and fluffy. Work in half of the flour mixture. Add the remaining flour in amounts that can be absorbed. Dough will be stiff. Turn out onto a lightly floured board. Divide dough in half. Knead and shape into a roll about 8 inches long. Wrap in plastic wrap. Repeat with other half of dough. Refrigerate until firm—about 8 hours. Will keep for 7 to 10 days in refrigerator. Slice and bake cookies for 8 to 10 minutes in a preheated 375-degree oven until lightly browned. Remove with a spatula.

Auriel Sandstead
Sterling, Colorado

Remember Mary Stanley's (1869-1955) contribution to Colorado quilt history in her terminology and use of "prairie points" for 2-inch or smaller folded squares used in finishing and decoration.

Pumpkin Cookies

- 1 cup packed brown sugar
- 1 cup mashed pumpkin (unspiced) (can used canned)
- 1/2 cup vegetable oil
- 1 teaspoon vanilla
- 1 teaspoon baking soda
- 1 teaspoon baking powder
- 1/2 teaspoon salt
- 2 cups flour
- 1/2 teaspoon ground cinnamon
- 1/2 teaspoon ground nutmeg
- 1/4 teaspoon ginger
- 1 cup raisins
- 1/2 cup chopped nuts

Preheat oven to 350 degrees. Beat together brown sugar, pumpkin, vegetable oil, and vanilla. Sift together dry ingredients and add to pumpkin mixture. Stir until smooth. Blend in raisins and nuts. Drop by spoonfuls onto greased cookie sheet. Bake for 12 to 15 minutes.

Notes:
These are best after they cool and ripen a few hours. They stay moist and delicious.

Janet Mount
Longmont, Colorado

German Christmas Cookies

Cookies:
- 1 cup honey
- 3/4 cup firmly packed brown sugar
- 1 egg, beaten
- 1 tablespoon lemon juice
- 2 1/4 cups all purpose flour
- 3/4 teaspoon ground cinnamon
- 1/2 teaspoon ground allspice
- 1/2 teaspoon ground nutmeg
- 1/4 teaspoon ground cloves
- 1/2 teaspoon salt
- 1/2 teaspoon baking soda
- 1/4 cup finely chopped almonds
- 1/3 cup finely chopped candied citron (fruitcake fruits work very well also)
- candied red cherry halves
- whole blanched almonds

Frosting:
- 1 cup plus 2 tablespoons sifted powdered sugar
- 1/4 cup plus 1 tablespoon rum or water

Heat honey in a medium saucepan just until warm. Stir in brown sugar, egg, and lemon juice and set aside. Combine dry ingredients in a large bowl. Add honey mixture, almonds, and citron; stir until blended. Cover and chill overnight.

Work with one-quarter of dough at a time, keeping remaining dough chilled. Roll dough to 3/8-inch thickness on a heavily-floured surface. Cut dough into 2 1/2-inch rounds and transfer to greased cookie sheets. Press a candied cherry half in center of each, and arrange five whole almonds radiating from center of each cherry. Bake for 12 minutes in a preheated 375-degree oven or until golden brown. Transfer to racks. For frosting, combine powdered sugar and rum; stir until blended. Immediately brush frosting over hot cookies. Let cool completely. Store in airtight container.

Notes:
When first baked, cookies are hard and crunchy; they are typically stored in an airtight container for 2 weeks to soften, although they may be eaten earlier.

Dorothy Main
Parachute, Colorado

Yield: 2 dozen cookies

Mother's Classic Coconut Cookie

- 1 cup (2 sticks) margarine
- 1 cup sugar
- 1 egg
- 1/2 teaspoon vanilla
- 1/2 teaspoon baking soda
- 1 cup flour
- 2 cups flaked coconut

Preheat oven to 350 degrees. Cream margarine and sugar; add egg and vanilla; stir in flour and baking soda; form dough into rolls or drop onto greased cookie sheet. Bake for 10 minutes.

Jerry Goddard
Loveland, Colorado

Lemon-Pecan Sugar Cookies

- 1 cup (2 sticks) margarine or butter, softened
- $1/2$ cup vegetable oil
- $3/4$ cup granulated sugar
- 1 cup powdered sugar
- 3 eggs, unbeaten
- 1 teaspoon lemon extract
- 4 cups flour
- 1 teaspoon baking soda
- 1 teaspoon cream of tartar
- $1/8$ teaspoon salt
- $1/2$ cup finely chopped pecans
- 1 teaspoon grated lemon peel
- $1/2$ cup sugar

Cream margarine and vegetable oil. Add $3/4$ cup granulated sugar and powdered sugar and mix well. Add eggs, lemon extract, flour, baking soda, cream of tartar, and salt. Stir in nuts and lemon peel. Cover dough and chill for 2 to 3 hours (optional).

Preheat oven to 350 degrees. Roll teaspoonfuls of dough into small balls. Dip tops of balls in bowl of $1/2$ cup granulated sugar. Place dough sugar side up on ungreased baking sheet. Flatten balls with a small glass or jar. Bake 6 to 8 minutes, until bottoms of cookies are lightly browned. The tops of cookies should be barely beige, not brown.

Naomi Luck
Aurora, Colorado

Family's Favorite Cookies

- 1/2 cup (1 stick) margarine, softened
- 1 1/4 cup sugar, divided
- 1 egg, beaten
- 1 1/2 cups flour
- 1 teaspoon cream of tartar
- 1/2 teaspoon baking soda
- 1/4 teaspoon salt
- 1 teaspoon ground cinnamon

Preheat oven to 350 degrees. Cream butter, add 3/4 cup sugar, and blend well. Add egg. Add flour, cream of tartar, baking soda, and salt. Mix well. In a small bowl, mix 1/2 cup sugar and cinnamon. Roll cookie dough into small balls. Roll balls in sugar mixture and place on an ungreased cookie sheet. Bake 8 to 10 minutes.

Deana Lovelace
Littleton, Colorado

Jeanne's Favorite Sugar Cookies

½ cup (1 stick) butter or margarine, softened
¾ cup sugar
1 egg, beaten
2 tablespoons milk
1 teaspoon vanilla
2 cups flour
1 teaspoon baking powder
¼ teaspoon salt

Preheat oven to 375 degrees. Cream butter and sugar. Add egg, milk, and vanilla. Sift and stir in flour, baking powder, and salt. Beat well. If necessary, add more flour to make a stiffer dough. Wrap in waxed paper and refrigerate. Later, roll out on floured board to ⅛-inch thickness. Using your favorite cookie cutter, cut cookies and place on lightly greased cookie sheet. Bake for 10 minutes, watching carefully.

Notes:
I make these for Valentine's Day and Easter, decorating them with the classic powdered sugar and butter frosting. You can find this frosting recipe on page 303—*Frosting for Cake and Sugar Cookies*.

Jeanne Creighton
Denver, Colorado

Marylou's Moist Cookies

- 1/2 cup butter-flavored vegetable shortening
- 3/4 cup packed brown sugar
- 3/4 cup granulated sugar
- 2 teaspoons flavoring*
- 2 large eggs
- 2 cups flour
- 1 teaspoon baking soda
- 1/2 cup flaked coconut
- 3/4 cup chopped pecans
- 1 8-ounce box chopped dates

Preheat oven to 350 degrees. Beat vegetable shortening, brown and granulated sugars, flavoring, and eggs on high speed for 1 minute. Add flour, baking soda, coconut, pecans, and dates. Mix well. Drop by heaping teaspoons onto greased cookie sheet. Bake until almost done—8 to 9 minutes. It is very important to take these out of the oven before they look done. They will finish baking on the cookie sheet. Cool completely. Store in an air-tight container.

Variations:
*I use different flavorings, such as butterscotch, butternut, butter pecan, or vanilla.

Notes:
You can have these mixed and baked and have the bowl cleaned up in half an hour.

Marylou Groves
Pueblo, Colorado

Yield: 2 1/2 dozen cookies

Peanut Butter 'n Chocolate Chip Cookies

- 3/4 cup margarine, softened
- 1 cup granulated sugar
- 1 cup firmly packed brown sugar
- 1/2 cup peanut butter
- 2 eggs
- 2 teaspoons vanilla
- 2 1/2 cups flour
- 1 teaspoon baking soda
- 1/2 teaspoon salt
- 1 11 1/2-ounce package chocolate chips

Preheat oven to 350 degrees. Cream margarine, granulated sugar, and brown sugar together until smooth. Add peanut butter and beat on medium speed of mixer until mixture is light brown and fluffy. Blend in eggs and vanilla. Mix in flour, baking soda, and salt. Stir in chocolate chips. Drop by rounded tablespoonfuls onto ungreased cookie sheet. Bake 10 to 12 minutes or until lightly browned. Cool 2 minutes; remove from cookie sheet onto wire racks to continue cooling.

Kathlyn Thompson
Colorado Springs, Colorado

Yield: 4 dozen

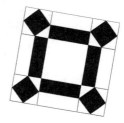

Chocolate Cookie Sheets
(Brownies)

    4 eggs
    2 cups sugar
    1 cup (2 sticks) butter or margarine, softened
    2 cups flour
    8 tablespoons cocoa
    1 teaspoon vanilla

Preheat oven to 350 degrees. In a large bowl, beat eggs. Add sugar and butter; mix well. Sift flour and cocoa; stir into mixture. Add vanilla and mix well. Spread onto a greased and floured cookie sheet with sides. Bake 15 to 20 minutes.

Variations:
Add nuts if desired. Frost with chocolate frosting if desired.

Shirley Franzen
Thornton, Colorado

Quilt Camp Brownies

- 4 eggs, beaten
- 2 cups sugar
- 1 cup (2 sticks) margarine, softened
- 1 teaspoon vanilla
- 2 cups flour
- 8 tablespoons cocoa powder
- 1 cup chopped nuts (optional)

Preheat oven to 350 degrees. In a large bowl, beat eggs. Add sugar, margarine, and vanilla. Mix until smooth. Add flour, cocoa, and nuts. Mix until smooth. Pour batter into a greased 9x13x2-inch pan and bake for 20 minutes.

Notes:
If you like your brownies frosted, use the old family recipe, the premade frosting in a tub from your grocery store. Leaves time for quilting.

Toni Fitzwater
Pine, Colorado

To remove odor from a quilt or a piece of fabric, place it in a plastic bag with a bar of Irish Spring or similar type of soap. Seal bag. Leave it for a couple of days.

Brownies

Brownies:
- 2 cups sugar
- 1/2 cup cocoa
- 1 cup (2 sticks) butter or margarine, softened
- 4 eggs
- 2 teaspoons vanilla
- 1 1/2 cups flour
- 1 teaspoon salt
- 1/2 cup nuts, chopped

Chocolate Frosting:
- 2 ounces unsweetened chocolate
- 1/4 cup butter or margarine
- 2 tablespoons milk
- 2 cups powdered sugar

Preheat oven to 350 degrees. For brownies, mix sugar and cocoa together; stir in butter, add eggs and vanilla, and beat well. Sift flour and salt together; stir into cocoa mixture. Fold in nuts. Pour into a greased 15x10-inch jelly roll pan. Bake for 25 minutes. Cool and then frost.

For frosting, melt chocolate, butter, and milk together. Stir in powdered sugar, adding more milk if necessary.

Variations:
Remove brownies from oven and immediately cover top with tiny marshmallows. If you use marshmallows on top of brownies, add extra milk to frosting so it is rather thin and can easily be spread over marshmallows.

Mary Biesecker
Grand Junction, Colorado

Chocolate Caramel Squares "Killers"

- 1 14-ounce bag caramels
- 2/3 cup evaporated milk, divided
- 1 18 1/2-ounce package German chocolate cake mix
- 3/4 cup butter or margarine, softened
- 1 cup chopped walnuts
- 1 6-ounce package semi-sweet chocolate chips

Preheat oven to 350 degrees. Combine caramels and 1/3 cup evaporated milk in top of double boiler; cook, stirring constantly, until caramels are completely melted. Combine cake mix, remaining 1/3 cup evaporated milk, and butter, mixing with electric mixer until dough holds together; add nuts. Press half of cake mixture into greased 9x13x2-inch pan. Bake for 6 minutes. Sprinkle chocolate chips over hot mixture; pour caramel mixture over chocolate chips; spread evenly. Crumble remaining cake mixture over caramel mixture. Return to oven and bake 15 to 18 minutes. Cool. Cut into bars. Serve warm or cooled.

Robin Anders
Fort Lupton, Colorado

Triple Chocolate Bars

2 cups milk
1 4-ounce package chocolate cook and serve pudding mix
1 18$^{1}/_{2}$-ounce package chocolate cake mix
1 6-ounce package mini chocolate chips

Preheat oven to 350 degrees. Combine milk and pudding and cook according to package directions. After pudding comes to a boil, pour dry cake mix into pudding. Mix well. Batter will be thick. Pour into greased 10x15-inch or 9x13x2-inch pan. Sprinkle chocolate chips on top. Bake for 20 to 30 minutes.

Notes:
No adjustments are necessary for high altitude.

Karen Scully
Colorado Springs, Colorado

Butterscotch Brownies

- ½ cup vegetable oil
- 2 cups packed brown sugar
- 2 eggs
- 1½ cups flour
- 2 teaspoons baking powder
- 1 teaspoon salt
- 1 teaspoon vanilla
- 1 cup chopped nuts

Preheat oven to 350 degrees. Blend all ingredients by hand (do not use an electric mixer). Blend vegetable oil and sugar in large bowl. Stir in eggs. Blend in dry ingredients, then vanilla and nuts. Bake in a greased 9x13x2-inch pan for 28 to 30 minutes. Do not over bake.

Chris Mooney
Longmont, Colorado

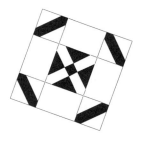

Butterscotch Chewies

1 cup (2 sticks) butter or margarine, softened
2 1/2 cups (1 pound) packed brown sugar
3 eggs
1 teaspoon vanilla
2 1/2 teaspoons baking powder
2 scant cups flour
1 teaspoon salt
2 cups nuts, chopped

Preheat oven to 325 degrees. Cream softened butter and brown sugar together. Add eggs, one at a time, beating after each addition until well blended. Stir in vanilla. Combine baking powder, flour, and salt. Mix well. Add to creamed mixture. Fold in chopped nuts. Bake in an 8x10-inch pan for 45 minutes. Allow to cool. Store tightly wrapped.

Marti Thomas
Salida, Colorado

Oatmeal Marble Squares

- 1/2 cup (1 stick) butter or margarine, softened
- 6 tablespoons granulated sugar
- 6 tablespoons brown sugar
- 1/2 teaspoon vanilla
- 1/4 teaspoon water
- 1 egg
- 3/4 cup flour
- 1/2 teaspoon baking soda
- 1/2 teaspoon salt
- 1 cup uncooked oatmeal
- 1/2 cup walnuts or pecans, chopped
- 1 cup chocolate chips

Preheat oven to 375 degrees. Cream granulated sugar, brown sugar, softened butter, and vanilla together until smooth. Add vanilla, water, and egg. Mix well. In a separate container, combine flour, baking soda, and salt. Mix well. Add flour mixture to creamed mixture, blending until smooth. Stir in oatmeal and nuts. Put dough into a greased 9x13x2-inch pan. Sprinkle with chocolate chips. Bake for 1 to 2 minutes. Remove from oven and run knife through dough to marble it. Return to oven and bake for 12 to 14 minutes. Cool and cut into squares.

Judy Veyera
Conifer, Colorado

Seven-Layer Bars

- ¼ cup butter or margarine
- 1 cup graham cracker crumbs
- 1 cup shredded coconut
- 1 6-ounce package chocolate chips
- 1 cup chopped nuts
- 1 6-ounce package butterscotch chips
- 1 14-ounce can Eagle Brand sweetened condensed milk (no substitutes)

Preheat oven to 350 degrees. Melt butter in a 9x13x2-inch baking pan or dish. Sprinkle graham cracker crumbs evenly over butter. Tap side of pan to evenly distribute crumbs. Sprinkle on coconut and chips. Pour condensed milk on top evenly. Sprinkle nuts on top and press lightly into pan. Bake for 30 minutes. Cool and cut into bars.

Variations:
Use peanut butter chips in place of butterscotch chips.

Notes:
It is best to cut bars before they get too hard. I usually store these in the refrigerator after cutting.

Janette Nash
Grand Junction, Colorado

Nana's Date Squares

- 1 cup sugar
- 2 eggs
- 1 teaspoon vanilla
- 1/2 cup milk
- 1 cup flour
- 1 teaspoon baking powder
- 1/2 teaspoon salt
- 1 scant cup chopped nuts
- 1 cup chopped dates
- powdered sugar

Preheat oven to 250 degrees. Cream sugar, eggs, vanilla, and milk together. Add flour, baking powder, and salt. Mix well. Stir in nuts and dates. Spread in a greased 9x13x2-inch pan. Bake for 50 minutes. When cool cut into small squares and roll in powdered sugar.

Gerry Phenix
Littleton, Colorado

Quasi-Lemon Bars

Crust:
- 1 18½-ounce package yellow cake mix
- ½ cup (1 stick) margarine, softened
- 1 egg, beaten

Topping:
- 1 8-ounce package cream cheese, softened
- 2 eggs
- 1 16-ounce box powdered sugar
- 1 teaspoon vanilla

Preheat oven to 375 degrees. Combine cake mix, margarine, and egg. Mix until crumbly and press dough into ungreased 9x13x2-inch pan.

For topping, combine cream cheese, eggs, powdered sugar, and vanilla. Mix until smooth. Spread over top of crust. Bake for 25 to 30 minutes.

June Staab
Longmont, Colorado

Danish Apple Bar

Dough:
- 2 1/2 cups flour
- 1 teaspoon salt
- 1 cup vegetable shortening
- 1 egg yolk (egg white used later in recipe)
- water

Filling:
- 1 cup corn flakes, crushed
- 8 cups peeled, sliced apples
- 1 cup sugar
- 1 teaspoon ground cinnamon
- 1 egg white, beaten until frothy

Frosting:
- 1 cup confectioners sugar
- 3 to 4 tablespoons milk

Preheat oven to 375 degrees. Combine flour and salt, and cut in vegetable shortening. In a 1-cup measuring cup, beat egg yolk and add enough water to fill measuring cup to 2/3 cup. Stir into flour mixture and mix. Roll half of dough on floured surface to fit bottom and part way up sides of 10x15x1 1/2-inch greased pan.

Sprinkle crushed corn flakes over dough. Top with sliced apples. In a separate container, mix cinnamon and sugar together. Sprinkle over apples. Roll out remaining dough to fit pan. Place over apples and seal edges. Wet edges of dough with water and press together as you would to seal a pie crust. Cut slits in top of crust. Brush egg white on top of crust with pastry brush. Bake about 50 minutes until done.

For frosting, combine confectioners sugar with milk. Drizzle over warm bar. Cut into 2-inch squares.

Doris Graf
Fort Collins, Colorado

Yield: 35 squares

Judy's Lemon Bars

Crust:
- 1 cup plus 2 tablespoons flour
- 1/4 cup powdered sugar
- 1/2 cup (1 stick) butter or margarine, softened

Lemon Filling:
- 2 eggs
- 3 tablespoons lemon juice
- 2 teaspoons grated lemon rind
- 1 cup sugar
- 3 tablespoons flour
- 1 1/2 teaspoons baking powder

Preheat oven to 350 degrees. Mix flour, powdered sugar, and butter together with a pastry blender. Pat evenly into an 8-inch pie pan. Bake for 15 minutes.

Mix eggs, lemon juice, lemon rind, sugar, flour, and baking powder. Spread over top of crust. Return to oven for 25 minutes.

Cool and sprinkle with additional powdered sugar.

Judy Hying
Denver, Colorado

Lemon Bars

Crust:
- 2 cups flour
- 1/2 cup powdered sugar
- 1 cup (2 sticks) butter or margarine, softened

Filling:
- 4 eggs
- 1/2 cup flour
- 2 cups sugar
- 4 tablespoons lemon juice
- 1 teaspoon baking powder
- 1/2 teaspoon salt

Preheat oven to 350 degrees.

For crust, combine all crust ingredients and press into 9x13x2-inch greased cake pan. Bake for 15 minutes.

For lemon filling, combine all filling ingredients and mix well. Pour over baked crust. Bake for 25 minutes. Cool and cut into squares.

Notes:
You get the best results with this recipe when you use an electric mixer.

If I went to a potluck and did not bring these lemon bars, I would hear about it.

Louise Bergman
Silverton, Colorado

Blondies

- 1/2 cup (1 stick) butter or margarine
- 2 cups firmly packed brown sugar
- 2 eggs
- 2 teaspoons vanilla
- 2 cups flour
- 2 teaspoons baking powder
- 1 teaspoon salt
- 1/4 cup chopped walnuts or pecans (optional)

Preheat oven to 375 degrees. Melt butter in a medium-sized saucepan over medium heat. Remove from heat and stir in sugar; add egg and vanilla and beat until well combined. Stir in remaining ingredients. Spread batter in a greased 9x13x2-inch pan. Bake for 20 to 25 minutes. Cool in pan on rack. Cut into 2-inch squares. Store airtight.

Variations:
Use only 1 1/2 teaspoons baking powder at high altitudes.

Cardwell Spiller
Colorado Springs, Colorado

Raspberry Bars

Crust:
- 4 eggs
- 1 cup sugar
- 1 cup vegetable oil or vegetable shortening
- 2 cups flour
- 1 teaspoon baking powder
- 1/2 teaspoon salt
- 1/2 teaspoon vanilla

Filling:
- 2 to 3 cups raspberries
- 1 cup sugar

Frosting:
- 1 cup powdered sugar
- 1/2 teaspoon vanilla
- 2 tablespoons butter or margarine, softened
- 1 tablespoon milk

Preheat oven to 375 degrees. For crust, combine eggs, sugar, and vegetable oil. Add flour, baking powder, salt, and vanilla. Spread a little more than half this mixture over the bottom of a 9x13x2-inch pan.

For filling, combine raspberries and sugar; mash together. Spread filling over bottom crust, then dribble remaining dough over filling. Bake for 30 to 40 minutes. Cool competely.

For frosting, blend all ingredients until smooth. Spread over cooled bars.

M. Susan Danielson
Golden, Colorado

Special Notes:

Pies, Puddings, & Other Desserts

Special Notes:

Vermont Apple Pie

- 6 to 8 large tart apples
- 1 9-inch unbaked pie crust
- 1/2 cup sugar
- 1/2 teaspoon ground cinnamon
- 3/4 cup gingersnap crumbs
- 1 tablespoon flour
- few grains salt
- 1/2 cup chopped walnuts
- 1/4 cup melted butter or margarine
- 1/3 cup maple syrup

Preheat oven to 350 degrees. Core and pare apples; slice thin. Spread about half the apple slices in pastry shell. Combine sugar, cinnamon, gingersnap crumbs, flour, salt, walnuts, and melted butter. Mix well. Spread half of this mixture over apples in pastry shell. Add remaining apple slices. Spread remaining crumb mixture evenly over top. Bake for about 50 minutes. Heat maple syrup to boiling point. Pour evenly over pie. Bake 15 minutes longer.

Yvonne Prendergast
Denver, Colorado

Yield: 8 to 10 servings

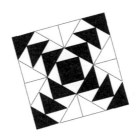

Glazed Peach Pie

   4 cups sliced fresh peaches, divided
 1/2 cup water
   1 cup sugar
   3 tablespoons cornstarch
   1 tablespoon butter or margarine
   1 9-inch baked pie shell

Crush enough peaches to make 1 cup of crushed peaches with juice, leaving the rest of the peaches sliced. In a saucepan combine crushed peaches with water, sugar, and cornstarch. Bring to a boil. Cook over low heat, stirring constantly until clear—2 or 3 minutes. Add butter; stir until melted. Cool.

Line pie shell with fresh peach slices and pour glaze over peaches. Chill. Serve with a dollop of whipped cream.

Bev Zabloudil
Buena Vista, Colorado

Fresh Peach Upside Down Pie

Crust:
- pastry for 2-crust 9-inch pie
- 2 tablespoons butter or margarine, softened
- 2/3 cup (4 ounces) toasted sliced almonds or pecans
- 1/3 cup packed brown sugar

Filling:
- 5 cups sliced fresh peaches
- 3/4 cup granulated sugar
- 1/4 cup packed brown sugar
- 2 tablespoons tapioca
- 1/2 teaspoon ground nutmeg
- 1/4 teaspoon ground cinnamon

Preheat oven to 450 degrees. Line 9-inch pie pan with 12-inch square of foil, allowing excess to hang over the edge. Spread the foil with butter; press in nuts and brown sugar. Fit bottom crust into pan over nuts and sugar. Mix the ingredients for the filling. Pour into crust. Cover with top crust. Seal, flute, and prick crust with a fork. Brush crust lightly with milk. Bake at 450 degrees for 10 minutes, then turn temperature down to 375 degrees and continue baking for 35 to 40 minutes. Let pie cool. Turn upside down on serving plate. Remove foil.

Jeanene Nehren
Aurora, Colorado

Strawberry Glacé Pie

- 1 9-inch pie shell, baked
- 6 cups fresh strawberries
- 1 cup sugar
- 3 tablespoons cornstarch
- ½ cup water
- 1 3-ounce package cream cheese, softened
- whipping cream or yogurt (to garnish)

Mash enough strawberries to measure 1 cup. You will have whole berries left over. Reserve the whole berries for later. Stir together the sugar and cornstarch. Gradually add the water and mashed berries. Put into a pan and cook mixture over medium heat, stirring constantly, until mixture thickens and boils. Cook and stir 1 minute more. Cool.

Beat cream cheese until smooth. Spread on the bottom of the baked pie crust. Fill the bottom of the pie shell with the remaining whole berries. Pour berry mixture over all. Chill 3 hours.

Serve with whipped cream or drizzle with yogurt.

Jan DeBellis
Woodland Park, Colorado

Strawberry Cream Pie

Crust:
- 1¼ cups vanilla wafer crumbs
- ¼ cup margarine, melted

Filling:
- 1 3-ounce package cream cheese, softened
- ¼ teaspoon almond extract
- 1 8-ounce container frozen non-dairy whipped topping, thawed
- ¾ cup sugar
- 2 cups fresh halved strawberries

Mix crust ingredients well and pat into the bottom of a 10-inch pie plate. Mix together the cream cheese, almond extract, non-dairy whipped topping, and sugar until well blended. Fold in halved strawberries. Pour over crust and refrigerate for 4 to 6 hours.

Variations:
Can substitute peaches for strawberries.

Virginia Lewis
Denver, Colorado

Strawberry Rhubarb Pie

1¼ cups sugar
⅓ cup flour
⅛ teaspoon salt
2½ cups strawberry halves
2½ cups rhubarb, cut into 1-inch pieces
2 unbaked 9-inch pie shells
butter or margarine

Preheat oven to 425 degrees. In a bowl, combine sugar, flour, and salt. Mix well. Combine strawberries and rhubarb. Pour half of the strawberry-rhubarb mixture into a pie shell. Sprinkle half sugar-flour mixture over the strawberry-rhubarb mixture. Repeat layers. Dot with butter. Top with the second pie shell. Cut slits in top crust. Brush with cold water and then sprinkle with sugar. Bake for 50 to 60 minutes.

Chris Mooney
Longmont, Colorado

Yield: one 9-inch pie

French Cherry Pie

Crust:
- 3 egg whites, beaten stiff
- 1 cup sugar
- 18 soda crackers, crushed
- 1 teaspoon vanilla
- 1 teaspoon vinegar
- 1/2 cup chopped pecans
- 1 teaspoon baking powder

Filling:
- 1 cup cream, whipped
- 6 ounces cream cheese, softened
- 1/2 cup powdered sugar
- 1 1/2 teaspoons vanilla
- 1 21-ounce can cherry or berry pie filling

Preheat oven to 325 degrees.

For crust, fold sugar into beaten egg whites; add remaining ingredients and mix together. Spread into a 9x13x2-inch pan and bake for 20 minutes.

For filling, mix together whipped cream and cream cheese. Add powdered sugar and vanilla. Pour into pie shell. Cover with pie filling and chill for 5 hours or longer.

Debbie Dilley
Gilcrest, Colorado

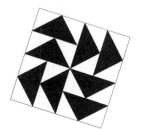

Mom's Raisin Pie

- 2 cups raisins
- 2 tablespoons sugar
- 1 teaspoon cornstarch
- 2 cups thin cream
- 2 eggs, well beaten
- 1 9-inch pie shell, unbaked

Preheat oven to 350 degrees. Soak raisins in warm water for about 15 minutes. Drain and grind. Mix sugar and cornstarch together; add ground raisins, cream, and beaten eggs and mix well. Pour into unbaked pie shell. Bake for 30 to 40 minutes or until knife comes out clean when inserted in center of pie.

Notes:
This recipe is one that my mother concocted during World War II when sugar was rationed. She used heavy cream but I just use half and half.

Rose McCullough
Pueblo, Colorado

Millionaire Pie

- 1 12-ounce can sweetened condensed milk
- 1/4 cup lemon juice
- 1 7-ounce package angel flake coconut
- 1 20-ounce can crushed pineapple, well drained
- 1 cup chipped pecans
- 1 13- to 16-ounce container frozen non-dairy whipped topping, thawed
- 2 graham cracker pie crusts

Mix condensed milk and lemon juice with electric mixer. Add coconut, pineapple, and pecans. Fold in non-dairy whipped topping. Pour into pie crusts. Chill.

Notes:
A hit with everyone and very easy to make.

Bev Zabloudil
Buena Vista, Colorado

Yield: two 9-inch pies

Fudge Sundae Pie

- 1 cup sweetened condensed milk
- 6 ounces semi-sweet chocolate chips
- 1 cup miniature marshmallows
- vanilla wafer cookies for crust
- 1 quart vanilla ice cream, softened
- 1 6-ounce jar maraschino cherries
- pecans

Combine milk, chocolate chips, and marshmallows in a heavy saucepan. Stir over medium heat until chocolate and marshmallows melt completely and mixture thickens. Cool to room temperature.

Line the bottom and sides of a 9-inch pie pan with vanilla wafers.

Spoon half of ice cream over wafers. Cover with half of chocolate mixture. Repeat with rest of ice cream and chocolate mixture. Garnish with maraschino cherries and pecans.

Freeze for 3 to 5 hours.

Variations:
Can substitute spumoni for ice cream.

Laroletta Petty
Evergreen, Colorado

When threading size 12 betweens, cut the quilting thread at a slight angle as it comes off the spool and thread the needles with that end. When done in this manner, it is unusual for the thread to fray or balk at going through the eye of the needle.

Classic Chocolate Cream Pie

1 9-inch pastry shell, baked, or use a crumb crust

Filling:
- $2^1/_2$ ounces unsweetened baking chocolate
- 3 cups milk, divided
- $1^1/_3$ cups sugar
- 3 tablespoons flour
- 3 tablespoons cornstarch
- $^1/_2$ teaspoon salt
- 3 egg yolks
- 2 tablespoons butter or margarine, softened
- $1^1/_2$ teaspoons vanilla

Meringue:
- 3 egg whites, at room temperature
- $^1/_4$ teaspoon cream of tartar
- 6 tablespoons sugar

Preheat oven to 350 degrees. If you use a pastry shell, bake shell and set aside to cool. For pie filling, melt chocolate with 2 cups of milk in medium saucepan over medium heat, stirring constantly. Cook and stir just until mixture boils; remove from heat. Combine sugar, flour, cornstarch, and salt in small mixing bowl. Blend egg yolks with remaining cup of milk. Add to dry ingredients and blend into chocolate mixture in saucepan. Cook over medium heat, stirring constantly until mixture boils. Continue boiling and stirring for 1 minute. Remove from heat; blend in butter and vanilla. Pour into cooled shell.

For meringue, beat egg whites and cream of tartar in small bowl until foamy. Gradually add sugar; beat until stiff peaks form. Spread meringue onto hot pie filling, carefully spreading meringue to the edge of the crust. Bake 8 to 10 minutes or until browned. Cool to room temperature. Chill several hours or overnight.

Kea Blair
Arvada, Colorado

Try Vinegar Pie

- 2 egg yolks
- 1 1/2 cups water
- 1/2 cup cider vinegar
- 1 tablespoon butter or margarine, melted
- 1 1/4 cups sugar
- 1/3 cup flour
- 1/2 teaspoon vanilla
- 1/2 teaspoon lemon extract
- 1 single-crust pie shell, baked

Combine egg yolks, water, vinegar, and melted butter in a saucepan. In a separate bowl, mix sugar and flour together and add to egg mixture, stirring until smooth. Cook over low heat, stirring constantly, until mixture comes to a boil and thickens. Cool slightly. Stir in vanilla and lemon extract. Cool, but before the filling sets, pour into a cooled, baked pie shell. Refrigerate until firm. Cut and serve.

Notes:
This recipe was my grandmother's who, with grandpa and family, homesteaded in 1910. Vinegar pie was a welcome substitute for lemon pie for Colorado homesteaders at the turn of the century. They lived in remote areas away from a source of lemons and before the Watkins salesman toured the countryside door-to-door with his extracts and remedies.

Auriel Sandstead
Sterling, Colorado

Beetle Nut Pie

- 3 eggs
- 1 cup sugar
- 1/4 cup butter or margarine, softened
- 1 cup milk
- 3 tablespoons flour
- 1 teaspoon vanilla
- 1/4 cup maple-flavored syrup
- 1/4 cup uncooked oatmeal
- 1/4 cup chopped pecans
- 1/2 cup grated coconut
- 1 unbaked 9-inch pie shell

Preheat oven to 350 degrees. Combine eggs, sugar, butter, milk, flour, vanilla, and syrup; beat well. Add the oatmeal, pecans, and coconut and pour into pie shell. Bake for 45 to 55 minutes. Will be dark-gold honey color when done.

Nancy Orth
Kiowa, Colorado

Pumpkin Cheesecake Pie

Pastry:
- 3/4 cup unbleached white flour
- 1 cup rolled oats
- 1/4 cup vegetable oil
- 1/4 teaspoon almond extract
- 1/4 to 1/3 cup unsweetened fruit juice

Filling:
- 1 1/2 cups cottage cheese
- 1 1/2 cups pumpkin, cooked, drained, and mashed
- 3 eggs
- 1 teaspoon ground nutmeg
- 1 teaspoon ground cinnamon
- 3 tablespoons unbleached white flour

Topping:
- 2 cups heavy cream
- 1 teaspoon vanilla extract

Preheat oven to 350 degrees. For pastry, combine flour, rolled oats, vegetable oil, and almond extract until well blended. Gradually add fruit juice, adding just enough to form a soft dough. Press dough evenly in lightly oiled 9-inch pie pan.

For filling, combine all ingredients in a blender and blend well. Pour into pastry-lined pie pan. Bake for 50 minutes or until custard has set. Cool and refrigerate.

For topping, shortly before serving, whip heavy cream and vanilla extract together in a small bowl until light and fluffy. Do not over beat. Spoon over pie and serve.

Jeanne Arnoldy
Littleton, Colorado

Yield: 8 servings

Buttermilk Pie

- 3 eggs
- 1 cup buttermilk
- 1 teaspoon vanilla
- 1 cup sugar
- 3 rounded tablespoons flour
- 1/4 cup butter or margarine, melted
- 1 9-inch unbaked pie shell
- 1/4 teaspoon ground nutmeg to sprinkle on top

Preheat oven to 375 degrees. Beat together eggs, buttermilk, vanilla, sugar, flour, and butter. (This can be done in a blender.) Pour into unbaked pie crust and sprinkle top with nutmeg. Bake for 40 to 50 minutes or until inserted knife comes out clean. Serve chilled.

Jayne Pritko
Colorado Springs, Colorado

Yield: 6 to 8 servings

Cornmeal Pie

- 1 cup packed brown sugar
- 1 cup granulated sugar
- 2 tablespoons flour
- 1 tablespoon cornmeal
- 2 eggs, beaten
- 1/2 cup milk
- 1 teaspoon vanilla
- 4 tablespoons butter or margarine, melted
- 1 single-crust pie shell
- 1/4 cup slivered almonds
- 1/4 cup coconut

Preheat oven to 350 degrees. Mix the brown sugar, granulated sugar, flour, and cornmeal together. In a separate bowl, mix the eggs, milk, and vanilla. Combine the two mixtures. Add melted butter. Pour into single-crust pie shell. Sprinkle almonds and coconut on the top. Bake for 35 minutes.

Lois Andis
Denver, Colorado

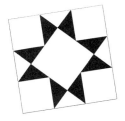

Cherry Pudding

- 1 12-ounce can Dole's Mountain Cherry frozen fruit juice concentrate
- 3 cups water
- 1/2 cup tapioca
- 1 to 2 16-ounce packages frozen dark sweet cherries, thawed

Cook frozen fruit juice concentrate, water, and tapioca over low heat until tapioca is clear and mixture is thickened, stirring occasionally. Fold in cherries and refrigerate.

Variations:
To dress it up for guests, make layers in parfait glasses using the cherry pudding, fresh or canned fruit, cookie crumbs, and whipped topping.

Try other fruit juice concentrates combined with other fresh or frozen fruits.

Notes:
This is good for your kids. Store individual servings in covered containers for snacks.

Use your slow cooker for this recipe and let it cook unwatched while you quilt.

Julie Callahan
Buena Vista, Colorado

Zwieback Pudding

Crust:
- 1 6-ounce package zwieback
- 1/2 cup (1 stick) butter or margarine
- 1/2 cup sugar
- 1 teaspoon ground cinnamon

Custard:
- 3 eggs yolks (whites will be used in meringue)
- 3 tablespoons sugar
- 3 cups milk
- 3 tablespoons cornstarch
- 1 teaspoon almond extract or flavoring

Meringue:
- 3 egg whites
- 1/2 teaspoon vanilla
- 1/4 teaspoon cream of tartar
- 1/3 cup sugar

For crust, grind the zwieback in a food processor. Melt butter; add sugar and cinnamon. Combine with zwieback crumbs and pat crumb mixture into bottom of 2- to 3-quart casserole dish.

To make a soft custard, in a 2-quart saucepan blend yolks with sugar (using a wire whisk); slowly stir in milk and cornstarch. Over medium-low heat, cook the mixture, stirring constantly, until it just coats back of metal spoon, about 15 minutes (do not boil). Remove from heat and stir in almond extract. Chill. Pour custard mix into crumb crust.

For meringue, have egg whites at room temperature. In a small bowl with mixer at high speed, beat egg whites, vanilla, and cream of tartar until soft peaks form. At high speed, sprinkle in sugar, 2 tablespoons at a time, beating after each addition until sugar is dissolved.

(continued)

Zwieback Pudding
(continued)

Rub a bit of meringue between fingers; if it doesn't feel grainy, sugar is dissolved. Whites should stand in stiff, glossy peaks. With back of spoon, spread meringue over custard filling. Seal to edge of casserole. Bake in a preheated 400-degree oven for 10 minutes or until golden. Cool away from drafts.

Notes:
In the late 1920s our next-door Swedish neighbors gave this recipe to my mother. It has been my favorite dessert ever since.

Zweiback is a kind of biscuit that is sliced and toasted after baking. Should be able to find it in your grocery store around the baby food. It is a baby cookie/cracker.

Elizabeth Govan
Estes Park, Colorado

Hot Fudge Pudding

   1 cup flour
   2 teaspoons baking powder
   ¼ teaspoon salt
   ¾ cup sugar
   ¼ cup plus 2 tablespoons cocoa, divided
   ½ cup milk
   2 tablespoons vegetable oil
   1 cup nuts, chopped
   1 cup packed brown sugar
1¾ cups hot water

Preheat oven to 350 degrees. In a 2-quart casserole dish, blend flour, baking powder, salt, sugar, and 2 tablespoons cocoa. Stir in milk, vegetable oil, and nuts. In a separate bowl blend brown sugar and ¼ cup cocoa. Sprinkle sugar mixture over top of batter. Pour hot water over top; **do not mix**. Bake for 45 minutes.

Notes:
This recipe is great for chocolate lovers.

Barbara Dyer
Fort Collins, Colorado

Lemon Snow Pudding

Lemon Mixture:
- 1 3-ounce package lemon gelatin
- 1/8 teaspoon salt
- 2 tablespoons sugar
- 1 cup boiling water
- 3/4 cup cold water
- 1/4 cup lemon juice
- 1/2 teaspoon grated lemon rind (optional)
- 1 egg white

Custard Sauce:
- 1 egg yolk
- 1/4 cup sugar
- 1/2 teaspoon cornstarch
- 1/8 teaspoon salt
- 1 cup milk
- 1 teaspoon vanilla

Mix gelatin, salt, sugar, and boiling water together. Stir until gelatin and sugar have dissolved. Add cold water, lemon juice, and lemon rind. Chill until thickened. Add 1 egg white; beat until fluffy. Chill until firm.

To make custard, combine egg yolk, sugar, cornstarch, and salt. Beat together. Scald milk and add to mixture. Heat until mixture thickens, stirring constantly. Stir in vanilla and cool. Serve custard over chilled gelatin.

Peggy Sparks
Glenwood, Colorado

Bread Pudding with Whiskey Sauce

Bread Pudding:
- 1 loaf French bread
- 1 quart (4 cups) milk
- 3 eggs
- 2 cups sugar
- 2 tablespoons vanilla
- 1 cup raisins
- 3 tablespoons margarine or butter, melted

Whiskey Sauce:
- 1 cup sugar
- 1/2 cup (1 stick) margarine or butter
- 1 egg
- whiskey, to taste

Preheat oven to 350 degrees. Break up bread and soak bread in milk. Crush with hands until well mixed. Add eggs, sugar, vanilla, and raisins. Stir well. Pour margarine in bottom of 9-inch square pan. Pour bread mixture over margarine. Bake for 60 minutes or until very firm. Let cool. Cube pudding and put in individual dessert dishes. When ready to serve, add Whiskey Sauce and heat under broiler.

To make sauce, cream sugar and butter. Place in a double boiler and heat until very hot and sugar is well dissolved. Beat egg and add to butter mixture. Whip real fast so egg does not curdle. Let cool and add whiskey to taste.

Peggy Sparks
Glenwood Springs, Colorado

Apple Crumble

Filling:
- 5 medium apples, pared and sliced
- 1/3 cup water
- 2 tablespoons lemon juice
- 3/4 teaspoon ground cinnamon

Topping:
- 3 tablespoons flour
- 3/4 cups rolled oats
- 1/3 cup packed brown sugar
- 1/3 cup peanut butter
- 2 tablespoons butter or margarine, softened

Preheat oven to 300 degrees. Sprinkle sliced apples with water, lemon juice, and cinnamon. Place in an 8x8-inch oiled baking dish. In a separate bowl combine flour, rolled oats, brown sugar, peanut butter, and butter. Mix well. Crumble over apples. Bake for 50 minutes until top is brown and apples are tender.

Donna Sandy
Colorado Springs, Colorado

Apple Cheese Crisp

    6 apples, peeled and sliced
    1 tablespoon lemon juice
  1/2 cup light corn syrup
    1 teaspoon ground cinnamon
  1/2 cup sugar
  2/3 cup flour
      pinch salt
  1/4 cup butter or margarine, softened
  1/4 pound (1 cup) grated Cheddar cheese

Preheat oven to 350 degrees. Arrange sliced apples in a greased 9x13x2-inch dish. Individually sprinkle lemon juice, corn syrup, and cinnamon over apples.

In a bowl, combine sugar, flour, and salt. Add butter and blend until mixture resembles corn meal. Lightly blend in grated cheese. Sprinkle mixture over top of apples. Bake for 1 hour.

Notes:
This is an old family recipe that has always been in my mother's file. It is perfect for that quick dessert and the taste is out of this world. The Western Slope of Colorado has always been known for its great apples and this recipe makes good use of those from the old orchards.

Patricia Joy
Colorado Springs, Colorado

Fresh Peach Cobbler

Peach Filling:
- 1½ tablespoons cornstarch
- ¼ to ⅓ cup packed brown sugar
- ½ cup water
- 4 cups sweetened, peeled, and sliced peaches
- 1 tablespoon butter or margarine
- 1 tablespoon lemon juice

Batter Topping:
- ½ cup flour
- ½ cup granulated sugar
- ½ teaspoon baking powder
- ¼ teaspoon salt
- 2 tablespoons butter or margarine, softened
- 1 egg

Preheat oven to 400 degrees. For peach filling, in a saucepan mix cornstarch, brown sugar, and water. Add peaches and cook until mixture is thickened. Add butter and lemon juice. Stir until butter has melted. Pour into an 8-inch round baking dish.

For batter, combine all ingredients and mix well. Drop by spoonfuls over hot peach mixture. It will spread out during baking. Bake for 40 to 50 minutes.

Notes:
Very good served warm with ice cream.

Fern Hayes
Denver, Colorado

Peach Cobbler

- ¼ cup butter or margarine
- 1 cup flour
- 1 cup sugar
- dash salt
- 1 tablespoon baking powder
- ⅔ cup milk
- 1 29-ounce can sliced peaches
- ¼ teaspoon ground nutmeg
- ¼ teaspoon ground cinnamon

Preheat oven to 350 degrees. Melt the butter in a shallow 7x11-inch baking dish. In a separate bowl, sift the flour, sugar, salt, and baking powder together and blend in milk. Pour mixture into baking dish. Place peaches and juice on top. Do not stir. Sprinkle nutmeg and cinnamon over peaches. Bake for about 40 minutes or until golden brown. Serve warm.

Mary Biesecker
Grand Junction, Colorado

Fruit Cobbler

- 1 cup sugar
- 1 cup flour
- 3 teaspoons baking powder
- 1/2 teaspoon salt
- 3/4 cup milk
- 1/2 cup (1 stick) butter or margarine
- 1 29-ounce can sliced peaches

Preheat oven to 350 degrees. Combine sugar, flour, baking powder, and salt. Add milk and mix until smooth. Melt margarine in a deep-dish casserole. Pour batter over melted butter. Then pour peaches with juice over top of batter. Bake uncovered approximately 1 hour or until top is golden brown and bubbly.

Topping this off with vanilla ice cream, canned milk, or half and half makes it extra yummy!

Variations:
Any fruit will do. I sometimes use two cans of pie filling (any flavor). To make sure its juicy, always include the liquid. If you use unsweetened frozen fruits, pour fruit over batter while it is still frozen. You can substitute either whole wheat flour or bread flour for half the regular flour. Gives it a nice texture.

Notes:
This is a family "staple" from my childhood. It makes an excellent last-minute dessert. It is "fool-proof" and easy to make. This recipe doubles very well.

Debi Nichols
Lyons, Colorado

Rhubarb Crunch

Filling:
- 6 cups rhubarb, cut in small pieces
- 1 1/2 cups granulated sugar
- 1/4 cup flour

Topping:
- 1 1/2 cups packed brown sugar
- 1 1/2 cups uncooked oatmeal
- 2 1/4 cups flour
- 3/4 cup margarine
- 3/4 cup vegetable shortening

Preheat oven to 375 degrees. Combine the rhubarb, granulated sugar, and flour and press into a greased 9x13x2-inch pan. In a bowl, mix the remaining ingredients until crumbly, then sprinkle over the top of the rhubarb mixture, covering the rhubarb completely. Bake for 40 minutes.

Lori Anderson
Wellington, Colorado

Cherry Rhubarb Crunch

- 1 cup rolled oats
- 1 cup packed brown sugar
- 1 cup all-purpose flour
- 1/4 teaspoon salt
- 1/2 cup (1 stick) butter or margarine
- 4 cups diced rhubarb
- 1 cup granulated sugar
- 2 tablespoons cornstarch
- 1 cup water
- 1 teaspoon almond extract
- 1 21-ounce can cherry pie filling
- 1/2 cup finely chopped walnuts

Preheat oven to 350 degrees. In a large mixing bowl, combine rolled oats, brown sugar, flour, and salt. Stir well. Cut in butter until crumbly. Pat 2 cups of mixture into a greased 9x13x2-inch baking pan. Cover with rhubarb. In a saucepan, combine granulated sugar and cornstarch. Stir in water. Cook over medium heat until mixture is thickened and clear. Stir in almond extract and cherry pie filling. Spoon over rhubarb. Combine nuts with reserved crumb mixture. Sprinkle over cherries. Bake for 40 to 45 minutes.

Notes:
Great served alone or with ice cream.

Sandi Fruehling
Aurora, Colorado

Yield: 12 to 15 servings

Almond Cheesecake

- 1 1/2 cup uncooked oatmeal
- 1/2 cup chopped almonds
- 1/3 cup packed brown sugar
- 1/3 cup margarine, melted
- 2 8-ounce packages cream cheese, softened
- 1/2 cup granulated sugar
- 1 teaspoon almond extract, divided
- 1 teaspoon vanilla extract
- 3 eggs
- 1 16-ounce container sour cream, divided
- 2 tablespoons granulated sugar

Preheat oven to 350 degrees. Grease bottom and sides of springform pan. Combine oatmeal, almonds, brown sugar, and margarine. Mix well and press onto bottom and sides of pan. Bake 18 minutes. Cool. Beat cream cheese, granulated sugar, 1/2 teaspoon almond extract, and vanilla extract at medium speed of electric mixer until fluffy. Add eggs, one at a time, beating well after each. Stir in 1 cup sour cream. Pour into crust. Bake 50 minutes. Combine remaining 1 cup sour cream, 1/2 teaspoon almond extract, and 2 tablespoons granulated sugar and spread over cheesecake. Continue baking 10 minutes. Cool. Loosen rim of pan and remove. Chill.

Naomi Bennett
Aurora, Colorado

Great Cheesecake

  2 pounds cream cheese, softened
1 1/2 cups sugar
  4 eggs
  1 teaspoon vanilla or almond extract

Preheat oven to 250 degrees. Beat cream cheese and sugar until well mixed. Add eggs, one at a time, mixing well after each addition. Add vanilla and mix well. Pour into a springform pan. Place springform pan into another pan with 2 inches of water. Bake for 2 hours. Refrigerate overnight. Add your favorite topping just before serving.

Donna Preston
Denver, Colorado

Cherry Cheesecake

    4 large eggs
1 1/2 cups sugar
    3 tablespoons flour
    3 tablespoons cornstarch
    4 8-ounce packages cream cheese, softened
    2 teaspoons vanilla
  1/2 cup (1 stick) margarine or butter, softened
    1 pint dairy sour cream
    1 21-ounce can cherry or blueberry pie filling

Preheat oven to 350 degrees. Beat eggs in large mixer bowl. Blend in sugar, flour, and cornstarch. Add remaining ingredients (except pie filling) and beat at medium speed until smooth. Pour into 9-inch springform pan and bake for 1 hour and 15 minutes. Turn off heat, open door, and leave cake in oven 1 hour. When cake is cool, remove from pan and refrigerate. Serve with pie filling spread on top.

***Naomi Bennett**
Aurora, Colorado*

Yield: 12 servings

Cheesecake

Cheesecake Filling:
- 1 8-ounce package cream cheese, softened
- 3/4 cup sugar
- 2 eggs
- 1 teaspoon vanilla

Crust:
- 1 prepared graham cracker crust

Topping:
- 1 8-ounce container sour cream
- 1 teaspoon vanilla
- 2 tablespoons sugar

Preheat oven to 350 degrees. For filling, beat cream cheese and sugar until creamy. Add eggs, one at a time, and beat well. Add vanilla. Pour into graham cracker crust. Bake for 25 minutes. Remove from oven.

In a separate bowl, combine sour cream, vanilla, and sugar for topping and spread over top of cheesecake filling. Bake for 5 minutes more at 450 degrees.

Janette Nash
Grand Junction, Colorado

Light Cheesecake

- 1 graham cracker crust for 8- to 9-inch pie
- 2 8-ounce packages light cream cheese, softened
- ½ cup sour cream
- 1 tablespoon lemon juice
- ½ cup sugar
- 1 8-ounce container of frozen light non-dairy whipped topping, thawed
- sliced strawberries (optional)

Mix together cream cheese, sour cream, lemon juice, and sugar. Fold in non-dairy whipped topping. Spread over graham cracker crust. Refrigerate until set. Serve plain or with sliced strawberries.

Judy Kiser
Grand Junction, Colorado

Cheese Cupcakes

- 2 eggs
- 1 cup sugar
- 2 teaspoons vanilla
- 2 8-ounce packages cream cheese, softened
- 1 12-ounce box vanilla wafers
- 1 21-ounce can pie filling or 1 20-ounce can crushed pineapple, drained

Preheat oven to 350 degrees. Beat eggs; add sugar and vanilla. Mix well. Add cream cheese and mix together until smooth. Line cupcake tins with paper liners. Place one or two vanilla wafers on the bottom of each liner. Fill with mixture. Heap it on because it settles as it cools. Bake for 35 minutes.

After the cupcakes have cooled, place favorite pie filling in each center.

Variations:
For mini-muffin size, put part of a vanilla wafer on the bottom of paper lining. Do not use candy cups because they are not bake-proof. Fill and bake for 15 to 20 minutes.

Notes:
These freeze well. Add fruit when ready to serve.

Joyce Smiley
Boulder, Colorado

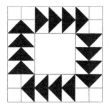

Pineapple Cheesecake Squares

Crust:
- 2 cups flour
- 2/3 cup margarine or butter, softened
- 1/2 cup finely chopped and toasted almonds
- 1/2 cup powdered sugar

Filling:
- 2 8-ounce packages cream cheese, softened
- 1/2 cup sugar
- 2 eggs
- 2/3 cup unsweetened pineapple juice

Topping:
- 1/4 cup flour
- 1/4 cup sugar
- 1 20-ounce can crushed pineapple, well drained (reserve 1 cup of juice)
- 1/2 cup whipping cream

Preheat oven to 350 degrees. To make crust, toss all ingredients in a medium bowl with fork until crumbly. Press firmly and evenly into an ungreased 9x13x2-inch pan. Bake until set, 15 to 20 minutes.

To make filling, beat cream cheese in medium bowl until smooth and fluffy; beat in sugar and eggs. Stir in pineapple juice. Pour cream cheese mixture over hot crust. Bake just until center is set, about 20 minutes. Cool completely.

To make topping, mix flour and sugar in a 2-quart saucepan. Stir in reserved pineapple juice. Heat to boiling over medium heat, stirring constantly. Boil and stir 1 minute. Remove from heat; fold in pineapple. Cool completely. Beat whipping cream in chilled bowl until stiff. Fold into pineapple mixture. Spread carefully over dessert. Cover loosely and refrigerate for 4 hours. Cut into 3-inch squares.

Gerry Phenix
Littleton, Colorado

Yield: 12 squares

Kay's Trifle

- 1 6-ounce package raspberry gelatin
- 1 3 3/4-ounce package* banana instant pudding
- 1 3 3/4-ounce package* chocolate instant pudding
- 1 12-ounce container* frozen non-dairy whipped topping
- 1 6-ounce package dried apricots
- 1 12-ounce box vanilla wafers
- 1 18-ounce large jar raspberry preserves
- 1 11-ounce can mandarin oranges, drained
- 1 6-ounce package chocolate chips
- 1 to 2 bananas, sliced
-    fresh strawberries, sliced and/or raspberries
- 1 2-ounce package slivered almonds
-    Southern Comfort to taste

The night before you assemble the trifle, make raspberry gelatin, banana pudding, and chocolate pudding; thaw non-dairy whipped topping, and stew dried apricots.

Next day (the day you will be serving the trifle), spread vanilla wafers on bottom of trifle bowl or deep glass container. Sprinkle the wafers with Southern Comfort until lightly moistened. Spread half jar of raspberry preserves on wafers and stand more wafers around side of bowl. On top of wafers, layer banana pudding, chocolate pudding, non-dairy whipped topping, gelatin, and some of the fresh fruit (if you like). Add another layer of non-dairy whipped topping, more vanilla wafers, more Southern Comfort, then the other half of the jar of raspberry preserves. Add more layers of banana pudding, chocolate pudding, gelatin, and non-dairy whipped topping. Top trifle artistically with stewed dried apricots, banana slices, strawberry slices, mandarin oranges, chocolate chips, and slivered almonds. Chill until time to serve, or serve immediately.

Notes:
*or 2 packages, depending on the size of your trifle bowl. Once you dip a spoon into this work of art it looks like slop, but it's a tasty slop!

Kay Jesse
Conifer, Colorado

Yield: 6 to 8 servings

Twinkie Torte

- 1 6-ounce package chocolate chips
- ¼ cup sugar
- 2 tablespoons water
- 5 eggs, separated
- 12 Twinkies, cut up
- 2 cups whipping cream, whipped

In a saucepan, melt chocolate chips with sugar and water. Don't stir the chips while they are on the heat. Chips will be shiny when melted but will retain their shape. Remove from heat and add 5 egg yolks, one at a time, stirring constantly as they are added to keep eggs from cooking. Cool.

Beat egg whites until stiff. Add the egg whites to the chocolate mixture. Put Twinkies in springform pan. Pour chocolate mixture over Twinkies. Refrigerate. Spread whipped cream over top just before serving.

Margie McCandless
Arvada, Colorado

Butterfinger Torte

- 3 3.8-ounce Butterfinger candy bars
- 4 egg yolks
- 2 cups powdered sugar
- 1/2 cup (1 stick) margarine
- 2 16-ounce container frozen non-dairy whipped topping, thawed
- 1 18-ounce angel food cake

Crush candy bars. Using an electric mixer, mix yolks, sugar, and margarine well. Fold in non-dairy whipped topping. Crumble half the angel food cake into serving bowl. Spoon half the sugar mixture over cake. Spoon half the crumbled candy mixture over the top. Repeat these three layers one more time. Chill well.

Gwen Moore
Littleton, Colorado

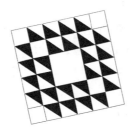

Pumpkin Torte

Crust:
- 24 graham crackers, crushed
- 1/2 cup (1 stick) margarine or butter, softened
- 1/2 cup sugar

First Layer:
- 2 eggs
- 3/4 cup sugar
- 2 8-ounce packages cream cheese, softened

Second Layer:
- 1 16-ounce can (2 cups) pumpkin
- 3 egg yolks
- 3/4 cup sugar, divided
- 1/2 cup milk
- 1/2 teaspoon salt
- 1/2 teaspoon ground cinnamon
- 1 envelope unflavored gelatin
- 1/4 cup cold water
- 3 egg whites

Topping:
- whipped cream topping of your choice

Preheat oven to 350 degrees. Mix graham crackers, margarine, and 1/2 cup sugar together. Pat lightly into a 9x13x2-inch pan. Beat eggs, 3/4 cup sugar, and softened cream cheese. Spread over top of crust. Bake for 20 minutes. Cool.

In a saucepan, combine pumpkin, egg yolks, 1/2 cup sugar, milk, salt, and cinnamon. Cook until thick—about 3 or 4 minutes. Remove from heat; add gelatin and cold water. Cool well.

Beat egg whites until stiff; add 1/4 cup sugar and continue beating until sugar is dissolved. Fold into pumpkin mixture. Pour into baked crust. Let set. Top with favorite whipped cream topping just before serving.

Jerry Sommer
Denver, Colorado

Strawberry Jello Torte

    2 packages jelly cake roll (about 24 ounces)
    1 20-ounce package frozen strawberries, thawed
    1 6-ounce package strawberry gelatin
1½ cups whipping cream

Slice cake roll ¼-inch thick and line bottom and sides of springform pan. Drain strawberries and save juice. Add enough water to reserved strawberry juice to make a total of 3½ cups liquid. Heat this liquid to boiling and dissolve gelatin. Refrigerate gelatin until it is slightly thick. Whip gelatin until frothy.

Whip cream and fold into gelatin along with strawberries. Chill overnight. Remove outer ring of pan before serving.

Notes:
This dessert not only tastes great, it looks great!

Margie McCandless
Arvada, Colorado

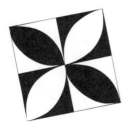

Escalloped Apples

    4 cups apples, peeled, cored, and cut into large pieces
1/2 cup sugar
1/2 teaspoon ground cinnamon
    2 tablespoons flour
1 to 2 tablespoons butter or margarine

Preheat oven to 350 degrees. Combine apples with sugar, cinnamon, and flour. Place in greased casserole. Dot with butter, cover, and bake for 50 to 60 minutes.

Notes:
Any cooking apple will do, but hard ones are best.

Beverly Giffin
Pueblo West, Colorado

Freezer Peaches

    1   cup honey
    3   cups hot water
6 to 8   fresh peaches, sliced

Dissolve honey in hot water. Chill. Add to sliced peaches. Pack in freezer containers, leaving head space. Freeze.

When ready for use, thaw and serve warm or cold or use as you would use peaches in any recipe.

Notes:
This easy recipe is a great way to enjoy those delicious Colorado peaches all year long.

Leann Woertman
Denver, Colorado

Pineapple Souffle

- 6 slices white bread, crusts removed, cubed
- 4 eggs, beaten
- 1 20-ounce can crushed pineapple in juice
- 1/2 cup (1 stick) butter or margarine, softened
- 2/3 cup sugar

Preheat oven to 350 degrees. Grease a 2-quart casserole with butter or margarine. Combine all ingredients. Pour into casserole. Mixture will be very soupy. Bake 40 minutes or until top is golden brown. Serve warm.

Notes:
Goes great as a side dish with ham or as a dessert.

Virginia Berger
Wray, Colorado

Mandarin Orange Jello

Filling:
- 1 6-ounce package orange gelatin
- 2½ cups boiling water
- 1 6-ounce can frozen orange juice
- 1 11-ounce can mandarin oranges, drained
- 1 15¼-ounce can crushed pineapple, drained

Topping:
- 1 2.9-ounce package instant lemon pudding
- 2 cups milk
- 1 8-ounce container frozen non-dairy whipped topping, thawed
- 1 cup grated Longhorn cheese

Dissolve gelatin in boiling water. Add frozen orange juice, oranges, and pineapple. Stir until orange juice is melted. Pour into a 9x13x2-inch pan and refrigerate until firm.

To make topping, combine pudding with milk. When mixture thickens, mix in non-dairy whipped topping. Spread topping mixture over mandarin orange gelatin mixture. Top with grated cheese.

Maxine Tamlin
Fort Collins, Colorado

To make an inexpensive portable pressing table, obtain an empty bolt board from your local quilt shop. Pad the bolt board with a piece of cotton batting (I used an old mattress pad) and pellon fleece. Then wrap cotton fabric around the padding. Tape or staple in place.

Pumpkin Supreme

- 1¾ cups graham cracker crumbs
- ¼ cup sugar
- ½ cup (1 stick) butter or margarine, melted
- 1 8-ounce package cream cheese, softened
- 2 eggs, beaten
- ¾ cup sugar
- 2 3¾-ounce packages vanilla instant pudding mix
- 1 cup milk
- 2 cups cooked, mashed pumpkin
- ground cinnamon to taste
- ground nutmeg to taste
- 1 12-ounce container frozen non-dairy whipped topping, thawed, divided
- ½ cup chopped pecans

Preheat oven to 350 degrees.

Combine graham cracker crumbs, sugar, and melted butter. Press into a 9x13x2-inch baking dish. Set aside.

Combine cream cheese, eggs, and sugar. Beat until fluffy. Spread over crust. Bake for 20 minutes. Cool.

Combine pudding mix and milk. Beat 2 minutes at medium speed of electric mixer. Add pumpkin, cinnamon, and nutmeg. Mix well. Stir in half of non-dairy whipped topping. Spread over cooled cream cheese layer. Cover with remaining non-dairy whipped topping. Sprinkle with nuts. Refrigerate.

Theresa Clouse
Littleton, Colorado

Yield: 15 servings

Caramel Corn
(Microwave)

         brown paper bag
         non-stick cooking spray
     6   quarts popped corn
     1   cup packed brown sugar
    1/4 cup light corn syrup
    1/2 cup (1 stick) margarine
         pinch of salt
    1/2 teaspoon baking soda

Spray the inside of a brown paper bag with non-stick cooking spray. Place popped corn in bag.

In a casserole dish, mix brown sugar, corn syrup, margarine, and salt. Cook in microwave on high for 2 minutes. Remove and add baking soda. Stir until foamy.

Pour caramel mixture over corn. Shake; microwave popcorn on high for 1 1/2 minutes. Shake bag again and microwave popcorn on high for another 1 1/2 minutes. Shake popcorn one more time and microwave on high for 1/2 minute.

Pour popcorn onto waxed paper to cool. Enjoy!

Mary Christofferson
Littleton, Colorado

Banana Dessert

Crust:
- 1 cup flour
- 2 tablespoons sugar
- 1/2 cup (1 stick) margarine, softened
- 1/2 cup nuts, chopped

First Layer of Filling:
- 1 cup frozen non-dairy whipped topping, thawed
- 1 8-ounce package cream cheese, softened
- 1 cup powdered sugar

Second Layer of Filling:
- 3 bananas, sliced

Third Layer of Filling:
- 2 3 3/4-ounce packages instant vanilla pudding
- 3 cups milk

Fourth Layer of Filling:
- 2 cups frozen non-dairy whipped topping, thawed
- 1/2 cup chopped nuts

Preheat oven to 350 degrees. Mix flour, sugar, margarine, and 1/2 cup nuts together. Press into a 9x13x2-inch pan and bake for 15 minutes. Let cool.

Mix 1 cup of non-dairy whipped topping, cream cheese, and powdered sugar together and spread over top of crust. Place sliced bananas over top of first layer. Mix milk and pudding and spread over bananas. Spread 2 more cups of non-dairy whipped topping on top of pudding and sprinkle with 1/2 cup chopped nuts. Refrigerate.

Judy Hying
Denver, Colorado

Party Rhubarb Dessert

Crust:
- 3/4 cup butter or margarine, softened
- 1 1/2 cups flour
- 2 tablespoons powdered sugar
- dash of salt

Filling:
- 6 egg yolks
- 2 cups sugar
- 1 cup whipping cream
- 4 tablespoons flour
- 5 cups cut-up rhubarb

Topping:
- 6 egg whites
- 2 tablespoons water
- 12 tablespoons sugar
- 1 teaspoon vanilla

Preheat oven to 325 degrees. Mix butter, flour, powdered sugar, and salt. Press into bottom of 9x12-inch glass cake pan. Mix egg yolks, sugar, and whipping cream. Add in flour and fold in rhubarb. Bake for 1 hour; test for doneness with knife inserted in center.

For topping, beat egg whites with water until stiff. Add sugar 1 tablespoon at a time. Add vanilla. Spread over top of dessert, covering completely. Brown under broiler. Watch carefully as it browns quickly.

Notes:
This is a very pretty dessert and I guarantee everyone will want your recipe.

JoAnn Roemer
Grand Junction, Colorado

Yield: 12 servings

Fruit Pizza

Pizza Crust:
- 1 18 1/2-ounce package yellow cake mix
- 1/4 cup water
- 2 eggs
- 1/4 cup butter or margarine
- 1/4 cup packed brown sugar
- 1/2 cup chopped nuts

Suggested Toppings:
- frozen non-dairy whipped topping, thawed
- strawberries
- green grapes
- bananas
- kiwi
- pineapple

Glaze: (optional)
- 1/2 cup apricot preserves
- 2 tablespoons water

Preheat oven to 350 degrees. Combine all crust ingredients together in a large bowl and mix well. Place on a greased pizza pan and cook for 15 to 20 minutes. Allow to cool. Slice fresh fruit of your choice and arrange on top of a layer of non-dairy whipped topping. If you prefer, you can add a glaze made by combining the apricot preserves with the water. Spoon it over the top of the prepared fruit.

Jan Shuping
Pueblo, Colorado

Flower Pot Dessert

20 ounces chocolate sandwich cookies
1/4 cup margarine or butter
1 8-ounce package cream cheese, softened
1 cup powdered sugar
1 6-ounce package instant pudding mix
3 cups cold milk
1 12-ounce container frozen non-dairy whipped topping, thawed

Crush cookies; set aside. Cream margarine, cream cheese, and powdered sugar, mixing until smooth. Mix pudding and milk, add non-dairy whipped topping, and mix well. Add cream cheese mixture to pudding mixture. Mix well.

Using a new 8-ounce flower pot, place a layer of cookie crumbs in bottom of pot. Now add a layer of filling. Add another layer of cookie crumbs and another layer of filling. Top with another layer of cookie crumbs. Store overnight in refrigerator. Just before serving, stand artificial flowers in pot. Serve with a clean trowel.

Variations:
May place a few gummy worms under top layer of cookie crumbs.

Peggy Sparks
Glenwood Springs, Colorado

Easy Dessert

1 12-ounce can sweetened condensed milk
1 21-ounce can cherry pie filling
1 20-ounce can crushed pineapple, drained
1 12-ounce container frozen non-dairy whipped topping, thawed
1 graham cracker pie crust
  nuts (optional)

Combine sweetened condensed milk, pie filling, pineapple, and non-dairy whipped topping together and mix well. Pour into graham cracker crust. Sprinkle nuts on top. Refrigerate 1 to 2 hours.

Maxine Tamlin
Fort Collins, Colorado

Vanilla Wafer Refrigerator Dessert

3/4 12-ounce box vanilla wafers, rolled fine, divided

Bottom Layer:
- 1 cup powdered sugar
- 1/2 cup (1 stick) butter or margarine, softened
- 3 egg yolks, well beaten
- 1/2 teaspoon vanilla
- 2/3 cup chopped nuts
- 3 egg whites, stiffly beaten

Top Layer:
- 1/2 cup cocoa
- 1 cup powdered sugar
- 2 tablespoons boiling water
- 3 egg yolks, well beaten
- 3 egg whites, stiffly beaten

For bottom layer, cream powdered sugar and butter together, add well beaten egg yolks, and mix thoroughly. Add vanilla and nuts. Fold in stiffly beaten egg whites.

For top layer, combine cocoa and powdered sugar. Add the boiling water; add well beaten yolks and mix well. Fold in stiffly beaten egg whites.

Cover the bottom of a 9-inch square pan with one-third of vanilla wafer crumbs. Pour the bottom layer mixture over crumbs. Cover this with one-third of vanilla wafer crumbs. Spread top layer mixture over these crumbs. Top with remaining one-third of vanilla wafer crumbs. Allow to stand in refrigerator for 24 hours. Cut into squares and serve with whipped cream.

Notes:
Absolutely the best dessert ever.

Janice White
Colorado Springs, Colorado

Frozen Orange Tarts

2 cups crushed vanilla wafers
¼ cup finely chopped walnuts or pecans
6 tablespoons butter or margarine, melted
½ cup sugar
¼ cup frozen orange juice concentrate, thawed
1 egg white
1 cup sour cream

Combine wafer crumbs and nuts. Stir in melted butter. Place 12 paper baking cups in muffin tins. Press crumb mixture into cups covering sides and bottom. In mixing bowl, combine sugar, orange juice concentrate, and egg white. Beat at medium speed until soft peaks form and tips turn over—approximately 7 minutes. Carefully fold in sour cream. Spoon into prepared cups. Cover with foil and freeze until firm. Let stand at room temperature for about 10 minutes before serving.

Marcia Potter
Denver, Colorado

Yield: 12 tarts

New Peanut Butter Crispy Treat

- 1 cup light or dark corn syrup
- 1 cup sugar
- 1 cup creamy or super chunky peanut butter
- 6 cups puffed rice cereal

Grease 9x13x2-inch baking pan. In large saucepan over low heat stir together corn syrup, sugar, and peanut butter. Stirring constantly, bring to a boil. Boil 3 minutes. Remove from heat. Add cereal and toss to coat well. Press into pan. Cool. Cut into 2x2-inch squares.

Cami Termer
Pueblo, Colorado

Yield: 32 squares

Peanut Butter Balls

- 2 pounds powdered sugar
- 2 cups peanut butter
- 1 1/2 cups (3 sticks) melted margarine, melted
- 2 to 3 ounces dipping chocolate or chocolate candy coating, melted

Stir powdered sugar, peanut butter, and margarine together until smooth. Roll into 1-inch balls and place on foil. Dip each peanut butter ball into melted chocolate. Cool on foil at room temperature. Store in an air-tight container in the refrigerator.

Notes:
You may need more dipping chocolate than suggested. Just melt a little at a time in the microwave as needed.

Lois Andis
Denver, Colorado

Yield: 80 to 100 balls

Candy Bar Pizza

- 1   20-ounce package refrigerated sugar cookie dough
- 2   cups miniature marshmallows
- 1   Snickers candy bar
- 1   Milky Way candy bar
- 1   cup M&M's candies
- 1/3 cup chopped walnuts (optional)

Preheat oven to 325 degrees. Cut candy bars in half lengthwise and then cut each half into slices. Grease 14-inch pizza pan or 10x15-inch jelly roll pan. Press sugar cookie dough into bottom of pan and bake 12 to 15 minutes. Sprinkle evenly with marshmallows and return to oven for 3 to 4 minutes until marshmallows are puffed and golden. Remove from oven and sprinkle with candy and nuts. Cool and cut into wedges or rectangles to serve.

Variations:
Substitute any candy and leave out the nuts if your kids hate nuts.

Jeanne Creighton
Denver, Colorado

Cherry Mash Candy

- 2 cups sugar
- 2/3 cup evaporated milk
- 12 regular marshmallows
- 1 6-ounce package cherry chips
- 1 teaspoon vanilla
- 1/2 cup (1 stick) margarine
- 1 12-ounce package chocolate chips
- 3/4 cup creamy peanut butter
- 1 12-ounce can salted peanuts, crushed

Combine sugar, milk, marshmallows, and margarine. Cook over medium heat for 5 minutes after mixture comes to a boil, stirring frequently. Remove from heat; add cherry chips and vanilla. Mix well. Pour into buttered 9x13x2-inch pan. Refrigerate until cool. Cooling overnight may be best because this mixture needs to be pretty hard before adding chocolate. Melt chocolate chips in a double boiler. Add peanut butter and mix well. Add crushed peanuts. Pour over cherry mixture and allow to cool. Cut into 1-inch-square pieces.

Toni Fitzwater
Pine, Colorado

Dairy State Fudge

- 1 8-ounce package cream cheese, softened
- 2 tablespoons butter (no substitutes)
- 2 pounds white almond bark
- 1 cup chopped nuts

In a mixing bowl, beat cream cheese until fluffy; set aside. In top of double boiler, melt butter. Add almond bark; heat and stir until melted and smooth.

Pour over the cream cheese; beat until smooth and glossy, about 7 to 10 minutes. Stir in nuts. Pour into a greased 9x9-inch square pan. Store in the refrigerator.

Gwen Moore
Littleton, Colorado

Yield: 64 pieces, approximately 1-inch square

Home-Made Ice Cream

    4 eggs, beaten
2¼ cups sugar
    4 cups cream
    4 cups half and half
4½ teaspoons vanilla
    ½ teaspoon salt
    1 cup favorite fruit purée (optional)

In a large bowl beat eggs. Gradually add sugar, beating until mixture is very stiff. Mix in cream, half and half, vanilla, and salt. Add your favorite fruit purée if desired. Pour mix into ice cream freezer and freeze, following the manufacturer's instructions.

Toni Fitzwater
Pine, Colorado

Cappuccino Ice Cream

1¼ cups double-strength coffee or espresso
  ¾ cup sugar
  ½ cup dark corn syrup syrup
   2 tablespoons dark rum
  ½ teaspoon ground cinnamon
   2 cups heavy cream

Stir together coffee, sugar, corn syrup, rum, and cinnamon until sugar dissolves. Stir in heavy cream. Put in freezer and freeze until mushy. Remove from freezer and beat thoroughly with mixer. Refreeze.

Charlotte Miller
Monument, Colorado

Yield: 2 quarts (approximately)

Peanut Butter Chocolate Chip Ice Cream

- 6 eggs, separated
- 2 cups sugar
- 1 tablespoon vanilla extract
- 1 pint whipping cream
- 1 pint half and half
- 12 ounces (1½ cups) peanut butter
- 6 ounces mini chocolate chips
  milk

Beat egg whites and yolks separately and then fold together. Add sugar, vanilla, cream, and half and half. Add peanut butter. Pour into ice cream freezer. Put in paddle. Add chocolate chips and milk, as needed. Freeze according to manufacturer's directions.

Charlotte Seaton
Fort Lupton, Colorado

Yield: 1 gallon

Index

Special Notes:

INDEX 409

$10,000 Cookies, 307
8:30 a.m. Bread, 77
All Day Chuck Roast, 199
Alma's Chocolate Cake with Icing, 294
Almond Cheesecake, 376
Amish Dressing, 157
Appetizers 5, 7-14
   Cheddar Chutney Cheese Snacks, 7
   Chicken Nacho Supreme, 9
   Crisp Spiced Walnuts, 12
   Glazed Baked Brie, 8
   Hot Canapes, 7
   Party Swedish Meatballs, 11
   Praline Quaker Oat Squares, 14
   Sesame Chicken Wings, 10
   Tortilla Rollups, 12
   Vegetable Bars, 13
Apple and Banana Salad, 132
Apple Bundt Cake, 279
Apple Cheese Crisp, 370
Apple Crumble, 369
Apple Dapple Cake, 285
Applesauce Cake, 280
Applesauce Salad, 133
Apricot Pine Nut Pilaf, 158
Aunt Margaret's French Stew, 107
Aunt Sukey's Choice Cake, 266
Bailey's Chicken, 179
Baked Corn, 143
Baked Italian Spaghetti, 209
Baked Potato Soup, 98
Banana Dessert, 394
Banana Zucchini Cake, 278
Barbeque Beef Sandwiches, 196
Barbequed Hamburgers, 27, 211
Barbequed Meatballs, 216
Barbequed Spareribs, 200
Barley and Black Bean Salad, 109
Bear's Paw Black Bean Soup, 92
Beef, 11, 16, 100, 102, 104-108, 194-226, 245
   All Day Chuck Roast, 199
   Amish
   Baked Italian Spaghetti, 209
   Barbeque Beef Sandwiches, 196
   Barbequed Hamburgers, 27, 211
   Barbequed Meatballs, 216
   Barbequed Spareribs, 200
   Beef Samovar, 194
   Broccoli-Cheese Stromboli, 217
   Cabbage Bread, 225
   Chili Pizzeria Bake, 214
   Dorothy's Sloppy Joes, 205
   Enchilada Pie, 202
   Fancy Beans, 219
   Flat Brisket of Beef, 198
   French Bread Surprise, 222
   Grilled Island Teriyaki, 201
   Hearty Rice Casserole, 208
   Hero Burger, 226
   Jan's Mexican Manicotti, 220
   Meat and Potato Puff Casserole, 223
   Mexican Casserole, 221
   Mexican Lasagna, 203
   Mexican Manicotti, 207, 220
   Picnic Pizza, 212
   Salsa-Garlic Flank Steak, 197
   Salsburg Steak, 224
   Spaghetti Pie, 215
   Stuffed Peppers, 213
   Swiss Hamburger Onion Pie, 206
   Swiss Steak, 195
   Talerini, 218
   Zucchini Lasagna, 204
Beef Samovar, 194
Beetle Nut Pie, 359
Best-Ever Chocolate Cake, 300-301
Best-Ever Chocolate Cake Frosting, 301
Best-Ever Dinner Rolls, 74
Better-Than-Sex Cake, 291
Beverages, 5, 19-21
   Fireside Coffee, 20
   Fruit Slush, 21
   Hot Buttered Lemonade, 20
   Juice Shake, 19
   Orange Julius, 19
Big D's Famous Chili, 86
Biscochitos, 318
Black Bean Salad, 109, 111
Black Beans and Rice (Feijao), 160
Blender Pancakes, 45
Blondies, 342
Blueberry Coffee Cake, 41
Blueberry Salad, 134
Brazilian-Style Rice, 156, 160
Bread Pudding with Whiskey Sauce, 368
Breads & Rolls, 57, 59-82
   8:30 a.m. Bread, 77
   Best-Ever Dinner Rolls, 74
   Breakfast/Brunch Rolls, 35
   Butter Dips, 60
   Corn Muffins, 61
   Cranberry Apple Bread, 64
   Easy Caramel Rolls, 35
   Eggnog Quick Bread, 71
   Family Reunion Rolls, 75
   Guadelupe Oatmeal Muffins, 63
   Landin's Pretzels, 76
   Mandarin Scones, 59
   Oatmeal Honey Bread, 73
   Orange Glazed Pumpkin Bread, 66
   Peachy Peach Bread, 67
   Poppy Seed Tea Bread, 68
   Pretzels, 18, 76, 79
   Prussian Cinnamon Rolls, 36-37
   Pumpkin Bread, 65-66
   Pumpkin Muffins, 62
   Refrigerator Rolls, 82
   Rosemary Focaccia, 72
   Two-Hour French Bread, 78
   Whole Wheat Banana Bread, 70
   Whole Wheat Bread, 80-81
   Zucchini Bread, 69
Breakfast/Brunch Rolls, 59
Breakfast Casserole, 51
Broccoli Cheese Soup, 97
Broccoli-Cheese Stromboli, 217
Broccoli Cream Soup, 96
Broccoli Squares, 140
Brownies, 259, 328-343
Brownies & Other Bars, 259, 328-343
   Blondies, 342
   Brownies, 259, 328-343
   Butterscotch Brownies, 333
   Butterscotch Chewies, 334
   Chocolate Caramel Squares, 331
   Danish Apple Bar, 339
   Judy's Lemon Bars, 340
   Lemon Bars, 340-341
   Nana's Date Squares, 337

410 INDEX

Oatmeal Marble Squares, 335
Quasi-Lemon Bars, 338
Quilt Camp Brownies, 329
Raspberry Bars, 343
Seven-Layer Bars, 336
Triple Chocolate Bars, 332
Brunch, 33, 35-56
　Rolls, Coffee Cakes, & Muffins, 35
　　Blueberry Coffee Cake, 41
　　Breakfast/Brunch Rolls, 35
　　Cinnamon Coffee Cake, 44
　　Easy Caramel Rolls, 35
　　Prussian Cinnamon Rolls, 36-37
　　Quick Cinnamon Coffee Bread, 40
　　Quick Coffee Cake, 39
　　Raw Apple Coffee Cake, 43
　　Streusel Coffee Cake, 42
　Main Dishes, 45
　　Blender Pancakes, 45
　　Breakfast Casserole, 51
　　Cheesy Spinach (or Broccoli) Quiche, 56
　　Egg and Ham or Sausage Brunch, 50
　　Egg Baskets with Hollandaise Sauce, 49
　　Egg Casserole, 54
　　Greek Spinach Pie, 55
　　Ham and Swiss Breakfast, 53
　　Kitchen Scrambler and Country Fries, 52
　　Overnight Apple French Toast with Spiced Applesauce, 46
　　Overnight Breakfast, 48
　　Pineapple-Cream Cheese Sandwiches, 47
Bug Juice, 27
Busy Day Cookies, 314
Butter Dips, 60
Butterfinger Torte, 385
Buttermilk Chicken Potpie, 166
Buttermilk Pie, 361
Butterscotch Brownies, 333
Butterscotch Chewies, 334
Buttery Grated Carrots, 142
Cabbage Bread, 225
Cabbage Salad, 112

Cakes, 41, 259, 261-300
　Alma's Chocolate Cake with Icing, 294
　Apple Bundt Cake, 279
　Apple Dapple Cake, 285
　Applesauce Cake, 280
　Aunt Sukey's Choice Cake, 266
　Banana Zucchini Cake, 278
　Best-Ever Chocolate Cake, 300-301
　Better-Than-Sex Cake, 291
　Carrot Cake with Cream Cheese Frosting, 275
　Chocolate Cake, 263, 271, 294, 297-302, 331-332
　Chocolate Chip Cake, 289, 296
　Chocolate Cola Cake with Frosting, 293
　Chocolate Eclair Cake, 288
　Chocolate Sheet Cake with Frosting, 295
　Fresh Rhubarb Cake, 282
　Fruit Cocktail Cake and Frosting, 284
　German Biscuit, 262
　Grandma's Chocolate Cake and Icing, 297
　Hurry-Up Chocolate Cake, 299, 302
　Italian Cream Cake, 272
　Janet's Chocolate Chip Cake, 289
　Jello Lightning Cake, 265
　Lemonade Cake, 268
　Mayonnaise Cake, 287
　Moon Cake, 270
　Oatmeal Cake with Broiled Frosting, 267
　Pineapple Carrot Cake, 276
　Pineapple Paradise Cake, 283
　Poppy Seed Sherry Cake, 269
　Pound Cake, 261-263
　Pumpkin Jelly Roll, 264
　Rhubarb Cake, 281-282
　Rum Cake and Sauce, 274
　Rum Cake Jubilee, 273
　Spicy Bean Cake, 277
　Strawberry Cake, 286
　Turtle Cake, 271
　Whipped Cream Devil's Cake, 292
　White Russian Chocolate Pound Cake, 263

　Wonder Cake, 290
Candy Bar Pizza, 402
Cappuccino Ice Cream, 405
Caramel Corn, 393
Carrot Cake with Cream Cheese Frosting, 275
Cauliflower Salad, 119
Cheddar Chutney Cheese Snacks, 7
Cheese Cupcakes, 381
Cheese Pie, 151
Cheesecake, 360, 376-380, 382
Cheesecakes, 376-382
　Almond Cheesecake, 376
　Cheese Cupcakes, 381
　Cheesecake, 360, 376-380, 382
　Cherry Cheesecake, 378
　Great Cheesecake, 377
　Light Cheesecake, 380
　Pineapple Cheesecake Squares, 382
Cheesy Spinach (or Broccoli) Quiche, 56
Cherry Cheesecake, 378
Cherry Mash Candy, 403
Cherry Pudding, 363
Cherry Rhubarb Crunch, 375
Chicken and Black Bean Tamale Pie, 181
Chicken and Sausage Jambalaya, 182
Chicken Casserole, 165, 168, 185
Chicken Chili, 88
Chicken Cordon Bleu, 183
Chicken Divan, 180
Chicken Enchiladas, 167, 184
Chicken Glop, 176
Chicken in Wine Sauce, 178
Chicken Nacho Supreme, 9
Chicken-with-Dressing Casserole, 172
Chili Cheese Dip, 16
Chili Con Queso, 15
Chili Pizzeria Bake, 214
Chilies Rellenos Jose, 251, 256
Chinese Coleslaw, 113
Chocolate Cake, 263, 271, 294, 297-302, 331-332
Chocolate Caramel Squares, 331
Chocolate Chip Cake, 289, 296
Chocolate Chipper Champs, 309

INDEX   411

Chocolate Cola Cake with Frosting, 293
Chocolate Cookie Sheets, 328
Chocolate Covered Cherry Cookies, 304
Chocolate Eclair Cake, 288
Chocolate Marshmallow Cookies, 305
Chocolate Sheet Cake with Frosting, 295
Cinnamon Coffee Cake, 44
Classic Chocolate Cream Pie, 357
Cobblers, Crisps, Crumbles, & Crunches, 369-375
  Apple Cheese Crisp, 370
  Apple Crumble, 369
  Cherry Rhubarb Crunch, 375
  Fresh Peach Cobbler, 371
  Fruit Cobbler, 373
  Peach Cobbler, 371-372
  Rhubarb Crunch, 374-375
Coffee Cakes, 39
  Blueberry Coffee Cake, 41
  Cinnamon Coffee Cake, 44
  Quick Cinnamon Coffee Bread, 40
  Quick Coffee Cake, 39
  Raw Apple Coffee Cake, 43
  Streusel Coffee Cake, 42
Cold Veggie Salad, 126
Cookies, 259, 303-327, 356, 397
  $10,000 Cookies, 307
  Biscochitos, 318
  Busy Day Cookies, 314
  Chocolate Chipper Champs, 309
  Chocolate Cookie Sheets, 328
  Chocolate Covered Cherry Cookies, 304
  Chocolate Marshmallow Cookies, 305
  Cornmeal Cookies, 313
  Cowboy Cookies, 311
  Family's Favorite Cookies, 324
  Fudge Cookies, 310
  German Christmas Cookies, 321
  Grandmother's Oatmeal Cookies, 316
  Jeanne's Favorite Sugar Cookies, 325

  Lemon-Frosted Pecan Sandies, 317
  Lemon-Pecan Sugar Cookies, 323
  Marylou's Moist Cookies, 326
  Monster Cookies, 306
  Mother's Classic Coconut Cookie, 322
  New England Fruit Cookies, 312
  No-Bake Chocolate Cookies, 308
  Oatmeal Whole Wheat Cookies, 315
  Peanut Butter n Chocolate Chip Cookies, 327
  Pumpkin Cookies, 320
  Slice-and-Bake Almond Cookies, 319
Corn Muffins, 61
Cornmeal Cookies, 313
Cornmeal Pie, 362
Country Potpie, 192
Cowboy Cookies, 311
Cranberry Apple Bread, 64
Creamy Baked Chicken, 155, 174
Crisp Spiced Walnuts, 12
Crock Pot Baked Beans, 162
Cuban Style Black Bean Soup, 93
Cucumbers, 32, 115
Curry of Chicken, 170
Dairy State Fudge, 404
Danish Apple Bar, 339
Deanna's Sweet and Sour Pork, 234
Deep-Dish Cheese/Sausage Pizza, 246
Dips, 15-18, 60
  Chili Cheese Dip, 16
  Chili Con Queso, 15
  Fruit Dip, 15
  Hot Artichoke Dip, 17
  Ranch Dip-Low Calorie, 18
Dorothy's Sloppy Joes, 205
Dressings, 23, 25-32
  Honey Dressing for Spinach Salad, 29
  Piquant Italian-Style Dressing, 30
Easy Caramel Rolls, 35
Easy Dessert, 398
Easy Oven Stew, 108

Easy Rice Pilaf, 154
Egg and Ham or Sausage Brunch, 50
Egg Baskets with Hollandaise Sauce, 49
Egg Casserole, 54
Eggnog Quick Bread, 71
Enchilada Pie, 202
Escalloped Apples, 388
Escalloped Pineapple, 153
Family Reunion Rolls, 75
Family's Favorite Cookies, 324
Fancy Beans, 219
Farofa, 159-160
Fired-Up Chili, 85
Fireside Coffee, 20
Fish & Seafood, 238-243
  Impossible Tuna Pie, 239
  Orange Roughy, 240
  Seafood Fettucini, 243
  Shrimp Boats, 241
  Shrimp Creole, 242
  Tuna Fish Casserole, 238
Flat Brisket of Beef, 198
Flower Pot Dessert, 397
Freezer Peaches, 389
French Bread Surprise, 222
French Cherry Pie, 353
French Rice, 155, 174
Fresh Broccoli-Mandarin Salad, 118
Fresh Peach Cobbler, 371
Fresh Peach Upside Down Pie, 349
Fresh Rhubarb Cake, 282
Frosting for Cake and Sugar Cookies, 303, 325
Frostings, 301-303
  Alma's Chocolate Cake with Icing, 294
  Best-Ever Chocolate Cake Frosting, 301
  Carrot Cake with Cream Cheese Frosting, 275
  Chocolate Cola Cake with Frosting, 293
  Chocolate Sheet Cake with Frosting, 295
  Frosting for Cake and Sugar Cookies, 303, 325
  Fruit Cocktail Cake and Frosting, 284
  Fudge Frosting, 299, 302
  Oatmeal Cake with Broiled Frosting, 267

412 INDEX

Frozen Orange Tarts, 400
Fruit Cobbler, 373
Fruit Cocktail Cake and Frosting, 284
Fruit Dip, 15
Fruit Pizza, 396
Fruit Salad, 38, 55, 131, 135
Fruit Slush, 21
Fudge Cookies, 310
Fudge Frosting, 299, 302
Fudge Sundae Pie, 356
Garlic Dill Pickles, 32
Gazpacho Mold, 127
German Biscuit, 262
German Christmas Cookies, 321
Glazed Baked Brie, 8
Glazed Peach Pie, 348
Golden Dobbin Chicken Casserole, 165
Grandma's Chocolate Cake and Icing, 297
Grandmother's Oatmeal Cookies, 316
Great Cheesecake, 377
Greek Spinach Pie, 55
Green Chili Potatoes, 146
Grilled Island Teriyaki, 201
Guadelupe Oatmeal Muffins, 63
Ham and Swiss Breakfast, 53
Ham-Potato Au Gratin, 237
Ham Shredded Wheat Casserole, 235
Hamburger Vegetable Soup, 100
Harvest Corn Chowder, 91
Hearty Rice Casserole, 208
Herb Chicken Casserole, 185
Hero Burger, 226
Home-Made Ice Cream, 405
Honey Dressing for Spinach Salad, 29
Hot , 15-18, 46, 183, 187, 235, 318, 323, 383, 401
Hot Artichoke Dip, 17
Hot Buttered Lemonade, 20
Hot Canapes, 7
Hot Fudge Pudding, 366
Hot Fudge Sauce, 25
Hurry-Up Chocolate Cake, 299, 302
Imperial Chicken, 187
Impossible Tuna Pie, 239
Italian Cream Cake, 272

Jan's Mexican Manicotti, 220
Janet's Chocolate Chip Cake, 289
Jeanne's Favorite Sugar Cookies, 325
Jello Lightning Cake, 265
Judy's Lemon Bars, 340
Juice Shake, 19
Kay's Trifle, 383
Kitchen Scrambler and Country Fries, 52
Kung Pao Chicken, 177
Landin's Pretzels, 76
Layered Vegetable Salad with Dressing, 125
Lemon Bars, 340-341
Lemon-Frosted Pecan Sandies, 317
Lemon-Pecan Sugar Cookies, 323
Lemon Snow Pudding, 367
Lemonade Cake, 268
Light Cheesecake, 380
Lynda's Chicken Enchiladas, 184
Lynda's Patchwork Crock Pot Rice, 258
Macaroni and Cheese, 249
Main Dishes & Casseroles, 163, 244-258
All Day Chuck Roast, 199
Amish
Bailey's Chicken, 179
Baked Italian Spaghetti, 209
Barbeque Beef Sandwiches, 196
Barbequed Hamburgers, 27, 211
Barbequed Meatballs, 216
Barbequed Spareribs, 200
Beef Samovar, 194
Broccoli-Cheese Stromboli, 217
Buttermilk Chicken Potpie, 166
Cabbage Bread, 225
Chicken and Black Bean Tamale Pie, 181
Chicken and Sausage Jambalaya, 182
Chicken Casserole, 165, 168, 185
Chicken Cordon Bleu, 183
Chicken Divan, 180
Chicken Enchiladas, 167, 184

Chicken Glop, 176
Chicken in Wine Sauce, 178
Chicken-with-Dressing Casserole, 172
Chili Pizzeria Bake, 214
Chilies Rellenos Jose, 251, 256
Country Potpie, 192
Creamy Baked Chicken, 155, 174
Curry of Chicken, 170
Deanna's Sweet and Sour Pork, 234
Deep-Dish Cheese/Sausage Pizza, 246
Dorothy's Sloppy Joes, 205
Enchilada Pie, 202
Fancy Beans, 219
Flat Brisket of Beef, 198
French Bread Surprise, 222
Golden Dobbin Chicken Casserole, 165
Grilled Island Teriyaki, 201
Ham-Potato Au Gratin, 237
Ham Shredded Wheat Casserole, 235
Hearty Rice Casserole, 208
Herb Chicken Casserole, 185
Hero Burger, 226
Imperial Chicken, 187
Impossible Tuna Pie, 239
Jan's Mexican Manicotti, 220
Kung Pao Chicken, 177
Lynda's Chicken Enchiladas, 184
Lynda's Patchwork Crock Pot Rice, 258
Macaroni and Cheese, 249
Meat and Potato Puff Casserole, 223
Mexican Casserole, 221
Mexican Lasagna, 203
Mexican Manicotti, 207, 220
Mexican Noodles, 171
Minestrone Chicken Dinner, 175
Navajo Tacos, 254
No-Meat Enchiladas, 252
Oat Burgers, 247
Orange Roughy, 240
Oriental Chicken Breasts, 169
Oriental Turkey Bake, 193
Picnic Pizza, 212
Pizza Burgers, 245

INDEX 413

Pork Chops and Amber Rice, 232
Pork Chops Supreme, 229
Pork Chops with Apples and Sauerkraut, 231
Premium Glazed Ham, 236
Quickie Lunch, 253
Red Beans and Rice, 257
Ruth's Chilies Rellenos Jose, 256
Salsa-Garlic Flank Steak, 197
Salsburg Steak, 224
Sausage Vegetable Dinner, 228
Seafood Fettucini, 243
Semolina Pizza Dough and Sauce, 244
Shrimp Boats, 241
Shrimp Creole, 242
Spaghetti Pie, 215
Spicy Bratwurst and Onions, 227
Stuffed Peppers, 213
Super Easy Super Shells, 250
Sweet and Sour Pork, 230, 234
Sweet-Sour Chicken, 186
Swiss Hamburger Onion Pie, 206
Swiss Steak, 195
Talerini, 218
Tangy Grilled Turkey Tenderloins, 190
Tijuana Train Wreck, 233
Tuna Fish Casserole, 238
Turkey Enchiladas, 189
Turkey Taco Filling, 191
Vegetable Lasagna Supreme, 248
Vegetable Tamale Pie, 255
Vince's Low-Fat Oven-Fried Chicken, 188
Zucchini Lasagna, 204
Mandarin Orange Jello, 391
Mandarin Scones, 59
Marinade for Chicken, 28
Marylou's Moist Cookies, 326
Mayonnaise Cake, 287
McCarthy's Caesar Salad, 122
Meat and Potato Puff Casserole, 223
Mexican Casserole, 221
Mexican Hominy Soup, 103
Mexican Lasagna, 203
Mexican Manicotti, 207, 220

Mexican Noodles, 171
Millionaire Pie, 355
Minestrone Chicken Dinner, 175
Mom's Raisin Pie, 354
Monster Cookies, 306
Moon Cake, 270
Mother's Classic Coconut Cookie, 322
Nana's Date Squares, 337
Navajo Tacos, 254
New England Clam Chowder, 90
New England Fruit Cookies, 312
New Mexico Chile Verde, 87
New Peanut Butter Crispy Treat, 401
No-Bake Chocolate Cookies, 308
No-Fat No-Sugar Lime Salad, 130
No-Meat Enchiladas, 252
Oat Burgers, 247
Oatmeal Cake with Broiled Frosting, 267
Oatmeal Honey Bread, 73
Oatmeal Marble Squares, 335
Oatmeal Whole Wheat Cookies, 315
Onion Casserole, 145
Orange and Romaine Salad, 124
Orange Glazed Pumpkin Bread, 66
Orange Julius, 19
Orange Roughy, 240
Orange Sherbet Salad, 138
Oriental Chicken Breasts, 169
Oriental Turkey Bake, 193
Other Desserts, 345, 388-406
  Banana Dessert, 394
  Candy Bar Pizza, 402
  Cappuccino Ice Cream, 405
  Caramel Corn, 393
  Cherry Mash Candy, 403
  Dairy State Fudge, 404
  Easy Dessert, 398
  Escalloped Apples, 388
  Flower Pot Dessert, 397
  Freezer Peaches, 389
  Frozen Orange Tarts, 400
  Fruit Pizza, 396
  Home-Made Ice Cream, 405
  Hot Fudge Sauce, 25

  Mandarin Orange Jello, 391
  New Peanut Butter Crispy Treat, 401
  Party Rhubarb Dessert, 395
  Peanut Butter Balls, 401
  Peanut Butter Chocolate Chip Ice Cream, 406
  Pineapple Cheesecake Squares, 382
  Pineapple Souffle, 390
  Praline Quaker Oat Squares, 14
  Pumpkin Supreme, 392
  Vanilla Wafer Refrigerator Dessert, 399
Oven Soup, 105
Overnight Apple French Toast with Spiced Applesauce, 46
Overnight Breakfast, 48
Party Rhubarb Dessert, 395
Party Swedish Meatballs, 11
Patchwork Quilt Salad, 117
Peach Cobbler, 371-372
Peachy Peach Bread, 67
Peanut Butter Balls, 401
Peanut Butter Chocolate Chip Ice Cream, 406
Peanut Butter n Chocolate Chip Cookies, 327
Pesto, 26
Pickles, 23, 25-32
  Cucumbers, 32, 115
  Garlic Dill Pickles, 32
Picnic Pizza, 212
Pies, 345, 347-362
  Beetle Nut Pie, 359
  Buttermilk Pie, 361
  Classic Chocolate Cream Pie, 357
  Cornmeal Pie, 362
  French Cherry Pie, 353
  Fresh Peach Upside Down Pie, 349
  Fudge Sundae Pie, 356
  Glazed Peach Pie, 348
  Millionaire Pie, 355
  Mom's Raisin Pie, 354
  Pumpkin Cheesecake Pie, 360
  Strawberry Cream Pie, 351
  Strawberry Glacé Pie, 350
  Strawberry Rhubarb Pie, 352
  Try Vinegar Pie, 358
  Vermont Apple Pie, 347
Pineapple Carrot Cake, 276

414 INDEX

Pineapple Cheesecake Squares, 382
Pineapple-Cream Cheese Sandwiches, 47
Pineapple Paradise Cake, 283
Pineapple Puff, 152
Pineapple Souffle, 390
Piquant Italian-Style Dressing, 30
Pizza, 60, 72, 212, 217, 244-246, 396, 402
   Candy Bar Pizza, 402
   Deep-Dish Cheese/Sausage Pizza, 246
   Fruit Pizza, 396
   Picnic Pizza, 212
   Pizza Burgers, 245
   Semolina Pizza Dough and Sauce, 244
Pizza Burgers, 245
Polish Potato Sausage Soup, 102
Poppy Seed Sherry Cake, 269
Poppy Seed Tea Bread, 68
Pork, 15, 152, 208, 217, 225, 227-237
   Deanna's Sweet and Sour Pork, 234
   Ham-Potato Au Gratin, 237
   Ham Shredded Wheat Casserole, 235
   Pork Chops and Amber Rice, 232
   Pork Chops Supreme, 229
   Pork Chops with Apples and Sauerkraut, 231
   Premium Glazed Ham, 236
   Sausage Vegetable Dinner, 228
   Spicy Bratwurst and Onions, 227
   Sweet and Sour Pork, 230, 234
   Tijuana Train Wreck, 233
Pork Chops and Amber Rice, 232
Pork Chops Supreme, 229
Pork Chops with Apples and Sauerkraut, 231
Portuguese Sausage Soup, 101
Pot Luck Potatoes, 148
Potsticker Salad, 116
Poultry, 165-193
   Bailey's Chicken, 179

   Buttermilk Chicken Potpie, 166
   Chicken and Black Bean Tamale Pie, 181
   Chicken and Sausage Jambalaya, 182
   Chicken Casserole, 165, 168, 185
   Chicken Cordon Bleu, 183
   Chicken Divan, 180
   Chicken Enchiladas, 167, 184
   Chicken Glop, 176
   Chicken in Wine Sauce, 178
   Chicken-with-Dressing Casserole, 172
   Country Potpie, 192
   Creamy Baked Chicken, 155, 174
   Curry of Chicken, 170
   Golden Dobbin Chicken Casserole, 165
   Herb Chicken Casserole, 185
   Imperial Chicken, 187
   Kung Pao Chicken, 177
   Lynda's Chicken Enchiladas, 184
   Mexican Noodles, 171
   Minestrone Chicken Dinner, 175
   Oriental Chicken Breasts, 169
   Oriental Turkey Bake, 193
   Sweet-Sour Chicken, 186
   Tangy Grilled Turkey Tenderloins, 190
   Turkey Enchiladas, 189
   Turkey Taco Filling, 191
   Vince's Low-Fat Oven-Fried Chicken, 188
Pound Cake, 261-263
Praline Quaker Oat Squares, 14
Premium Glazed Ham, 236
Pretzels, 18, 76, 79
Prussian Cinnamon Rolls, 36-37
Puddings, 345, 363-368
   Bread Pudding with Whiskey Sauce, 368
   Cherry Pudding, 363
   Hot Fudge Pudding, 366
   Lemon Snow Pudding, 367
   Zwieback Pudding, 364-365
Pumpkin Bread, 65-66
Pumpkin Cheesecake Pie, 360
Pumpkin Cookies, 320

Pumpkin Jelly Roll, 264
Pumpkin Muffins, 62
Pumpkin Supreme, 392
Pumpkin Torte, 386
Quasi-Lemon Bars, 338
Quick Cinnamon Coffee Bread, 40
Quick Coffee Cake, 39
Quickie Lunch, 253
Quilt Camp Brownies, 329
Quinoa-Almond Salad with Balsamic Vinaigrette, 121
Ranch Dip—Low Calorie, 18
Raspberry Bars, 343
Raw Apple Coffee Cake, 43
Red Beans and Rice, 257
Refrigerator Rolls, 82
Relish, 31
   Wesport Cranberry Relish, 31
Resort Fruit Salad, 135
Rhubarb Cake, 281-282
Rhubarb Crunch, 374-375
Rosemary Focaccia, 72
Ruby's Broccoli Casserole, 141
Rum Cake and Sauce, 274
Rum Cake Jubilee, 273
Ruth's Chilies Rellenos Jose, 256
Salads, 83, 109-139
   Apple and Banana Salad, 132
   Applesauce Salad, 133
   Barley and Black Bean Salad, 109
   Black Bean Salad, 109, 111
   Blueberry Salad, 134
   Cabbage Salad, 112
   Cauliflower Salad, 119
   Chinese Coleslaw, 113
   Cold Veggie Salad, 126
   Fresh Broccoli-Mandarin Salad, 118
   Fruit Salad, 38, 55, 131, 135
   Gazpacho Mold, 127
   Layered Vegetable Salad with Dressing, 125
   McCarthy's Caesar Salad, 122
   No-Fat No-Sugar Lime Salad, 130
   Orange and Romaine Salad, 124
   Orange Sherbet Salad, 138
   Patchwork Quilt Salad, 117
   Potsticker Salad, 116
   Resort Fruit Salad, 135

INDEX 415

Sour Cream Salad, 136
Spaghetti Salad, 115
Spinach Salad with Sweet
  and Sour Dressing, 128
Strawberry Salad, 129, 137
Strawberry Salad with
  Dressing, 129
Sweet and Sour Red
  Cabbage, 114
Three-Bean Salad, 110
Vegetable Salad, 123, 125
Wheat Berry Salad Primavera
  with Dijon Dressing, 120
Quinoa-Almond Salad with
  Balsamic Vinaigrette, 121
White Salad, 139
Salsa-Garlic Flank Steak, 197
Salsburg Steak, 224
Sauces, 23, 25-32
  Bug Juice, 27
  Hot Fudge Sauce, 25
  Marinade for Chicken, 28
  Pesto, 26
Sausage Vegetable Dinner, 228
Scalloped Potatoes, 147, 183
Scrap Soup, 104
Seafood Fettucini, 243
Semolina Pizza Dough and
  Sauce, 244
Sesame Chicken Wings, 10
Seven-Layer Bars, 336
Shrimp Boats, 241
Shrimp Creole, 242
Simply Super Tomatoes, 149
Slice-and-Bake Almond
  Cookies, 319
Soups, 60, 83, 85-108, 176
  Aunt Margaret's French
    Stew, 107
  Baked Potato Soup, 98
  Bear's Paw Black Bean
    Soup, 92
  Big D's Famous Chili, 86
  Broccoli Cheese Soup, 97
  Broccoli Cream Soup, 96
  Chicken Chili, 88
  Cuban Style Black Bean
    Soup, 93
  Easy Oven Stew, 108
  Fired-Up Chili, 85
  Hamburger Vegetable Soup,
    100
  Harvest Corn Chowder, 91
  Mexican Hominy Soup, 103
  New England Clam
    Chowder, 90
  New Mexico Chile Verde, 87
  Oven Soup, 105
  Polish Potato Sausage Soup,
    102
  Portuguese Sausage Soup,
    101
  Scrap Soup, 104
  White Bean and Roasted
    Tomato Soup, 94-95
  White Chili, 89
  Zucchini Soup, 99
Sour Cream Salad, 136
Spaghetti Pie, 215
Spaghetti Salad, 115
Spicy Bean Cake, 277
Spicy Bratwurst and Onions,
  227
Spicy Refried Beans, 161
Spinach Casserole, 150
Spinach Salad with Sweet and
  Sour Dressing, 128
Strawberry Cake, 286
Strawberry Cream Pie, 351
Strawberry Glacé Pie, 350
Strawberry Jello Torte, 387
Strawberry Rhubarb Pie, 352
Strawberry Salad, 129, 137
Strawberry Salad with
  Dressing, 129
Streusel Coffee Cake, 42
Stuffed Peppers, 213
Super Easy Super Shells, 250
Sweet and Sour Pork, 230, 234
Sweet and Sour Red Cabbage,
  114
Sweet-Sour Chicken, 186
Swiss Hamburger Onion Pie,
  206
Swiss Steak, 195
Talerini, 218
Tangy Grilled Turkey
  Tenderloins, 190
Three-Bean Salad, 110
Tijuana Train Wreck, 233
Tortilla Rollups, 12
Trifles and Tortes, 384
  Butterfinger Torte, 385
  Kay's Trifle, 383
  Pumpkin Torte, 386
  Strawberry Jello Torte, 387
  Twinkie Torte, 384
Triple Chocolate Bars, 332
Try Vinegar Pie, 358
Tuna Fish Casserole, 238
Turkey Enchiladas, 189
Turkey Taco Filling, 191
Turtle Cake, 271
Twinkie Torte, 384
Two-Hour French Bread, 78
Vanilla Wafer Refrigerator
  Dessert, 399
Vegetable Bars, 13
Vegetable Lasagna Supreme,
  248
Vegetable Salad, 123, 125
Vegetable Tamale Pie, 255
Vegetables & Side Dishes, 83,
  140-162
  Amish Dressing, 157
  Apricot Pine Nut Pilaf, 158
  Baked Corn, 143
  Black Beans and Rice
    (Feijoa), 160
  Brazilian-Style Rice, 156,
    160
  Broccoli Squares, 140
  Buttery Grated Carrots, 142
  Cheese Pie, 151
  Crock Pot Baked Beans, 162
  Easy Rice Pilaf, 154
  Escalloped Pineapple, 153
  Farofa, 159-160
  French Rice, 155, 174
  Green Chili Potatoes, 146
  Onion Casserole, 145
  Pineapple Puff, 152
  Pot Luck Potatoes, 148
  Ruby's Broccoli Casserole,
    141
  Scalloped Potatoes, 147, 183
  Simply Super Tomatoes, 149
  Spicy Refried Beans, 161
  Spinach Casserole, 150
  Zucchini Pie, 144
Vermont Apple Pie, 347
Vince's Low-Fat Oven-Fried
  Chicken, 188
Wesport Cranberry Relish, 31
Wheat Berry Salad Primavera
  with Dijon Dressing, 120
Whipped Cream Devil's Cake,
  292
White Bean and Roasted
  Tomato Soup, 94-95
White Chili, 89
White Russian Chocolate
  Pound Cake, 263
White Salad, 139

Whole Wheat Banana Bread, 70
Whole Wheat Bread, 80-81
Wonder Cake, 290
Zucchini Bread, 69
Zucchini Lasagna, 204
Zucchini Pie, 144
Zucchini Soup, 99
Zwieback Pudding, 364-365